teens
@ the library
series

Teen Book Discussion Groups

@ the Library

Constance B. Dickerson

Neal-Schuman Publishers, Inc.

New York   London

Published by Neal-Schuman Publishers, Inc.
100 William Street, Suite 2004
New York, NY 10038

The paper used in this publication meets the minimum requirements of American National Standard for Informational Sciences — Permanence of Paper for Printed Library Materials, ANSI Z39.48 — 1992

Printed and bound in the United States of America.

Library of Congress Cataloging-in-Publication Data

Dickerson, Constance, 1958-
      Teen book discussion groups @ the library / Constance Dickerson.
         p. cm. — (Teens @ the library series)
      Includes bibliographical references and indexes.
      ISBN 1-55570-485-9 (alk. paper)
         1. Young adults libraries — Activity programs — United States. 2. Teenagers — Books and reading — United States. 3. Young adult literature — Study and teaching (Middle school) — United States. 4. Young adult literature — Study and teaching (Secondary) — United States. 5. Book clubs (Discussion groups) — United States. I. Title: Teen book discussion groups at the library. II. Title. III. Series.

Z718.5.D53 2004
027.62'6 — dc22   2003044261

DEDICATION:

To the regulars with gratitude: Suzie, Rebecca, MaryLou, Becky, Patty, Caroline, Melissa, Beverly, and Lena.

TABLE OF CONTENTS

SERIES EDITOR'S FOREWORD

We librarians love to bring teens and books together. Finding "the right book for the right reader at the right time" is both challenging and rewarding. Matching a teen with the best book involves using all our talents, abilities, and intuition; we must assess his or her reading ability, interests, and specific needs. It requires a practical and theoretical knowledge of the developmental needs of teens, as well as a broad and current knowledge of contemporary young adult literature. The results are often rewarding. What could be better than a student saying, "I just read that book you recommended for me and it was GREAT! What should I read next?"

While working with a group of enthusiastic and diverse young teens in the after-school reading group at my junior high school, I encountered a somewhat different challenge. Leading these interesting discussions was akin to providing reader's advisory for each of them. The one-to-one interaction I was familiar with became a task of finding the best books to satisfy and meet the needs of many teens. Constance Dickerson's *Teen Book Discussion Groups @ the Library* would have definitely helped me to do a better job.

Whether you are a relative newcomer or a seasoned pro, Dickerson clearly takes you step-by-step through the system of creating a teen book discussion group. In the first part, she describes how to make a book discussion program work. In 15 steps she takes you through the entire process:

- from selecting books to creating questions,
- from making rules to steering the discussion,
- from recruiting group members by providing snacks to using online resources, and
- from establishing a group size to strategies for including more boys.

Her sensible ideas and thoroughly tested tips will ensure that you get started on the right foot.

Whatever your level of experience in leading teen book discussion groups, Dickerson's 50 discussion guides will prove to be informative and stimulating. She includes high quality, high interest, and highly discussable titles. No matter what the variety of genders, ages, or interests of your participants, I'm confident you'll find books to interest and challenge your readers. Whether her guides provide a springboard for your own ideas or you use her suggestions, you'll find teens eager to respond to the challenge.

And the payoff? You know how passionate teens can be about reading. Once you provide them a safe and secure venue to talk about books they love, stand back and prepare to be rewarded in excess for the effort you've put forth. They will not only talk about what the book means to them, they will also reveal their feelings. Their perceptions will surprise and inform you. When you expect more from them, ask more questions, and allow them to talk more, teens will open up in unexpected ways.

I'm constantly learning about what goes into creating a successful book discussion group. I know this latest addition to the teens@the library series will help me do my job better. Almost everyone who conducts teen book discussions ends up saying, "I get more out of it than the kids. I love to hear their thoughts and feelings about the books we discuss. They're amazing." Who wouldn't want more of that kind of reward in their professional lives?

Joel Shoemaker
teens@thelibrary Series Editor

PREFACE

Young people who engage in good conversation about interesting books grow to be critical and careful readers. They also gain invaluable experience expressing opinions in a group. Articulating ideas about a variety of interesting subjects is its own reward.

All too often, teenagers only talk about literature in the pressured environment of a formal classroom setting. The structured but informal meetings encouraged in *Teen Book Discussion Groups @ the Library* provide the freedom of a relaxed setting with no exact right or wrong answers. Students often say, "I've never thought about it that way before," in response to another's opinion or interpretation. Learning to respect and consider different points of view fosters global and empathetic thinking.

The adult who skillfully facilitates a discussion will witness its benefits firsthand. It is my belief that anyone, armed with a good set of questions, can lead a successful book discussion. I designed this step-by-step guide to provide teachers, librarians, and other concerned adults with the necessary how-to information for leading engaging and informal book discussions.

Part I, "15 Easy Steps to Creating Lively Book Discussions" examines the essential preparation and explores the benefits for both leaders and participants. It offers ways to

- Select the best books for sparking animated discussions.
- Come up with ideas to create provocative questions—complete with examples.
- Use online resources for enhancing and preparing for book discussions – with a listing of complementary online discussion venues.
- Learn how a group selects a book.
- Establish rules.
- Manage books discussions
- Increase the number of boys participating.

Part II, "50 Field-Tested Teen Book Discussion Guides," features ready-made reading group guides with insightful comments and provocative questions. Each guide includes the basic bibliographic information, a list of themes, the genre, the names and ages of the main characters, and general tips for presenting the book. Next is a summary of the book, a set of questions, and analyses of suggested discussion points.

I trust the guides will be a valuable resource to every discussion leader, from novice to veteran. The summaries and comments will help teachers and librarians find the right books to complement their curriculia and focus on issues that will interest the group. Following the guides are the author, title, and theme indexes for easy reference.

I have selected a variety of YA books from different genres featuring protagonists from various backgrounds. They all address issues that affect the lives of teenagers or are of special interest to teens; they have all been successfully "fieldtested" in real-life groups.

The guides are enhanced by the experiences of the librarians and teachers who replied to a survey I posted on the YALSA-BK listserv and by those with whom I spoke in person or by phone.

It is my hope that the resources in Teen Book Discussion Groups @ the Library will help novice leaders take the beginning plunge and help veterans to discover new inspiration.

ACKNOWLEDGMENTS

I am grateful to all the librarians and teachers who graciously responded to my survey and to those who took the time to talk with me in person or on the phone. I am also grateful to the many teens who have shared their opinions, fears, and dreams during book discussions.

My thanks to Joel Shoemaker, who helped me shape my proposal, and to my editor, Michael Kelley, for helping me develop a sense of order in my book and for keeping me smiling with his sense of humor.

Part I

FIFTEEN SURE-FIRE SUGGESTIONS FOR SUCCESSFUL BOOK DISCUSSIONS

1. UNDERSTAND THE VALUE OF BOOK DISCUSSIONS WITH TEENS

The teens are one of the most interesting times of life. Teens begin to look for answers about who they are. They begin to formulate opinions about the outside world and learn to apply and develop their values. To be a witness and confidante to these processes is a privilege. To offer encouragement and to be in a position to present and talk about problem-solving options with teens is also a privilege. To talk with young adults about the "big questions" is thrilling. Books reflect every aspect of life and provide fuel for discussion. Discussing books with teens provides an informal, comfortable opportunity for them to express their feelings and opinions on issues that arouse their fears, longings, and beliefs. If you work with teens or if teens are part of your life in any capacity, book discussions present a unique opportunity to learn more about them and establish rapport.

When budgets are being slashed and staffing is minimal, as they are during this time of economic uncertainty, we have had to set priorities and justify time spent in programming and preparing programs. Book discussions have always been one of the staple programs in libraries. Library customers expect them, and they are one of the best ways to foster positive feelings about libraries. Several years ago, during Teen Read Week, I hosted a book discussion in the main reading area of an urban library. Fifteen teens, mostly boys, sat around for an hour and talked about books. It was in a busy area that adults routinely pass through. We generated a lot of attention, and I'm sure that one reaction was surprise to find these teens in the library talking about books instead of in the parking lot on skateboards or smoking cigarettes. This program reflected very positively on the library.

The benefits to the individuals are even greater. Any positive group interaction can promote self-confidence in teens. Everything takes practice, and learning to express one's feelings in a group can be only a bonus in other settings.

In Response to the survey, Rosalie Olds, young adult librarian at Fairwood (Wash.) wrote, "Teens say that they feel like loners in school, but the book group is a place they feel welcome." There's no need to stress the importance of providing a place of belonging for kids who feel like outsiders at school.

Book discussions lead to critical analysis of literature, a skill that sharpens with practice and has obvious benefits on schoolwork. My neighbor, who is from Sri Lanka and has lived in England and the U.S. is critical of education in the United

States because he believes that critical thinking is not encouraged enough, that there's too much memorization and preparation for standardized tests. Critical thinkers are problem solvers, and problem solving is an attribute most worthy of being fostered in young people.

In her work on reader response, Kay E. Vandergrift (1995) describes how reading is a private event. The reader makes meaning from what she reads based on her own experience and understanding. The same story is interpreted individually, so that when readers share their responses an opening in understanding is created, and a subtle realization of many other possibilities occurs. Book discussions are an expansive experience. Caroline Ward (1998, p 28) cites the expansion of meaning as one of the most powerful benefits of group discussion. She warns against allowing members to express their initial likes and dislikes because they often change. It is not at all unusual to find a post-discussion appreciation for a book that you initially disliked. Discussions deepen understanding and provide exposure to other points of view. I think it's okay to express initial reactions with the understanding that they may change and that shift is one of the worthwhile effects of participating in a book group.

Not only is each initial individual interpretation unique, but each group experience is unique, as well. Librarian Natalie Emiliani of Mt. Lebanon (Penn) Public Library discusses the same book with separate groups of sixth, seventh, and eighth graders. She notes that each group responds so differently to the same book that she sometimes wonders if they've read the same book. In a sense they haven't. Just as each individual has his or her own response, each group does also based on its unique components. It would be interesting to study whether the group responses have some age-related similarities beyond individual interpretation and group dynamics.

The books we use for book discussions invite ethical debate. They allow teens to become thoughtful about social issues that may not directly impinge on their daily lives now, but that they will need to form opinions about as they mature.

Reading about other cultures and characters involved in very different experiences from the reader's own leads to a better understanding of others. Getting a glimpse of what it's like to step inside a character's shoes and understand their realities and motivations breeds empathy and compassion.

Parents and teens participating in book discussions together invariably wind up talking about issues they wouldn't have otherwise, and so they develop more understanding and appreciation of each other. Any adult who hosts a book discussion group for teens benefits in the same way. Book discussion provides a format for talking with teens about issues in an informal way that adults don't often have; this can be especially helpful to adults who work with teens as teachers or librarians.

Teens can go for years without choosing to read anything but books that are required by their schools. If the books that they read in school don't move them, they may not be inclined to read outside of classroom assignments. If a friend convinces them to come to a book discussion, even if they haven't read the book, the teens will witness a positive literary experience previously unimagined. There is always laughter. There are no wrong answers. All opinions are valued and respected. There are many books that *will* interest teens.

2. GET THE BOOKS

If you're lucky enough to have access to a large library system, getting books for a discussion group may be the least of your worries. Drawing from many branches or a network of libraries makes it easy to get enough copies to a central location for participants to check out. Some larger libraries have book discussion sets that may be borrowed, multiple copies of titles especially for group use. Smaller libraries have asked Friends groups to donate copies of books for discussion. Bookstores often give discounts to book groups or titles purchased in quantity.

3. SELECT THE PLACE

Most public libraries offer meeting and conference rooms that can be reserved for book groups. Some also offer outdoor areas, atriums and courtyards. Parks are refreshing. Local YMCAs and YWCAs or churches often have rooms to let. Bookstores offer space for discussions, though some don't have private rooms. Consider a local coffeehouse—somewhere you'd find teens anyway. Some lucky communities have youth centers or recreational facilities. Teachers can use an empty classroom, though I think the school library is more conducive to discussion because it doesn't import a formal, assigned, and to-be-graded feel discussion. Venues outside of the library or classroom have the added benefit of attracting teens who may not be library users yet.

Noise is a consideration. We want to encourage friendly disagreement and the passionate expression of ideas, and that can get quite loud. I recommend looking for a space away from quiet study areas or other potential sources of disapproval.

Whatever space you use, tables and chairs are about all that's needed. You can circle chairs. Tables are best for resting books, elbows, and snacks. If you work with teens, you know you can't underestimate the importance of food, so make sure your space is food friendly.

4. FEED THE BODY WHILE FEEDING THE MIND

Anyone who's worked with teens will testify to the fact that teens eat an astonishing amount. It's a no-brainer for anyone who works with teens: if you feed them, they will come. If you can swing pizza, you are golden, but popcorn (though messy, especially when spirits are high), cookies, and pretzels work well enough—with drinks of course. If your budget is challenged by the purchase of snacks, consider having brown-bag discussions, or even a potluck. Some books lend themselves to theme-oriented food. Bring fortune cookies or eggrolls and tea if your group is reading Mah's *Chinese Cinderella*. Bring meringue cookies when discussing *The Adventures of Blue Avenger*.

Food can be such a draw that Beth Galloway (Haverhill [Mass] Public Library,) calls her programs "Pizza and Pages." "Pizza and Pages" is printed in large, bold type on her flyers.

5. FIND A TIME THAT WORKS

Whether your book discussion group is school based or not, it's a good idea to have a copy of the school calendar when you're setting dates for your programs. Thursdays worked for a year with one of my discussion groups. Occasionally we met on a Thursday a week earlier than our customary monthly meeting, or a week later because of school events. But after a magical year, most of the teens in the group had a new responsibility, band practice, on Thursday evenings. This is when a group sometimes fades away. Other nights find one or two in dance class or at cheerleading practice, one is with a different parent from the one who brings her to the library, or you can't juggle your work schedule to be available on the night that seems most possible.

For unknown reasons, most group leaders have had little success planning more than a month ahead of time. Many of the survey respondents and people whom I've talked to have had the same experience and related many instances of cancelled programs. Most discussion leaders keep trying till they find an evening when three or more teens show up, then nurture that group, asking them to bring friends and trying to remain flexible in scheduling with that core group.

Almost no one with a regular book group holds discussions on Saturdays. There are too many other activities vying for those precious hours — lessons, errands, sports events, and shrinking social time. The majority of groups meet in the evening. If you have an after-school crowd, try that time slot. Actively recruit member's of the regular after-school crowd. Ask them to sit in even if they haven't read the book just to see if they may want to participate in the future.

A wonderful opportunity that some teachers and librarians have taken advantage of is school lunch periods. Brown-Bag groups have been gaining in popularity.

Home-schoolers are available during the day, which makes scheduling easy if you're in a library. During the school day is typically the least busy time in a public library.

Most libraries are closed on Friday evenings. If you've tried any type of after-hours programs, you've probably found a ready group of participants. After-hours programs are appealing for several reasons. Parents approve of the library and are willing to chauffeur their "pre-drivers." Parents like having a weekend activity in a safe, supervised environment. For teens the appeal includes being in a minimally supervised space doing something you normally can't do in the library. You can shout and eat. After-hours programs like poetry slams and mystery nights have drawn sizable crowds at many libraries. Book discussions are another matter, however. Despite the smaller turnout, they may still require the attendance of at least two staff members. The discussions may not be cost effective. An alternative is to schedule a Friday night meeting at a local coffeehouse or bookstore.

The crucial consideration in scheduling book discussions is to know what you're competing with. Be aware of when special events are happening in the community and at the schools. It's a definite advantage if your schedule allows you to be flexible from meeting to meeting.

6. ACHIEVE AN OPTIMAL GROUP SIZE

Most people who plan and offer programs for teens don't need to think about limiting reservations. We are often heard saying things to each other like, "Five is a *good* number. Maybe they'll bring friends next time." Attendance at teen programs can be disappointing. Five *is* a good number. Three or four are okay, but the smaller the number, the shorter the discussion. Likewise, be prepared to not get through all of your questions if your group swells. Sometimes four or five questions, particularly if they're provocative, are all you'll manage. On the sad occasion when two show up, it's your call on whether to proceed. I think that most of us would. Once, when only one teen came for the discussion, we sat at my desk and chatted.

You will want a rough idea of attendance, especially if it will affect the space you use and the amount of refreshments you purchase, so requiring registration may be advantageous. Of course, one of the natural laws of program registration is that usually half of the registrants will actually show up along with several teens who didn't register. Some group leaders call registrants the day before the program to remind them about it.

Fourteen or fifteen participants is the preferred maximum for an hour-long discussion. A few less is probably better. You want everyone to have the chance to say everything they want. It's harder to draw out shyer members when the numbers are large. Most adults who facilitate teen book discussions would view having a group so large that it had to be split into two as a very enviable situation. Dreamy even. However, our attention is usually taken with keeping the regulars coming and attracting new attendees.

7. PUBLICIZE AND BRIBE

Publicize your book discussions at all the places teens go. Put up flyers at schools, in bookstores and coffee shops, and at the library. Put the word on the community cable station. Write and submit a piece for the school's morning announcements or a blurb in the school newspaper. Contact home-schooling groups. Making an appearance at the school is a possibility. Librarians often visit schools to give booktalks or talk about upcoming summer programs. Make and distribute bookmarks announcing the book group. Curriculum nights offer an opportunity for parents to pick up flyers about your book discussions. Parents can have considerable sway in suggesting activities for their teens, especially if teens depend on them for transportation.

There are two ways of advertising your program: either by focusing on the book or focusing on the group. If the book is the draw, your publicity will be much like a short booktalk that teases the reader into wanting to read the book. Mina Gallo of Cuyahoga County (Ohio) Public Library (OH) created a very eye-catching and provocative flyer for her discussion of the book *Speak* by Laurie Halse Anderson. Text from the book is printed with the following phrases highlighted: are herded in, we fall into clans, wasted the last, don't have anyone. In the middle of the excerpt were the words "I am clanless," in red and several points larger than the rest of the text. There are no graphics on the page, just the colors of the yellow highlighted phrases, a block of orange surrounding the program particulars (date, time), and the words in red contrasting with the black text. It's perfect for this book.

The combination of the eye-catching format and engaging text draws bulletin-board browsers(survey response).

Most groups focus on the group when advertising. They advertise a series of brown-bag discussions, after-school discussions, sci-fi/fantasy-group discussions, or mother/daughter, to name a few. Some like the sci-fi/fantasy groups focus on a genre. In an attempt to attract more boys, I planned a series of discussions over a summer called "Blood and Guts." The red fliers for the programs listed titles in blood-drop print.

Feedback from discussion leaders suggests that the group *is* more important than the book or series of books in drawing attendees. One way of attracting a group may be to have teens bring a favorite book, so that the first meeting can be a general talk about favorite books. In this case you'd want to emphasize the social aspects of the program—meeting other teens who like to read, sharing literary interests, enjoying free pizza. Once you have two or three teens who are interested and you can figure out when they're available, the recruiting begins.

Those polled reported that regular members recruit many of their discussion attendees. Don't forget to ask them to bring a friend. One librarian even offered an incentive (bribery) for bringing a friend. Some group leaders have giveaways on hand—bookmarks or other inexpensive, hoarded things. Some groups have been able to give copies of the books they read to participants. You may want to hold a raffle at each discussion for a copy of the book or some other related item. Anyone who's had children knows that well-used bribery can produce positive effects, though it's not always a good strategy for attracting program attendees.

Sometimes teachers are willing to give students extra credit (serious bribery) if they attend a book discussion program. While this can really boost attendance, it doesn't necessarily foster good discussions. It's no pleasure having someone attend your program who doesn't want to be there or who is obviously there just for extra credit, and it can have a negative impact on the whole group dynamic. There is, however, the chance that, once there, unwilling participants will find that it's fun and undergo a conversion. You take your chances.

If your discussion is at a school during lunch hour, any alternative to the cafeteria may be incentive enough to attract some teens. Some school lunch groups enjoy the status of having been selected by a teacher to attend. C. J. Bott, a teacher at Shaker Heights (Ohio) High School wrote a grant to study books with strong female characters. The highly motivated students who participated were invited. Still, Bott's project attracted low numbers, which she credits to the many competing activities that high school students juggle.

8. DECIDE ON RULES

Setting ground rules for your group may seem superfluous. By the time children become teens, they've been domesticated enough to know that they should listen to and respect others. When an infraction occurs it is time to say, "I don't think that you mean Michael is stupid. How can you rephrase that?" However, if a formal set of rules makes the leader more comfortable or if the leader intuits that rules are necessary, by all means work with your group to have them create some. To be effective, teens must feel ownership of any ground rules, especially if they're about behavior.

Creating a set of rules may be one of your group's first activities. Some of the guidelines your group might adopt follow:

- Respect each other's opinions.
- Listen to the speaker.
- Welcome friendly disagreement.
- Put-downs are not allowed.
- There are no right answers.
- You must read the book to attend.

One might assume that those attending a book discussion will have read the book. Anyone who's regularly hosted or attended book discussions knows better. I once had three teens show up for a book discussion and two of them hadn't read the book. Because it was a book with some universal themes, we were able to discuss some of the ethical questions that the book engendered. The reader and I even summarized parts of the story to talk about plot and characters. The experience was worthwhile in the way that interacting with teens always is, but I don't know if you'd call it a successful book discussion. Whether or not reading and finishing the book is required may be a rule you'll want to consider. Unless someone who didn't read the book is being distracting, I wouldn't ban such a person from attending the discussion.

9. CHOOSE DISCUSSABLE BOOKS

You know when you've read a book that will be a great discussion book. It's well written, skillfully told; the characters are well developed and realistic; the situations are ones with which teens can identify and are curious about; the story is compelling. The best books are fraught with issues that can be debated. Unresolved issues also make for good discussions, endings that leave a reader hanging, like Sherryl Jordan's *The Secret Sacrament,* which ends with the words "the beginning," or Patricia Armstrong's *The Kindling*, which ends with the sighting of a mysterious woman in white, the first adult a group of children has seen in five years. These cliffhangers invite speculation about what will happen next.

In selecting discussion books for college freshman, William W. Anderson (1995) cites timelessness as criteria. He writes that he seeks relevant rather than trendy or politically correct books. I agree that books that address the eternal rather than the ephemeral questions are most intriguing and provide the most provocative discussion material. In her article "Having Their Say," Caroline Ward (1998) writes that successful book-discussion books are those that "tap into the big questions with which all ages grapple," which is why you can sometimes have great conversations when you include participants who haven't read the book. On the other hand, it's fun and engaging to talk about current issues and even whether or not a book will withstand the test of time and remain relevant. Furthermore, some of the big questions make some participants uncomfortable. When discussing Norma Howe's *Adventures of the Blue Avenger*, the issue of whether or not we have free will had some group members squirming. One teen bluntly stated that she didn't want to think about things like that.

So what happens when you seem to have chosen a dud? On the surface, *Waiting for Christopher* by Louise Hawes seemed to have discussion-rich content when I suggested it to my group. It's about a teenage girl who witnesses a toddler being abused by his mother on several occasions. She responds by kidnapping him. The problems were pretty straightforward and the issues didn't engage the group for long. Because there wasn't much to debate, however, the group went on to talk about how they thought that the book could have been more intriguing as well as other critical points. It turned out to be a good discussion—more about how the book was written than the issues it raised. Literary criticism can be an enjoyable part of the discussions.

Many groups limit their reading to one type of literature, particularly fiction, but biographies and poetry make for good discussion as well. One survey respondent reported that her group reluctantly ventured into nonfiction and tackled *The Life and Death of Adolf Hitler* by James Giblin and had the best discussion ever. Some groups have used graphic novels and humor. Margaret Cole of Oceanside (NY) Library used *There's a Hair in My Dirt* by Gary Larson with one of her book groups. Some groups read specific genres, especially fantasy or science fiction. Or groups may choose to read Printz, Alex, or other award winners or books from the "Best Books for Young Adults" or "Popular Paperbacks" lists composed by the Young Adult Library Association (YALSA) of the American Library Association.

10. CREATE INTRIGUING QUESTIONS

Good questions make for good discussions, and, obviously, the best questions and the bulk of your questions should

- be open-ended (can't be answered in a word).
- be speculative (they invite the reader to imagine alternative scenarios or what happens next).
- invite interpretation or evaluation (Why do characters act as they do; how effective are their actions; how effective is the author in telling the story?).
- elicit opinions.
- lead teens to make comparisons with their own experiences.

Generally avoid yes/no because they don't encourage readers to expand on their answers. Of course, some yes/no questions easily become interpretive and useful when you add a why/why not. Also avoid questions that test readers' retention of facts and seem too much like what happens in the classroom. One comparison I don't want teens to make is between this fun, informal book discussion and the worst of what sometimes happens in a classroom—what might be called the "beating-the-book-to-death syndrome." There is a tendency among some teachers or curricula to discuss a book to the point of joylessness by insisting that only one interpretation is valid. The best questions don't have right answers.

Yes/no and factual questions are sometimes useful as icebreakers, for example, "Did you like the book?" or "Let's recall the setting."

Some books are better than others for formulating good discussion questions. I usually bring a selection of books and book talk or read reviews and allow my group to select the next book, so sometimes they choose something I haven't read and it doesn't turn out to spawn great questions. There are some standbys to use in these situations. You can ask questions about preferences and style like those listed below:

- Who is your favorite character? Why?
- What is your favorite episode? Why?
- Are the characters realistic? Well developed?
- Why do you think the author chose the title? What title would you have chosen?
- Is there too much or too little description?
- Is there a lesson or moral?
- How important is the setting and time period? Could a different one have worked as well?
- Do any of the characters change?
- Is there anything that dates the book? Will it or has it withstood the test of time?
- Is the cover appropriate and eye-catching? Would you change the cover?
- Is there any part of the book that made your heart beat faster? Made your eyes tear? Made you laugh out loud?
- Is the end satisfying? How would you change it?

It is helpful to have these generic questions on hand in case you need some fillers or don't have a particularly meaty book.

Biographies invite questions about the subject's motivations and speculation about how things would have turned out differently had the subject made different decisions. It's also worthwhile to discuss how events might have been different if they had happened at a different time in history or in a different place. What if the gender of the subject had been different?

Besides the usual questions about story and characters, discussing graphic novels leads to questions about art and the effectiveness of the format for telling the story, comparisons with traditional novels, and whether or not the story would translate well to a traditional format. The distinctive features of *manga* versus American styles can also be an interesting discussion point. You may want to invite a local cartoonist to attend your program and talk about his or her experience.

Discussing humor encourages groups to consider what makes something funny and whether some things are universally funny. It also invites exploration of when humor is offensive, cruel, and critical. Comparison of various forms of humor from several books might be interesting. If time and opportunity allow, a short video of examples of different kinds of humor from popular TV shows may enhance your discussion.

The form of poetry offers many points for discussion, including how the rhythm reflects the subject, how the piece would translate into prose, words that the poet has selected for their economy of meaning, and, if the poem rhymes, whether the rhymes are natural. How does the collection fit together as a whole? Choose individual poems that provide a provocative subject for discussion. The layout of poems on the page can sometimes be significant. How does the form enhance the meaning of the poem?

If you have a regular group and can count on most of them to come back next month then you can ask each participant to bring a question that they would like to ask the group, but don't depend on them; some forget and some just don't take to the task.

You might want to try a technique developed for classroom book discussions by Harvey Daniels (2002) in his book *Literature Circles: Voice and Choice in Book Clubs and Reading Groups* in which group members assume the following roles:

- Work Wizard–looks up and shares meanings of new vocabulary.
- Illuminator–pulls out "big ideas."
- Connector–compares ideas in the book to other books and movies.
- Questioner–thinks up open-ended questions.
- Character Shrink–chooses one character from the book to "psychoana-lyze."
- Statesperson–gives facts about the locale of the book.
- Game Warden–devises a short, fun activity connected with the book.
- Gossip–tells something about the author.

Daniels' clever format is probably best suited to a classroom or school-library setting where one can be assured that assignees will return. Also, while interesting, the format is limiting and a lot more structured than you may want for an informal discussion. Some kids and groups thrive on structure. Take the pulse of your group. It's important that preparing for an informal book discussion not resemble a school assignment.

Most of the books you'll want to use for book discussions lend themselves to questions all on their own, and, while it's not recommended to book talk a book you don't like, this situation can be a boon to discussion. By demonstrating that it is okay to not like a book, you can open doors to teen members who may have been reticent to voice their private reservations. The discussion may become especially lively if the group is split in their opinions. Be ready to keep opinions from getting personal.

11. STEER THE DISCUSSION AND KEEP IT ON COURSE

Experience will help you recognize when the discussion is veering off course. Inevitably, the discussion sparks a memory in one of the participants that may seem related in his or her mind, but leaves the rest of the group puzzled. Sometimes the shift will leave you speechless, which carries the danger of opening the door for more discussion on the new, unrelated topic. Before the discussion spins out of control, gently steer it back on course, acknowledging the speaker. If possible, do this while connecting what she or he has said with the book. For example, so that person on your bus may have some compulsive behaviors like the character in the book. Or sometimes, when the thread has unraveled completely, one might say, we've digressed a bit, why don't we get back to the book?

It's crucial for the facilitator to acknowledge the value of each contribution. It a good idea to interject encouraging comments like "interesting point" or "good insight." If someone isn't participating, ask if he or she agrees with a point someone else has made. This makes it possible to answer with a simple yes or no, but still have the opportunity to expand on that answer if the person wishes. Sometimes more outgoing group members can dominate the discussion, and that's when it becomes necessary to draw in some of the others into the group. It's a good practice to restate a member's comments to clarify what was said. Your job is to establish a comfortable, safe environment where all opinions are heard and valued. There's nothing more rewarding than watching a shy teen become more comfortable in sharing his or her opinion with a group.

The balance may be a little trickier to maintain in the case of parent-teen groups. Adults may assume an authoritative role, but that can be averted by directly questioning the teens. Adults in these groups often query the younger generation directly. Mixed generation groups are extremely rewarding for their different points of view. The parents involved hear things from their teens that they wouldn't have heard otherwise, and they get to discuss topics that might not be as easy to talk about except in the context of a book discussion. The example that comes to mind is a discussion I hosted of Sonya Sones' book, *What my Mother Doesn't Know*. The character in the book has an online romance that turns ugly. During the discussion, the mothers in my group were enthusiastic about talking with their daughters about the dangers of meeting people online. They seemed very happy to have an opportunity to express their fears and give warnings. While the teens were weary of warnings they seem to get at every turn, the foray into this topic seemed to reassure parents that their teens were well informed.

Jackie Hemond, young adult librarian at Simsbury (Maine) Library has found that the adults in a mixed group can be overbearing, that they "ask questions and expect a certain answer," and that they sometimes talk among themselves to the distraction of the rest of the group (survey response). This situation requires a much more active leadership role in which the facilitator directs questions to and asks for comments from specific group members. When you assert yourself as the leader, there aren't too many adults who won't get the message.

Sometimes digressions from a discussion of the book are valuable and welcome. During an August book discussion of *The New You*, by Kathleen Leverich, in which a teen moves to a new town and school and seems to lose her identity, several teens who were about to enter high school expressed their worries about fitting in and how they would be treated by upper classmen. A couple of teens who were going to be sophomores talked about the fears they had had as beginning freshman and what really happened, and they offered advice. Needless to say, I wasn't about to steer away from this diversion too soon. Another time, while discussing Nancy Werlin's *The Killers Cousin* the subject of school violence arose. It was a short time after Columbine and we were all feeling raw and fearful. It was a relief to express those feelings.

A facilitator should never pronounce a reader's interpretation right or wrong. One of the wonderful things about this kind of book discussion is that there are no right or wrong answers, unlike some of the discussions in class. On the other hand, it's fine and exciting when members of the group disagree with each other and become passionate. At that point, it is helpful to restate each position along with the supporting arguments before moving on to another question. Often the members find their way back to questions they're not quite done with and may even return to them on their way out of the meeting.

The results of a survey I sent out in preparation for writing this book informed me that while most book discussion hosts compose questions prior to the meeting, quite a few wing it. Personally, I wouldn't dream of winging it because I don't always think well on my feet and do much better having thought for a few days about questions. It's nice to have something in print to rely on, especially if the group gets far off track. This is not to say that I would absolutely advise against winging it; it's a personality or style issue, and flexibility when conducting the discussion is essential. If you like the spontaneity of winging it, go for it. Most discussion leaders would feel more secure with at least some preparation to fall back on.

I suggest formulating questions by reading the book twice. The first time some basic questions will come to mind. The second time, read to look for questions. Try to finish at least a few days before the meeting to allow your brain time to mull ideas over. You're very likely to formulate additional questions and think of ways to supplement your discussion with background information on the author, setting, time period, and so forth.

One successful tactic is to distribute your set of prepared questions as the discussion begins. Frequently someone in the group comes in with a burning issue and the discussion begins immediately with that. It may or may not be on your list of questions. Be flexible. If discussion doesn't happen spontaneously, ask the group to read over your questions and see if there's something they want to start with. If no one speaks up, start with your first question. The first question often segues to another question. Don't try to stay in order. Follow the group's lead and skip back and forth, sometimes returning to a question with a new insight. You'll rarely get through all of your questions, and often you'll develop new questions during the course of the discussion. This is a very dynamic process. Follow your group's interest and gently lead them back when they wander too far afield. Don't be a slave to your questions. Be a guide, not a dictator.

Some groups need to begin with a device to warm them up and build trust. In these cases, use an icebreaker. An icebreaker gives everybody in the group a chance to get to know a little about each other and participate in a non-threatening way. This is especially helpful when your group meets for the first time, and, the members don't know each other. Try some of the following:

- Ask the teens to bring souvenirs from trips they have taken to share when they introduce themselves to the group. Favorite objects also work well.
- Ask the teens to give their names and the names of their favorite characters or the characters they could most relate to. They may explain why if they like.
- Ask the teens describe the places where they read the book or their favorite places to read.
- As people arrive poll the teens on whether or not they liked the book, whether if was a fast or slow read, or if they would recommend it.

Beth Galloway of Haverhill (Mass.) Library has used the following creative icebreakers:

- "Two truths and a lie" is a game that requires members to make three statements about themselves, two true statements and one a lie. The group has to figure out which of the three statements is the lie.
- Ask attendees to write their names. Then the leader using her knowledge gained from studying books on handwriting analysis (or an

expert guest), the leader interprets each teen's handwriting, verifying the correctness of her proclamations with the member.

• Pass around a bowl of M&Ms and ask participants for a fact about the book for each M&M they eat. (You can never go wrong using food as a motivator).

Remember that while icebreakers are fun in themselves, they should only take the first few minutes to get your group comfortable and not take too much time away from your discussion. You may want to use icebreakers when the group is new and progress to briefer introductions as the group continues. Whether you use formal icebreakers or casual conversation, it is important to establish a relaxed environment and if your group needs it, some kind of bonding experience can go a long way.

It is important to know each other's names. You may ask the group members to introduce themselves and simply give a thumbs up or down to the book. Your group might develop a rating system based on their own criteria and begin each meeting by given their names and ratings. If you're hopeless about remembering new names, fold-over paper nameplates are handy. You might ask them to put their ratings or single word to describe themselves on the other side.

You may want to name your group, or the group may enjoy selecting a name for itself. Among the names I've encountered are Lunch Bunch, Book Bistro, Pizza and Pages, Lunch-n-Lit, Book Time Together, and Novel Ideas. I don't think it's an accident that several have references to food in their names. One group chose the name Aquinas in honor of St. Thomas Aquinas, who is the patron saint of students, universities, and books, among other things. Most groups don't have formal names.

Finally keep an eye on the time so that the group has time to select a book and date for the next meeting.

12. ASSIST THE GROUP IN MAKING THEIR NEXT BOOK CHOICE

You might want to play it safe and only use books that you've already read. On the other hand, one of my survey respondents, librarian Carlie Kraft, pointed out that by selecting books you haven't read, you can kill two birds with one stone — increasing your knowledge of young adult literature while working on your discussion program. Although you may be hesitant to take a chance on books you haven't read, you can avert nasty surprises by using the many online resources available to read about candidates you have in mind for book discussion. Take five or six books and do a quick booktalk at the end of the session. Let the group decide what to read next. Read the book descriptions or journal reviews from Amazon (www.amazon.com) or you might work from one of the excellent lists prepared by Jennifer Hulbert (www.readinggrants.com) or Cathy Young (teen angst books at: www.grouchy.com). If you're pressed for time grab a selection of books off of the new bookshelf and read the descriptions from the book covers. When I did this, a group selected a book that I considered poorly written and excessively shallow. In a word, I hated the book, but, to my surprise, everyone else in the group liked it. I have a prejudice against romances, but I know from experience and my master's research that most girls do enjoy romance and this particular book was a romance. It was an all, girls group, but we'd read many books that had very little or no romance. For me their favorable reaction to the book was a call to humility; even though I've been working with teens and reading teen literature for more than ten years, I still can fail to be in tune with teen perspectives, especially when my own prejudices come into play. So try to be aware of your prejudices and respect the preferences of the teens you serve.

Another consideration when choosing books is whether anyone will be offended by the choice — usually language and explicit sex or violence are the culprits. Some parents read book discussion selections before allowing their children to read them. Most librarians have had the experience of parents, refusing to allow their child to read specific books and attend discussions because the parents found something offensive in the book. All librarians need to be comfortable defending their choices. Titles for discussion should be selected based on the librarian's knowledge of, and experience with, the needs of their patrons and the larger community. Gwen Kistner of Amherst Main Library at Audubon, New York, wrote that a teacher stopped endorsing her book discussion group and giving extra credit for attendance because "she decided the books I was picking were too controversial or the subject matter was too heavy for her to continue to recommend my group without getting herself in trouble with the school. Too bad, because we had developed a great relationship" (survey response). Too bad, indeed.

Young adult literature addresses issues with which teens are very familiar and curious. When they encounter these issues on their own, they have only their own rather brief life experiences to help them process the information. A book discussion provides a format for them to express their feelings about controversial topics and form opinions based on exposure to various points of view. One would be very naïve to believe that teens don't encounter every issue addressed in young adult literature in the media, through friends, or in their personal lives.

If you have a regular group, you begin to know their preferences, but that doesn't mean you can always predict their reactions. I had a regular group member who was very sensitive to language, the use of curse words. I realized that I overlook that kind of language unless it is somehow incongruent or unrealistic. She was always surprising me: she would take the language in a book to task when I hadn't even noticed it. Certainly one of the wonders of book discussions is having a member point out something that you totally missed. It allows us to learn something about ourselves, where some of our blind spots are.

A young mother-daughter group that I hosted chose to read Jane Yolen's *Briar Rose*. It was the same group with the girl who was sensitive to language. Most of the teens in the group were younger teens, sixth and seventh graders. After reading the book, I became concerned about how they would react to references to gay sex. No one blinked an eye about that, but, of course, there were the usual complaints about language.

One of the rewards of having a regular group is that over time they begin to trust you and will read things they wouldn't have chosen on their own. My mother-daughter group used to routinely reject books with any hint of angst. They wanted happy endings, and if a little romance was thrown in, so much the better. After we'd been together for a year or so I learned to present some meatier books to them in a way that I thought would appeal to them. Once they'd read a couple of these books and enjoyed discussing them, they became more open to reading different kinds of books. You, as a leader, have a wonderful opportunity to gently expand the reading interests of your group members.

I recommend steering clear of classics because they are perceived to be the kind of books that are used and often overdone in classrooms. Also, there is so much great contemporary young adult literature available that I want to do everything I can to get it into the hands of teens. Librarians fill the niche between busy classroom teachers and teens stumbling around the stacks on their own. As Natalie Emiliani (Mt. Lebanon [Penn] Public Library,) states, "the fact that we are reading books they haven't heard about in school emphasizes the fact that we are doing this for fun, that this isn't some kind of trick to get them to read books they 'should' be reading." (survey response).

Many of the survey respondents reported that they, as group leaders, select the books used for book discussion programs without input from a group. In this case, the book is really the draw, and your publicity to attract new members uses the book as the hook. You may want to consider, however, that having been part of the decision may make them more committed to returning.

Many group leaders bring a selection of suggestions, get input from the group, and make the final decision. One of the respondents, Jackie Hemond from Simsbury (Conn.) Public Library takes a formal vote, which is a fun and eagerly anticipated part of her group's meetings. Often groups amicably agree among themselves on what to read next. I suggest taking five or six books and allowing the group to debate among themselves. Make sure that the selection is varied: a contemporary "problem" novel or two, a mystery, a biographical fiction, a fantasy, a book about another culture.

Try a collection of poetry or short stories. I was keen to try a story collection because I hadn't used one before. As I was preparing for a book discussion one evening, I noticed David Almond's *Counting Stars* on the top of a stack of new books on my desk. I grabbed it not remembering much from reading the reviews, except than that it was a collection of stories. I was much more familiar with the other books that I booktalked that evening, so it was a surprise when one of the teens immediately suggested we read Almond's book.

"I like the cover," she admitted. Others agreed. I agreed, also; it is an especially beautiful cover. Sometimes it seems that only a few publishers are aware of how important attractive covers are to teens. I recall a whole program dedicated to the importance of cover art presented at an American Library Association conference. Maybe sometime in the future I will skip the booktalks and we will select a book based solely on cover appeal!

I was book talking *Gina. Jamie. Father. Bear* by George Ella Lyon, and one teen said it reminded him of *Tuck Everlasting* by Natalie Babbitt. There was a sprinkle of conversation about the upcoming movie opening, so I suggested we all see the movie and read the book for our next meeting so that we could compare them. My suggestion was met with enthusiastic approval. While Tuck isn't exactly a teen book, the movie was being aggressively marketed to the teen audience, and I had added the book with the cover from the movie to my teen collection. Book and movie comparisons are a good change of pace for your discussion groups. If the title is available on DVD or video and you can get a copy with performance rights, you might consider showing the movie during your (extra long) meeting.

Tuck brings to mind that fact that older readers don't read some of the very thought-provoking children's books, like *Tuck Everlasting* or *The Giver* by Lois Lowery, that offer much to discuss and issues that might be thought of differently depending on the level of maturity of the reader. Just as a group may, on occasion, read an adult book like *Girl with a Pearl Earing* by Tracy Chevalier or *The Lovely Bones* by Alice Sebold (both of which teens ask for), so, too, it would be an interesting exercise to have your group read a "children's book" that they may have read several years earlier and talk about any changes in their interpretations. For example, a simple view of the ending of *The Giver* would be the literal interpretation of Jonas reaching his destination. A more sophisticated interpretation is that he has died and is entering the afterlife.

13. CONSIDER BOYS

In teen book-discussion groups, as well as adult groups, females tend to make up the majority. In her book, *The New York Public Library Guide to Reading Groups* (Saal, 1995), Rollene Saal suggests several reasons for this phenomenon. She writes that women are inclined to build networks of friends, so cooperating in groups is natural. She thinks that cooperation is a key to the gender difference, surmising that men are competitive by nature and less likely to be satisfied with the differing points of view. Men are resolution oriented.

Frustrated with my own lack of success in attracting boys to book discussions, I publicized a three-part series of summer book discussions for the adventurous. The "Blood and Guts" series was intended to arouse the interest of boys using outdoor adventure, sports, and war-related books. I had a small group that included three or four boys a couple of years ago. I learned that part of the draw for a couple of the group members was a romantic interest in another member. Maybe if boys realized that the book discussion's were a good place to meet girls, more would attend. One survey respondent reported that one boy regularly attended her all girl group, and that she thought he enjoyed being surrounded by girls. Smart boy. My own mixed group attendance dwindled as the core group got older, until I decided to try a mother-daughter book discussion instead. That has been going strong for two years. From time to time, I have tried to launch an additional, more general book discussion, but have been unsuccessful. "Blood and Guts" held to that disappointing pattern.

Guts by Gary Paulsen was to be the first in the series. I had to notify the one boy who registered that we were canceling this month's discussion and that I hoped to see him next month when we would discuss *Soldier X* by Don L. Wulffson. I thought that *Guts* would be a good first in the series because it's short and most teens are familiar with Paulsen's books. I got flyers to the schools and talked about it during my end-of-the-year visits. Real live boys expressed interest! Parents who saw my flyers in the library expressed interest in having their boys attend.

Experience with summer programs based on a series of books suggests that their success hinges on the first one, when you try to get the few who attend to bring friends to the next one. Summer has an amnesiac effect on teens. It's very unlikely that in July they'll still remember something you came to their school and talked about in May. My "Blood and Guts" never materialized.

According to survey responses my experience is not unusual. Except for a few flukes or unless there is a group of homeschoolers or you do book discussions at a school where students are chosen to participate, the numbers of boys who attend book discussions are slim.

If you are lucky enough to have a number of boys in your group, or a group of boys, compose questions that deal with concrete issues. In general, boys seem more willing to express that they liked particular episodes or characters or that they would like to do some of the things that the characters do rather than analyze motivations or talk about philosophical issues. On his Guys Read Web site(2002), Jon Scieszka notes that our society hasn't encouraged boys to express their feelings, so it follows that boys are less willing to discuss emotional aspects of books. Boys are action oriented. We might be more successful having a discussion while walking with boys rather than sitting.

Another unfortunate fact reported by Scieszka is that boys don't have an abundance of male role models in their reading lives. Most of their teachers and librarians are women.

My master's research showed that while girls may prefer female protagonists, they are willing to read about male characters, while boys are less likely to choose books with female main characters.

As already mentioned, the importance of food should not be overlooked, and it's a good idea to advertise refreshments on your flyers. Though teens in general are remarkable eaters, boys usually outdistance girls in this regard.

Several years ago, I had a free-for-all book discussion to celebrate teen Read Week. I asked teens to bring any book they wanted to talk about. There was an active teen advisory group that was composed mostly of boys at the time, and I persuaded them to come. We started a bit late because, perhaps typical of teen preparedness, some of the attendees had to scan the shelves for a title that they could talk about. A couple of them talked about the books that had movie adaptations they had seen. A couple of them grabbed comics or magazines. Some picked up books that they had been required to read in school. Although it was a bit impromptu, the result was that fifteen teens, mostly boys, talked about books for an hour in a main area of the library while adults did double takes. It remains my favorite Teen Read Week celebration.

One survey respondent (one of the flukes) had a regular discussion group of mostly boys. Two books they discussed were *Dinotopia* by Scott Ciencin and *There's a Hair in My Dirt* by Gary Larson. Graphic novels would be a good choice, also. Several survey respondents reported success in drawing boys with fantasy and science fiction: Tolkien, Pullman, the Redwall series, Harry Potter, *The Hitchhikers Guide to the Galaxy*. The "Guys Read" links to discussions on the Readerville Web site are mostly of this genre.

The good news is that efforts to entice boys to read are paying off. The books I talked about to promote my "Blood and Guts" discussion program flew off the shelf. The plethora of graphic novels now offered at most libraries and bookstores are huge draws for boys. The backlash that brought a majority of female protagonists in new fiction is shifting and the protogonists are now becoming more balanced between the sexes. The secret that librarians know is that boys *are* reading, perhaps more than ever. They may not want to talk about it, but they are reading.

The reasons boys don't participate in discussion groups may simply be biological. Differences in communication styles between the genders are well documented. Females like to talk about "what ifs" and are comfortable with unresolved issues. Males are big on resolution and problem solving. When a problem is solved, there's no point in talking about it any more.

As with girls, there are many demands on the time of boys. They generally read less than girls and have different reading interests than girls. Their language skills develop later, and they tend to have more problems reading. In addition to biology, boys also have to overcome social stigma that conspires against participation in book discussion groups. Discussion groups may be perceived as being for braniacs, nerds, or girls. The advice to discussion leaders: keep the door open, keep the food, and never pass up the opportunity to attract boys.

14. INVESTIGATE ALTERNATIVES

The post-Oprah world is a book friendly place. Other celebrities are following in her footsteps, promoting reading and book discussion to new heights of coolness. In addition to what most of us think of as a book discussion group, several creative alternatives have surfaced.

Entire communities are reading and coming together to discuss books, as in the North Coast Neighbors Share a Book program sponsored by the Cleveland Area Metropolitan Library System (CAMLS), a cooperative that exists to assist member libraries. This year libraries throughout the region held discussions and programs related to the 2002 selection, *To Kill a Mockingbird*. Some programs showed the movie, and followed it with a comparative discussion of the book and movie. Teens and adults were involved in the programs. The CAMLS Web site (www.camls.org) has information about the program, information and links about moderating book discussions, and an outline for setting up teen coffeehouse discussions. The community voted on the selection for 2003 at local libraries and selected Ray Bradbury's *Fahrenheit 451* for 2003. Other cities and communities are hosting similar programs.

The community-wide programs are attractive in that they have the potential to bring together adults and teens. Pat Schnack, formerly of South East Junior High in Iowa City, implemented another innovative, intergenerational program. "Partners in Reading" involved teens and the greater community in reading and discussing books. Volunteers from the community, including business people, police officers, firefighters, club members, and seniors, were paired with a student and corresponded about one or more books during a five-week period. Students selected the books and their partners agreed to find copies. Participants wrote reactions and questions for their partners in a notebook that was transported back and forth once a week. Partners benefited from the intergenerational exchange not only in sharing an enriching reading experience but also in gaining a new understanding and appreciation for the older or younger generation. In her survey response, Pat shared many testimonials that addressed the benefits of the experience for those involved. Kudos to Pat for conceiving and facilitating an exciting, rewarding alternative book discussion experience. She is now retired, but during her last year at South East, 300 community volunteers and 300 students participated. Pat hopes that her colleagues will continue the program. Electronic correspondence might be an option for making the notebook exchange easier.

Librarian Laurel Erchul of Cuyahoga County (Ohio) Public Library piloted another innovative book discussion program. Reading teachers from her local middle school contacted her to help create a grant-funded supplemental reading experience for "at-risk" readers. Laurel visited the school four days per week during study halls and met with a group of sixth graders and a group of eighth graders selected by teachers. The first session was spent selecting a book that group would read and discuss, but Laurel quickly found that that independently reading a whole book in time for the meeting was beyond their capabilities. In subsequent sessions she used essays, newspaper stories, short stories, poems, and picture books that were read aloud during the session and discussed. There are many picture books that can be appreciated by audiences years beyond the typical picture-book crowd. Laurel used *Baseball Saved Us* by Ken Mochizuki and *Squids Will Be Squids* by Jon Scieszka. Laurel moderated the program for six months, and then she was promoted to a position at another library. The enthusiasm of the participants and having given them a positive literary experience made the project rewarding for Laurel. One of the teachers reported that skills improved in the participants. One boy's father commented that previously he hadn't enjoyed reading with his son because of the halting manner in which his son read; the improvement in his son's reading made reading together a pleasurable experience. This literary endeavor was successful on many levels, including as an example of school-public library cooperation (survey response).

Another imaginative means of conducting a book discussion was conceived of by librarian Maggie Snow of Austin (Minn.) Public Library. For her Saturday Serials program, she had her local paper print a book chapter each Saturday, then once a month her group met to discuss four chapters. She commented that she would like to do it again, perhaps as a weekly, instead of monthly program (survey response). This is an especially creative way of dealing with the problem of having enough copies for everyone in your group.

In their article, "Book Club on a Budget," Linda Jaeger and Sheila N. Demetriadis (2002) found another creative way of dealing with having enough copies. They decided to hold theme discussions in which participants read different books on a specific theme, like black history, instead of all reading the same book.

The book and movie comparison is a viable alternative to traditional book discussions. Showing a movie attracts those who haven't read or finished the book and allows them to discuss the salient issues addressed in the book, which are often translated adequately from book to movie.

Many discussion leaders mentioned having what I call a reading free-for-all, in which participants bring a book they've enjoyed and share it with the group. It's not a book discussion per se, but a book discussion group can easily start from this kind of a program.

It's good to remember that even if you've been disappointed by unfruitful efforts at starting a book discussion group, there are always new things to try. Be creative and willing to take a risk and try out something for the first time. Don't be afraid to think "outside the box."

15. EXPLORE ONLINE RESOURCES

The Internet is an awesome resource for book discussion groups. Adult groups fare best with a wealth of prepared reading group guides available from publishers' Web sites, bookstore sites, and other sites dedicated to book groups. The young adult reading group guide is still a rarity, but more are being published than ever before, and there are some other resources that can help to make formulating questions easier.

For a teen discussion group, the Internet is most helpful for finding background information about the author, subject or time period, and in looking for good discussion books. Thematic lists of reviews by young adult literature mavens, lists of award books, and library and teen sites with reviews by teen abound online.

Online book discussion groups allow teens a place to express their opinions about what they read. These sites usually have a time period when a particular title is open for discussion. Users can also respond to archives. Usually the group leader posts a question to get the discussion started, but users may post any thoughts they have about the book. The most successful online "discussions" lead users to respond to each other. Many of the online discussion sites flounder. The immediacy that comes with being in a live group is missing, so it's hard to sustain interest. Missing also is the dynamic that comes from human interaction. It's almost a misnomer to call these online groups discussion groups in the same sense as a group of live, warm bodies. The Chapter a Day book club sends a chapter to members via email each day. There is very little posting by teens happens with this group, and understandably. I know that trying to keep up with this daily dose of reading quickly overwhelmed me.

REVIEWS AND BOOKLISTS

Many public libraries have Web sites with young adult pages including book reviews and/or booklists. An especially nice one is the Multnomah County (Ore.) Library site: www.multcolib.org/outer/books.html.

leep.lis.uiuc.edu/seworkspace/rebrenner/304LE/gn/index.html
     graphic novels reviews and info.

www.ala.org/yalsa/booklists
     American Library Association's Young Adult Best Books, Award books, Quick picks, etc.

www.bn.com/
     Barnes & Noble online bookstore, reviews including *Horn Book* and *Alan Review*, reader reviews.

http://www.bookloon.com.HandHTML/teens.html/
     a hodgepodge of interesting teen reading related stuff including a significant collection of book reviews written by teens.

www.hbook.com/mag.shtml/
     the *Horn Book Magazine*, first-rate reviews of the best in young adult and children's literature.

www.grouchy.com/angst/
    Cathy Young's topical reviews written with "heart, humor and a careful eye," links to cool author sites.

tln.lib.mi.us/~amutch/jen/index.html/
    Jennifer Hubert Swan's most excellent site, clever topical lists and reviews, links.

www.mcdougallittell.com/disciplines/lang.cfm/
    Novel guides with summaries and related activities intended for the classroom, author profiles.

www.penguinputnam.com/statis/packages/us/yreaders/guysread/
    A literacy initiative by Jon Scieszka; a great resource for supporting boy readers.

www.teenreads.com/
    Reviews, a large selection of author interviews, reading group guides (adult books for teens and classics).

www.amazon.com/
    Online bookstore, reviews from *Publishers Weekly*, *School Library Journal*, and *Booklist*, customer reviews, customer lists.

www.powells.com/
    Online bookstore, excerpts from reviews including *Kirkus* and *Horn Book*, author interviews (mostly adult).

novelist4.epnet.com/default.asp/
    A subscription* database, lists, readalikes, and some discussion guides for bona fide young adult literature.

AUTHOR INFORMATION

ccpl.carr.org/authco/index.htm/
    Links to author sites.

sharyn.org/author.htm/
    Comprehensive list of links to author web pages.

www.scils.rutgers.edu/~kvander/AuthorSite/authorc.html/
    Extensive links to author pages.

www.authors4teens.com/
    A subscription* database, Don Gallo's incisive and comprehensive interviews including photos.

RESOURCES FOR CREATING QUESTIONS

novelist4.epnet.com/default.asp/
    A subscription* database, lists, readalikes, and some discussion guides for bona fide Young Adult literature.

---

*BY SUBSCRIPTION (Often available at public libraries. Some libraries also offer home use of their databases for cardholders.)

www.multcoplib.org/talk/guides/html/
> A selection of children's and teen reading group guides developed by Multnomah County Public Library.

www.readinggroupguides.com/
> At last look this site has 960 available guides, no specific YA titles but some adult titles that would appeal to teens. There is a sidebar link to Teens that doesn't go anywhere. Keep checking.

www.harpercollins.com/hc/readres/
> Guides to some "perennial classics," but basically guides to adult books.

www.randomhouse.com/teachers/guides/
> Many guides useful for developing discussion questions, author info.

ONLINE BOOK DISCUSSIONS

rite.ed.qut.edu.au/oz-teachernet/projects/book-rap/
> Australian online book club.

www.chapteraday.com/
> The many club choices include a young adult chapter-a-day sent to your e-mail with questions.

www.geocities/com/adbooks/
> listserv-type book discussion venue, booklists, links to author websites.

www.readerville.com/WebX?13@210.Q0Fxa2YegWG.1@f024863www.read/
> A fiesta of book discussions including Young Adult and Guys Read offerings; easy and attractive with significant activity.

www.yread.org/
> Drew Carey funded online book group launched and maintained by Cleveland Public Library.

Part II

THE GUIDES

The following guides are intended to familiarize you with the books so that you can determine whether you want to use them with your group and also to provide you with ready-made, provocative questions (many already tested) for your discussion. Themes, main characters, and genres are included along with comments to help you guide the discussions. You'll find ideas for exploring some questions in greater depth and suggested resources to supplement discussions. You'll want to pick and choose the questions that resonate with you and your group. Remember to let the group dictate the order. So, choose a comfortable place, bring the refreshments, and enjoy.

1

THE ADVENTURES OF BLUE AVENGER
BY NORMA HOWE

Bibliographic information: Holt, 1999; 230 pages.

Themes: Identity, fate versus free will, the rewards of performing good deeds, responsibility, gun control, chaos theory/determinism.

Genre: Fable.

Main characters: David Schumacher, Blue Avenger

Tips: There may be teens who are uncomfortable with some of the deep philosophical issues. While the story is entertaining and provides some excellent points for discussion, some readers won't like the implausibility of the story. You may want to explain allegory and fable.

SYNOPSIS:

David Schumacher decides to change his name and change his life. He assumes the identity of Blue Avenger and pursues his goals of helping those in need, discovering something new and wonderful as well as a perfect lemon meringue, solving the "gun problem" and the problem of people who can't afford medical care, and figuring out whether we are "truly the masters of our fate or merely actors on a stage, playing our parts in a predetermined cosmic drama over which we have no control." Blue manages to reach most of his goals and win the heart of Omaha Nebraska Brown to boot. Howe has rendered a smart and highly humorous story that invites readers to ponder some very big questions.

DISCUSSION QUESTIONS/LEADER POINTS

1. When David Schumacher decides to change his life and his name, he chooses the name Blue Avenger after a comic book character that he created. He wants to be as righteous as his character. What name would you choose and what aspect of your personality or aspirations would it reflect?

Teens are in the thick of defining themselves and making decisions about who they want to be in the future. Deciding what name they'd choose might take a little more thought than an on-the-spot question. It might be a good question to give before they read the book so that they have time to think about it.

2. How would you react to Blue Avenger if he were one of your classmates? How do people react to someone who is in-your-face different?

The character of Blue is nerd to the degree of cool and would have a tough time getting respect in most American high schools. Wearing his costume to school, the formal way he speaks, his obsession with making the perfect lemon meringue pie, and even his decision not to spend a penny of his reward check on himself make Blue an unusual teen. He is quite entertaining, however, and perhaps a more salient question is whether teens would *like* to have someone like Blue in their school.

3. What would you do if someone sent you a large check for an act of heroism like Blue's rescue of the principal?

After the fun of sharing the answers, ask whether it's appropriate to reward such an act, or if it is our duty as fellow human beings to look out for and protect one another.

4. Blue tells Omaha that he wants to help those in need and do it secretly whenever possible because the Blue Avenger wants no rewards. Is it possible to perform a good act without reward?

This question is meant to expose the reward implicit in the act. It's impossible to separate the two, whether the act is altruistically motivated or not. It makes us feel good to help others. Why does this happen? Does it make us feel like "good" people, or is it because we are all part of the same interwoven mesh of life? Why are people moved to rescue total strangers? Maybe when circumstances reduce us to our most basic level, we spontaneously realize we're part of one another.

5. After describing Omaha's relationship with and parting from Travis on page 45, the author writes, "If the cause of occasional uncontrolled fits of anger is unknown, does that mean they don't have a cause?" What do you think?

Can anything exist independent of other things? We may not know the causes, but everything is defined by what it's not. Without the "not" things, there would be no thing.

6. Blue and Omaha struggle with the question of whether we have free will or, are acting out a predestined script or as Omaha suggests, acting according to

some genetic pattern. What examples from the book support these ideas? In your experience, what notion seems most probable? Why?

The question of responsibility versus genetics is very intriguing. Do people act abnormally because their brains have abnormalities, or does the way people act change their brain patterns? If, as one of Omaha's clippings claims, alcoholism is genetic, then why are some alcoholics able to quit drinking? If they don't, are they being irresponsible?

On page 191, when Omaha says that nothing is anyone's fault, Josh asks if he can do anything he wants and have it not be his fault. Omaha responds by asking why people don't say, "I won't take credit for the good I do and I won't blame others for the bad they do?" She's talking about a Buddhist kind of acceptance and lack of ego—no judgment. We suffer because of ego and attachment. Ego makes us want to distinguish ourselves from others to make ourselves feel good. Attachment makes us want to make judgments about the actions of others. In discussing Hitler, Omaha admits that Hitler was an insane maniac. When Blue asks whether he wasn't responsible for the atrocities, Omaha counters with references to people who resisted and did the right thing. Ironically, Hitler was the catalyst for people acting with remarkable goodness.

7. Blue's act of kindness to Mike expands to include others. Can you think of other examples in the book, or in your life, where a kindness has had similar repercussions?

Kindness has a snowball effect. When you smile at someone, that person smiles back. Often the smile gets passed on and on, positively touching each person in a string of people. Blue's kindness to Mike touches Dr. Alvarez, which then causes him to extend kindness to many others. Those will then touch others and so on. Here's a case for practicing kindness. It multiples and makes the world a kinder place, like in the movie (or book) *Pay It Forward*.

8. How do Omaha's thoughts about fate help her to deal with her father's desertion and her brother's crime? Does it change how you feel about someone if you believe they are doing exactly what they're supposed to?

Omaha's beliefs make her accepting and nonjudgmental. She may not like the actions of these two, but their actions are a results of their own karma and circumstances. She can either suffer by thinking about the injustice of this, or accept it. Which is preferable?

9. Would you agree with Omaha that guns are improper toys? Why? Does the fact that we have toy guns show that American's are desensitized to violent images?

Toy guns certainly don't make criminals, but when one thinks about how many toys exist so that children can imitate adults, it's a dubious choice for a toy. Remind your group that, on the other hand, violent play may provide a harmless release for aggressive tendencies. Are there better ways to do this?

10. The author uses an allknowing (omniscient) point of view at times—we learn what is happening simultaneously in many places. What do you think her purpose is in doing this?

Howe has written humorously and skillfully about the relatedness of seemingly unrelated events, in other words, chaos theory. Perhaps the question isn't really whether we have free will, but how the free will of others affects us, or how the flap of a butterfly's wing can cause an earthquake on the other side of the world. Everyone can think of examples of how, when one looks back on a series of events, it's easy to see things that contributed to a final outcome that didn't seem related at the time or seemed highly coincidental.

11. The author maintains that "millions and billions and trillions of real-life 'coincidences' happen every day, but when they happen in books or movies, are blindly labeled 'contrivances of plot'." Can you think of examples from your own life that in retrospect seem too unlikely to be believed?

Here's an example from my life. My four-year-old daughter was taking an afternoon bath. When she got out of the tub, she asked if she could take a couple of the toy animals she'd been playing with in the tub to her room. I said okay and she dried them off and put them on her bed. I didn't notice which she'd taken. Later, we were walking around the neighborhood and stopped in front of a house where we always stop because they have a huge, old tree stump in the front yard where a changing collection of items is displayed, altar-like. There are crystals, a tiny Buddhist stupa, a statue of Shiva, candles, a miniature potted cactus. Today we observed that two small toy zebras had been added. Later when I put my daughter to bed, I saw the animals she had taken from the bath: two small toy zebras! If that wasn't enough, I was thinking about the "coincidence" the next day at work while waiting for a job to finish at the photocopier. When I looked down at the machine, I noticed that there are two zebras on the front of the photocopier.

Readers will think of similar coincidence as well as dramatic ones that have been in the news, like the person who has a series of incidents that make him late, and later he finds his tardiness has kept him from an accident or plane crash.

12. How do you think Blue's bullet exchange program would work?

Blue's bullet exchange program is on par with John Lennon's "Imagine." Teens will cynically and quickly point out that not all people would turn in their bullets, but what a nice world it would be if they would. You might ask what if guns were outlawed, allowing the group to reach the conclusion that guns will still be attainable for criminals.

13. What do you think of the way the author handles expletives?

Some readers will think that Howe's to use of symbols instead of expletives is "annoying" and "dopey," as some members of my group so eloquently stated. It may, however, make the book more appropriate for younger readers, which may be offset by the condom incident. The condom incident is very innocent though. It centers on the question of whether or not to have a diagram of how to put on a condom printed on the front page of the student newspaper, which Blue deftly averts.

The decision not to print the graphic condom instructions in the paper provides an opportunity to discuss the difference between sensationalism and good reporting, and that accusations of censorship shouldn't compromise that.

14. At the end of the book, we find Blue on the brink of reading something that would set into motion a series of events that could unite Omaha with her father. What do you think will happen next?

At the end of the story Blue is literally wrestling with the issue of whether he has the power to choose or is merely a puppet in a larger plan. The reader is left hanging. Will he go to sleep or read five more pages and set into motion a series of events that reunite Omaha with her father?

2

AMANDINE by ADELE GRIFFIN

Bibliographic information: Hyperion, 2001; 220 pages.

Themes: Loneliness, vulnerability to charisma, need to shock and control, uninvolved parents, moving, the irrevocable damage of slander, art as social or antisocial.

Genre: Realistic fiction.

Main characters: Delia and Amandine, both 14.

Tips: Suitable for tweens. High on girl appeal.

SYNOPSIS:

Shy and insecure, Delia feels lonely in her new, suburban school, but soon she is befriended by flamboyant Amandine, a gifted artist who keeps a notebook of drawings of the ugliest things she's ever seen, a dancer and actress who can improvise skits at the drop of a hat and can assume the identity of any character, a teller of tales too tall to believe. Delia's uneasiness about her friend is validated when Amandine plays a cruel trick on their mutual friend and blames Delia. When Delia stands up for herself, she learns just how disturbed and brutal Amandine can be. Amandine claims that Delia's father kissed her when he gave her a ride into town, striking a blow that changes the lives of Delia's family and eventually causes them to move.

DISCUSSION QUESTIONS/LEADER POINTS

1. What makes Delia so vulnerable? Do you think she had reasons early on to be wary of Amandine? Why or why not?

Amandine provides a good starting point for a discussion on trusting one's intuition. Being new and having low self-esteem makes Delia vulnerable. Although Delia is often uneasy about her new friend, she is desperate to have a friend and is an easy target for Amandine's charm. Here's a chance to talk about not mistaking charisma for sincerity, and how charismatic people can use their charm to manipulate others.

2. What do you think about Delia's mother's effort to control Delia's diet? How can a parent encourage a child to lose weight without hurting her self-esteem?

Offering children healthy foods and encouraging exercise are some ways that a parent might encourage a child to lose weight. Delia isn't obese, and her mother may be unduly concerned. Health is more important than someone's view of ideal weight. This is an especially tricky subject with girls who see, and are tempted to try to imitate, impossible standards in the media.

3. Why is it so easy for Delia to make up a brother?

Not only does Delia's loneliness make her vulnerable to Amandine, but it also makes it easy for her to manufacture a brother. She must have imagined many times how life had been if her brother had lived. Ask any "onlys" in the group whether they've fantasized about having a sibling.

4. Why would someone want to draw the ugliest things she ever (or never) saw?

Amandine is obviously starved for attention. Her parents don't pay any attention to her. One way she gets attention is to try to shock people. It's shocking to collect ugly images. It certainly sets one apart.

5. What motivates Amandine to act the way she does?

Amandine's parents are almost criminally self-involved. Dedicated to their art and offbeat lifestyle, their house shared by Amandine's mother's boyfriend, they don't care for each other or Amandine. Amandine has to be extreme just to get noticed. They don't seem real—just bad examples of parents who aren't involved enough in their child's life.

6. Delia calls Amandine's house the "Frightful Fun House" after a pop-up book she had when she was younger. Is this an appropriate name for Amandine's house? Why or why not?

While the nontraditional lifestyle and freedom Amandine enjoys in her house may seem attractive, it represents a lack of caring, so it is ultimately unenviable—a fun place to visit, but you wouldn't want to live there.

7. Why doesn't Delia tell her parents about Amandine's house?

Teens will likely relate to giving scant information about a friend's house for fear of being forbidden to return. Delia's parents are traditional and might frown on the liberal life-style practiced at the Frightful Fun House.

8. When Delia tries to blow fuzz off of Amandine's cheek when she's sleeping, Amandine says that Delia'a weird, that there's something wrong with her (p.97). Why does Amandine react this way, and what is wrong with Delia?

It's a tender expression, and so it's alien to Amandine and makes her uncomfortable. She strikes out to escape the tender moment. What's wrong with Delia is that she allows Amandine to make her question her own honest expression. Again, she is a victim of low self-esteem.

9. Are there any similarities between Delia's parents and Amandine's?

Like Amandine's parents, Delia's parents are lacking in empathy. Delia's mother is critical of her. They are so dazzled by Amandine that they ignore Delia when both girls are present. Both girls suffer from not enough positive support and attention, but it affects the girls in different ways. Amandine has a need to control others, and Delia with her lack of self-esteem becomes a victim. Ask readers which set of parents they would prefer and why.

10. Why does Amandine get so angry when Mary won't draw the ugliest thing she ever saw?

Of course, this is a control issue. Amandine has to be in control of the others. Also, in learning what the ugliest thing one can imagine is gives her even more control; she learns about someone's fears and can use that against the person.

12. Why does Delia take things?

Delia's only self-assertive act is her habit of stealing, and even her thievery is petty, things of little value.

13. Do you think that Delia's parents could have done anything to defuse the damage done by Amandine's lie? Were they hasty in their decision to move?

The most intriguing point of the book is how a simple lie can destroy lives, even if it is retracted. The seed of doubt always remains, especially in the case of inappropriate behavior by an adult toward a child. Ask readers if they think male teachers have to be more careful than female teachers in touching students. Has our culture become paranoid about touching others in some situations?

14. Delia asks Amandine why she doesn't use her talent by being in plays, designing the yearbook, and so forth (p.217), so that other people could see it. Amandine replies that she always has an audience. Is this true? How is the way Amandine shares her talent different from the way artists and performers share their talent?

Amandine uses her talents for purely selfish reasons. Artists who share their work are often motivated in their work by a sense of contributing to society. It's an outward rather than an inward expression. Amandine's sharing has to do with advancing her own agenda.

15. Mrs. Gogglio tells Delia, "Nobody learns anything from being happy." Do you agree or disagree? Why?

Mrs. Gogglio's wisdom in saying that no one learns anything from being happy is a reminder of how we learn the most and grow the most from overcoming adversity — or at least we have a great opportunity to do so. Seeing unwelcome events as challenges or opportunities is a skill we would all do well to practice.

3

BACKWATER by JOAN BAUER

Bibliographic information: Putnam's, 1999; 185 pages.

Themes: Independence, family expectations, the courage to be different, facing fears, the pros and cons of living outside society.

Genre: Realistic fiction.

Main characters: Ivy Breedlove, 16. Aunt Jo, the nontraditional, black sheep of Ivy's conservative family.

Tips: Bauer has created some interesting, strong female characters. There is a lot of humor in the book and some romance. Jack's humanity is refreshing. He has his own fears to overcome. Some readers may find the appearance of Jack and Mountain Mama when Ivy is crossing the ice a little too coincidental, but will enjoy the tension of the scene. Ivy's deprecating sense of humor can be annoying at times, but it's hard not to cheer her on when she faces and overcomes her fears.

SYNOPSIS:

Family expectations run high in the Breedlove family and toward the legal profession. Deviants are considered odd, possibly crazy like Aunt Jo, who bucked tradition and became a hermit in the Adirondack Mountains. Sixteen-year-old Ivy has a passion for history and becomes interested in her wayward aunt. She suspects they have more in common than their looks and their last names. Ivy embarks on a quest to find her aunt and finds out a lot about herself, as well. An accident and a heroic rescue reunite the wounded (doubly) Jo with the rest of the family. Transformed by her experience, Ivy is able to assert herself and demand the right to choose her own path.

DISCUSSION QUESTIONS/LEADER POINTS

1. Ivy is plagued by her father's expectation that she will become a lawyer. How important should family expectations be in considering your future plans?

Most teens will agree that career decisions should be left up to them. A parent's role is to expose children to various opportunities and help them develop their innate talents, but the ultimate decision must be the child's. Ask your group how they would handle a father like Ivy's, who tries to exert too much control? How can you distinguish between advice and control?

2. Fiona says, "When you've mastered time, you've mastered life." Is this true? Is it possible to master time?

Time is beyond our control and the best-laid plans are often set off course by unforeseen events. Readers will recognize Fiona as a control freak who misses some of the best things in life. Introduce the fact that thinking about time takes one out of the moment.

3. When Ivy sees the wreaths that Jo has left on her grandparents' graves, she remembers a quote by Georgia O'Keefe: "Nobody sees a flower really—it's so small. We haven't time and to see takes time, like to have a friend takes time." Do we take time to really see things? How would your life change if you took the time to really see things? How does this statement contrast with Fiona's idea of time?

The O'Keefe quote refers to giving things our full attention. Bring photos of extreme closeup photographs to illustrate this point. Common things are unrecognizable because we don't usually look at them that closely. It takes time to see details just like it takes time to know someone and cultivate a friendship.

4. Mountain Mama tells Ivy how she experienced being in the woods. she "Always felt more like myself than at any other moment," (p. 78). Is there a place where you feel this way?

While some readers won't be able to name a certain place where they feel more themselves, they will be able to think of an activity that produces that feeling. Ask them if they've experience "flow," the total absorption in an activity so that the mind's chatter seems to stop.

5. Mountain Mama also says that being in the woods has taught her not to be afraid of the unknown, and that is her definition of what makes a person free. Do you agree with her statement? How does fear create limits or barriers?

The experience of doing something frightening and the sense of freedom and elation it brings is an experience most people have had. Fear can keep life small and keep one from discovering talents and pleasures. Everyone is afraid of saying the wrong thing at times. Teens probably have that fear more often than older people. Ask your group what it would be like if they never feared saying the wrong thing again. How would it change their lives?

6. Is Jo crazy? Why do you or why do you not think so? Jo says that the best piece of advice she was given was to cultivate peace. How do you think one would go about cultivating peace?

Eccentric is probably a more accurate description of Jo than crazy. Quieter teens will be more sympathetic toward Jo, while the more extroverted will find her behavior in the range of strange to downright nuts. Compare Jo's life and the life of a contemplative and her wood carving to meditation. Her carving helps her to cultivate peace as do her birds. Many religious orders care for others by running hospitals, shelters, hospices, and so forth. Jo finds peace in caring for her birds.

The birds may bring some interesting comments. Readers (like my group) might wonder whether Jo's cabin was filled with excrement. Her dubbing herself the mayor of Backwater and creating a hospital and chapel will make some readers question her mental health, but it's really not very different from the way some people treat their pets. When I discussed this book one, member of the group brought a snapshot of herself with a wild bird sitting on her hand. She did swallow during the encounter, but it didn't upset the bird, thus disproving Jo's theory.

Most teens will find it surprising that someone would choose to live alone in the mountains as Jo does and have no idea what's going on in the world. Depending on the sophistication of the group, this could open the door for a philosophical discussion on how much reality is shaped by media and whether it's important it is to have information about things that will never directly affect you. Jo lives in the same world as the other characters do. Does it matter that Jo is unaware of the latest disaster? Would anything be gained by her knowledge of current events? Would anything be lost? On the other hand, the other characters have no knowledge of the events of Jo's world. Why is it more important to know what Nicole Kidman wore to the Golden Globes than that a creature gave birth in the woods? Do the events witnessed by some people have more weight than those witnessed by others, or if a tree falls in the forest and nobody hears it. …The subject may also spawn a discussion of how our society suffers from information overload, that people actually suffer a great deal of stress because they feel compelled to keep up with too much information.

7. Why do you think the ritual Jo and Ivy perform after mother's death is so healing? How do traditional death and burial customs help or hurt the bereaved?

Rituals honor significant people or events and are a basic human desire. The ritual that Jo and Ivy share after Ivy's mother's death is beautiful and gives Ivy needed, age. appropriate and needed closure. The freedom of the flying birds are a beautiful symbol for death and freedom. Do people adhere to death and burial customs that seem bizarre or disturbing because of tradition? For example, wouldn't it be more comforting to view photographs of the dead as they were rather than viewing their empty bodies that look so unlike them?

8. How does Ivy's quest change her?

In facing fear and discovering self-reliance, Ivy gains the confidence to steer her own course. Ask the group if they think part of what she learned came from being quiet and looking carefully.

4

BEYOND THE BURNING TIME
by KATHRYN LASKY

Bibliographic information: Blue Sky Press, 1994; 272 pages.

Themes: Mob mentality, man's inhumanity toward man, fear and superstition, the desire to blame.

Genre: Historical fiction.

Main character: Mary Chase, 12.

Tips: This book is a natural choice to accompany the study of this dark period in American history. It brings life to the well-researched facts. Advise readers to visit *National Geographic's* excellent, interactive Web site and find out if they would have survived being accused of witchcraft (www.nationalgeographic.com/features/97/salem/). Discovery also has a simple, attractive source of information (school.discovery.com/schooladventures/salemwitchtrials/story/index.html), which includes a short video and many useful links relating to the period and the book.

SYNOPSIS:

In 1691, when a strange malady strikes young girls in Salem Village, accusations of witchcraft begin to fly. When Mary Chase's independent mother is accused and sentenced to hang, Mary becomes determined to rescue her.

DISCUSSION QUESTIONS/LEADER POINTS

1. What factors contributed to the escalation of the witch-hunt?

There's a wealth of information on the factors that may have contributed to the Salem witch-hunt. These factors include economic hardships experienced by the village in contrast to the wealthier Salem Town. Puritan ethics and a desire to explain the hardships as having roots in lack of piety were also significant. Are there similarieties between what happened and the ancient religious practice of human sacrifice? Once the seed was planted, fear played a major role in the ensuing hysteria.

2. Why do you think that Tituba confessed?

Tituba is an interesting character and her confession prompts several theories. She was famous for telling stories. She may have been simple enough not to understand the consequences of her story spinning. She may have been mad. She may have been trying to provoke and scare her accusers.

3. Why do you think that the "afflicted" girls lied? Do you think that they realized the consequences of their actions? Should they be held accountable?

At first, the girls who started the hysteria were probably thrilled by their ability to stir up trouble and to get attention; then it was too late to turn back. Ask readers whether they have ever embellished the truth and had it spin out of control.

4. Was Gilly treated too harshly when he was caught looking in Virginia's window?

Virginia's reaction to Gilly's peeping seems, perhaps, a little out of character. Ask readers if the author might have used the incident to show the increasing tension and mistrust sweeping the town.

5. How can you explain the prosecutors' ability to ignore evidence that seemed to disprove the accusations of witchcraft, for example, George Burroughs' reciting the Lord's Prayer flawlessly, or the "witch's spirit" not being drawn back into Virginia when she touched the afflicted girls at her trial?

The prosecutors were so bent on getting convictions that they lost sight of the truth. Remind readers how many innocent people have been on death row.

6. Were there characters about whom you wanted more information? Should the author have supplied clear motivations for the characters' actions?

The motivations of those involved makes for interesting discussion. It's very difficult to understand how people could have acted in the way they did, accusing neighbors and sentencing them to death, incarcerating even a four-year-old. Lasky doesn't develop the minor characters enough to hint at their motivations. As when reading the historical record, we can only guess their true motivations.

7. Could something like what happened in Salem happen today? Can you think of examples of similar events in history?

It's easy to think something like this wouldn't happen today, but readers will easily recall modern examples like the Japanese internment and McCarthyism.

8. The author paid careful attention to historical records in telling the story. How did this affect readability?

Lasky's meticulous attention to historical facts and details weighs down the story, not that it makes the book less interesting or useful, but the it is a bit slow at times. Also there are a multitude of characters — many with similar names — and the scant details don't make them memorable. Still, it's a fascinating story and an important one.

9. Are Virginia's rescue and future believable? What lasting effects do you think her experience will have on her?

Virginia's rescue is the most exciting part of the story. The details of the physical effects of her internment are chilling. One might guess that she would suffer some kind of post-traumatic stress. Her experience certainly could make her cynical about human goodness.

10. Are the events of the Salem witch-hunt relevant for people today? How should we acknowledge them?

It's appropriate to acknowledge and mourn the victims. There are memorials to those killed during the witch hunt. I was moved just reading their names as they appeared on my computer screen. As with other human atrocities, we need to acknowledge the human potential for evil, lest we forget.

5

BLACK MIRROR
by NANCY WERLIN

Bibliographic information: Dial, 2001; 249 pages.

Themes: Self-esteem, guilt, suicide, responsibility to others, the influence of assumptions on point of view.

Genre: Mystery.

Main character: Frances Leventhal, 16.

Tips: Readers may find some elements of the story a little convoluted, but there's plenty of action, and the plot is compelling enough to hold the attention of teens. It's not predictable. Though incidental to the story, some readers may be offended by Frances' marijuana smoking or her finding condoms with her brother's things.

SYNOPSIS:

Outsider Frances Leventhal is most comfortable alone or with her art. She's a scholarship student in an exclusive prep school. What's more, she even looks different, half-Japanese and half-Jewish, looking not quite either. The only person she has ever felt close to was her brother, and now he's dead of an apparently deliberate heroin overdose. Could she have become so self-involved that she didn't notice Daniel was suicidal? When she is asked to work with the charity that Daniel was active in, Frances finds that things are not what they seem, and that Daniel just may have been murdered.

DISCUSSION QUESTIONS/LEADER POINTS

1. What makes Frances an outsider? Is it her choice?

The comments made by Frances' grandmother and the women in the grocery store have left an indelible mark on her; she feels like a freak. Her mixed heritage and her economic status further set her apart from her prep school classmates. Frances lacks support and attention from the adults in her life; she is left to fend for herself with her wounded self-esteem. It's easy to see why she would feel different from her classmates. She's smart enough to know that there are things she could do to fit in, but it's not in her nature.

2. When James says that Daniel was responsible for his own actions, Frances responds by asking if that was Cain's philosophy (p.38). Does Frances have some responsibility for Daniel's death?

Frances' reference to Cain and Abel lends itself to an ethical discussion of when one is responsible for others and when responsibility belongs to the individual. If James were dealing drugs, who has the greater responsibility, James or the buyer? Frances feels guilty for not noticing that her brother was suicidal. Tell your group that it's very common for friends and families of suicides to feel responsible for missing some clue. How are James' and Frances' responsibilities different?

3. James tells Frances not to create opportunities for violence for then it will occur (p.62). Do you agree? How does the world answer violent acts?

Spark the discussion on creating opportunities for violence with examples like road rage or the Middle Eastern conflict, where retaliation escalates violence. Is it ever correct to answer violence with violence? Doesn't that just add to the violence in the world? How can violence be transformed?

4. What impression do you get of Buddhism from this book?

Daniel and his mother manipulate Buddhist ideas to suit their own needs. Their mother justifies her selfishness. In his bitterness, Daniel cynically parodies her. Ask readers for other examples of how people use religion to justify irreligious actions.

5. In discussing Picasso with Ms. Wiles, Frances realizes, "If you think you already know what you're looking at, then you can't possibly see that something else is really there." What things are not what they seem in the book? Can you think of examples from your own life when someone was different from what he or she seemed?

Ms. Wiles comment (question 5) will bring a lot of examples from your group. Ms. Wiles and James aren't what they seem. Unity isn't what it seems. Daniel's death isn't what it seems. Although Frances thinks that James is an adult at one point, when she sees him eating French fries, she concludes that he really is a teen. Frances thinks she's unattractive because of comments others made years earlier; she is unable to see herself objectively. It's like when you have a pimple; you think that everyone is looking at it, but they probably don't even notice.

6. Andy shares his wisdom with Frances: when you're uncomfortable, you can get up and go. Nobody will stop you. Why is this such a liberating and surprising idea?

While I was using Andy's comment to get at why we sometimes stay in uncomfortable situations as if we didn't have a choice, teens might not be able to get beyond the idea of calling attention to themselves rather than leaving. Remaining in an unpleasant situation may be preferable to inviting scrutiny. Ask if they feel different if they have a very good reason for leaving, like to be on time for a babysitting job. Does this change how self-conscious they feel?

7. Struggling with her decision about whether to work with Unity, Frances laments, "Art doesn't help anyone" (p 107). Is this statement true? Why or not?

Assuming that basic needs are met, art is important. Remind teens of how important music is to them, how it can soothe or change their moods. Doesn't art make life more tolerable? Creative expression is a natural desire. It heals. It also broadens understanding. It can inform viewers about important issues and educate about other cultures and situations. Art may be one of the things that separates us from lower animals.

8. Is Saskia a hero? Do you think she acted out of concern for others or revenge?

I was surprised at how strongly my discussion group disliked Saskia. Remind your group that we are seeing Saskia through Frances' eyes. While your group may not believe that Saskia had an altruistic motive in shutting down Unity, ask them if she had had an altristic motive, would it have been worth killing Daniel to save many others? How could she have avoided killing Daniel without revealing her plan?

Your group may not pick up on the implication that Saskia and Patrick may have had an intimate relationship and a falling out that caused her to seek revenge. If not, you'll want to talk about how this possibility changes their interpretation of Saskia's actions.

9. Does Frances cover the mirror for Daniel or herself? When Frances finally regards herself in the mirror, she concludes that she's not beautiful, not pretty, but interesting looking. Can we be objective judges of how we look?

Frances does undergo a change, signified by her undraping the mirror, looking into it, and finding that she is interesting looking. Until then, she is unable to see herself objectively. Not only is her view of herself colored by the comments of others, it is also colored by her feelings of guilt for not saving her brother. When she undrapes the mirror, she is giving up her guilt.

Her experience of persevering to discover what really happened to Daniel has given her a sense of accomplishment and self-reliance. She has done something good and is able to look at herself a little more objectively, without so many negative filters. Ask readers if we ever see ourselves the way others see us.

10. Why is it meaningful that Frances keeps the white cashmere sweater?

Accepting the gift of the white sweater from her father — something pretty when she previously rejected pretty clothes — is another sign of her healing. Does wearing something pretty call attention to yourself? How would you dress if you wanted to be unnoticed?

11. Does James regret saying goodbye to Frances?

James seems to truly like Frances. Her narrative seems melodramatic and whiny at times, but Werlin does a good job of capturing the kind of defeating internal dialog that goes on in someone with low self-esteem. Readers may not even like Frances. Ask if they would like her better if, as with James, they didn't know her every thought.

12. How does the first person narrative affect your feelings about Frances? Does it weigh down the story at times? Would it have been better told from a different point of view?

Some readers will find Frances melodramatic and whiny, but remind them that usually we don't know someone's thoughts. Ask readers if they've had thoughts like Frances'. How would they feel if someone could read their thoughts? A different point of view may have made Frances seem less whiny, but it would also have given us less insight into a very complex character and would have given us much less to talk about. Nonetheless, it still would be a good mystery.

6

BLIND SIGHTED
by PETER MOORE

Bibliographic information: Viking, 2002; 262 pages.

Themes: Underachievement, alcoholism, blindness.

Genre: Realistic fiction.

Main character: Kirk Tobak, 16.

Tips: Teens may want to talk about the cover. In addition to its mediocrity, the boy looks pretty beefy to be Kirk, whose smallness is a major part of his persona. Discussion leaders may want to compare Kirk's poem that Mr. Brody reads in class to the poem it parodies, Allen Ginsberg's "Howl." Strong language, underage drinking, and sexual situations may make this book more appropriate for mature readers.

SYNOPSIS:

When brilliant loner and underachiever Kirk Tobak is demoted from honors English to "Loserville" English, he is unexpectedly befriended by a burn-out who happens to be a talented guitarist interested in collaborating with Kirk, a gifted writer. Even more surprising to Kirk is that another classmate, a.k.a. Parole Girl, actually wants to go out with him. His new job reading to a blind woman turns out to be interesting and the source of another new friendship. Just when life seems to be taking an upturn for Kirk, his alcoholic mother runs off to California with her boyfriend, decides to stay, and expects Kirk to follow. Kirk relates his insecurities and adventures with an honesty that teens will relate to and humor that readers will appreciate.

DISCUSSION QUESTIONS/LEADER POINTS

1. Kirk comments that he likes books because they're reliable (p. 9). What effects do his reading habit's have on his life and relationships?

Books are Kirk's consolation. In them he can find solace, escape from his less-than-perfect life, and find examples of normal, predictable behavior. Since Kirk has an absent father and an uninvolved mother, what he knows about relationships he's had to learn from books. Also, he can go back to the relationships in books again and again, and they will always be the same.

2. Blind sight is the ability of the blind to see light sources. Why is this a good title? How is Kirk blind sighted?

Although Kirk seems to be stumbling blindly along and have little control over his life in some areas, he finds friends and activities that help to fill some of the holes in his life. In this way he is blind sighted. His demotion to a different English class was his own doing, and the results are surprisingly positive because he's found friends and a teacher who encourages and appreciates him. Callie is certainly a source of light, giving Kirk new perspectives and support.

3. Kirk is obviously very bright. Why does he choose to fail?

Kirk may not be able to see the benefit of succeeding in school because he receives no encouragement or praise from his mother. Mr. Brody is the first teacher who thinks there's more going on with Kirk than meets the eye. Also, his failing at school is a way of being rebellious, one of the few things in his life he has control over.

4. Does Lauren love Kirk? Why does Lauren say that they're both too intense to be together?

Lauren seems to enjoy the excitement of having a new boyfriend and falling in love more than having a serious relationship. Her intensity and experience cause Kirk to question her genuineness. He is more attracted to Callie's maturity and sees Callie as an example of what is more appealing, although he wrongly confuses his appreciation for her with love. Callie may be the only mature female Kirk has ever encountered, since his mother fails in that area.

Lauren probably says that she and Kirk are just both too intense to be good together to save face. Kirk is the one who's lost interest. Does it also save face for Kirk?

5. On page 69, Kirk says that sometimes good things just happen to you and he believes that sometimes you should leave something for someone else to keep the balance. What do you think about this idea? Does this work in your own life?

It's interesting to learn whether others observe a karmic balance in life, whether they feel a responsibility to keep the balance and where they think that these notions come from. Is it something one just intuits? Does the feeling come from a religious tradition that one practices? Why does good fortune make people want to share good fortune with others? Are people who don't have that reaction less healthy or evolved? Kirk shows genuine goodness in his desire to leave something for others. It may be surprising considering the raw deal he's been given. Another interesting discussion point might be why some people do or don't turn cynical or bitter living in less than ideal circumstances.

6. Should Kirk have answered his mother's phone calls, given her plan a chance?

7. Does it matter that Kirk's mother stopped drinking? Should he be more supportive of that?

It might seem natural for Kirk to accept his mother's behavior since she's all he's ever known. He doesn't have anything to measure her impulsiveness and irresponsibility against, except maybe characters in books or later Callie. Somehow he's gone past the stage of feeling responsible for her, which may be a more typical reaction to her parenting style (or lack thereof). It's a good thing that he doesn't get trapped into trying to keep her sober. Maybe the reader is supposed to surmise that Callie's influence has made the difference. Questions 6 and 7 are meant to provoke discussion about how sometimes people try to make a fresh start by moving and changing jobs, or even getting married. However, what's wrong is really inside them and exterior changes probably won't have a long-term impact, for example Kirk's mother may not stay sober.

8. Should Callie have acted differently when she found out that Kirk's mother had left him alone? Should she have alerted the authorities?

The debate about whether to follow the letter of the law or the language of the heart is always an interesting discussion starter. There will be teens who will be bothered by Callie's not reporting Kirk's mother's abandonment and his deception at school, possibly even by his driving without a license and underage drinking.

9. Why does Kirk antagonize Lauren's new boyfriend? Why can't he stop when he's getting beat up?

In antagonizing Graham, at first Kirk seems to be acting out the hurt he feels when he realizes that to Lauren guys like him are a dime a dozen. All the anger he had to bottle up toward his mother combines with the frustration over Lauren and takes him beyond sensibility; he can't stop fighting.

10. What does Kirk learn from Callie? On page 259, Kirk says he's a "work in progress." What does he mean, and what does this statement tell us about his state of mind?

The references to Callie's eastern-influenced philosophy of life may be a little too subtle, but I think that the author meant for readers to assume that her influence brings Kirk to a more peaceful acceptance of being a work in progress. He has goals he hasn't reached yet, but it's fine to be right where he is. Ask readers how they feel about being works in progress. Do they need to develop more patience with themselves or more discipline?

11. Should Callie be more cautious in opening her home to Kirk after his declaration of love?

The resolution, the decision that Kirk will live with Callie while he finishes the school year seems a little too neat and unrealistic, especially after his declaration of love. One might expect Callie to be a little more cautious even though Kirk has displayed remarkable maturity in recognizing that his feelings were misplaced.

7

BREATHING UNDERWATER
by ALEX FLINN

Bibliographic information: HarperCollins, 2001; 272 pages.

Themes: Dating violence, child abuse, popularity, social status.

Genre: Realistic fiction.

Main character: Nick Andreas, 16.

Tips: The scene in which Nick beats Caitlin is shocking and may disturb some readers, but the story is realistically told and not sensationalized. It's important in that it depicts how controlling behavior can accelerate insidiously.

Breathing Underwater is an important book. It brings a classic example of abuse to a teen level without being didactic. It's an issue the author obviously cares about a great deal, and she has skillfully set it in a very realistic teen world of class distinctions in upper-class suburbia. It's hard to read this without hoping that at least one teen reads it and begins to recognize unhealthy, controlling behavior and is able to avoid violence.

See Alex Flinn's Web site for an alternate set of discussion questions and a teachers' guide (www.alexflinn.com).

SYNOPSIS

Popular and affluent, Nick has never had any trouble dating. Then he falls hard for the new improved Caitlin, who can't seem to shed her feelings of inferiority as easily as the 35 pounds she's lost. Nick becomes increasingly possessive, imagining Cat is with other guys whenever he doesn't know where she is. His fear of losing her causes him to keep close tabs on her, try to control whom she sees, make cruel remarks, and eventually to hit her. The story is told by Nick in journal entries ordered by a judge who has issued a restraining order against Nick after he brutally beats Cat. He is also ordered to attend a family violence class. Both activities lead him to recognize his problem and deal with his abusive father.

DISCUSSION QUESTIONS/LEADER POINTS

1. Why is *Breathing Underwater* a suitable title?

The title brings to mind lots of images: being in over one's head, drowning, being deprived of air. Teens will think of more.

2. Is Tom's family as nice as Nick imagines? Are they as bad as Tom imagines?

Perceptions of the lives of others is an interesting topic, the assumptions we make based on what we see. Tom knows that Nick's father isn't warm and nurturing, but he never suspects that he beats Nick. Nick idealizes Tom's family, and, probably, for Nick it is an ideal family. There is also the ideal we carry in our psyches about what a family should be—some TV-Land family that is completely free of dysfunctional behavior. It's important for teens to realize that this image is unrealistic but they also need to be able to identify behaviors that are harmful and dangerous.

3. What do you think of Cat's reaction when Nick beats Dirk at the party? Does Cat care more about Nick or being in Nick's group?

Cat seems like a good person who is overwhelmed by her sudden ascension to the "it" group. She has little self-esteem and a huge amount of insecurity. She still sees herself as fat, something that Nick cruelly uses to his advantage, and she accepts his controlling demands on her. She's flattered that Nick would stand up for her when even he can see he'd lost control in beating up Dirk. Because the story is told from Nick's point of view, it's hard to know whether she truly loves him. It is clear that the kind of testing he does is pathological. However, it's not clear whether she acquiesces because she's afraid of losing him or losing everything that being his girlfriend includes. After breaking up with Nick, she quickly finds a new boyfriend in Saint, which may indicate that dependency is still an issue for her. Cat needs to become a person who sets her own course and doesn't compromise herself for others. She worries that she's being selfish in wanting to go to the game when Nick is home "sick." You may want to delve into the issue of how females are socialized to put others first, to think that being selfish is bad. Does this make it hard for girls and women to be selfish in healthy ways?

It's important for teens to realize that judgments belong to the person who judges, and doing what *you* think is right is best. There's no reason to pass on something you want to do unless it endangers someone or is illegal.

4. Cat criticizes Zack for blowing off his old friends when his family becomes wealthy, then says she'd like to be in the position of blowing people off for once. Later she does blow off her friends under pressure from Nick. It may be for a different reason, but how is it similar? Do you think this is a typical reaction?

Chances are members of your group will have known people who blew off old friends when they made it into a new group. Becoming wealthy may be more rare, but the result is similar. How does wealth change status? What about when a friend starts dating someone. Do old friends get abandoned?

5. When Nick is home "sick" after his father beats him, he shames Cat into not going to the game. Cat relents and stay home, but she feels selfish for wanting to go. Is it selfish of her to want to go to the game without Nick?

Because Nick was so afraid of losing Cat's love, he keeps her from doing what was good for her. It's important for teens to realize that healthy love wants the loved one to have what makes him or her happy and to take advantage of opportunities. If Nick loved Cat in a mature way, he would celebrate her singing talent and want her to take advantage of the opportunities it brought. He would most certainly want her to be homecoming princess if that would make her happy. He'd also want her to go to the game without him and have fun.

6. Why doesn't Nick vote for Cat for homecoming princess?

Nick is afraid of having others admire Cat. That's also why he puts her down. It wouldn't be unusual for someone with his issues to dictate what his girlfriend can and can't wear. If she's attractive to others, he stands a greater chance of losing her. He may want to punish her for being attractive.

7. What's your reaction to how the group treats the street musician who throws his arms around Saint when Saint gives him a five-dollar bill? What are some other examples of class and social status in the book?

This book provides a lot of material for talking about class differences and popularity. The group treats the street musician disrespectfully—certainly not as someone on the same level of humanity as they are. Zack drops his old friends when his family becomes wealthy. The group accepts Zack, not because they like him, but because of his stuff. Liana's parents persuade her that Tom is using her because he's a gringo. The girls criticize Cat's mother for the way she dresses. Cat abandons her best friend because Elsa is a geek. Why is it sometimes easy for people to disregard the courtesy of respecting elders or to forget religious teachings or the "golden rule?"

8. When they're talking about Nick's losing his virginity, Tom says that he's glad Nick was first because he had so much more to prove. What does Nick have to prove and why?

A parent's job is to empower the child. Nick's father does just the opposite; even worse he's diminished him. Tom astutely knows that Nick has something to prove.

9. Why does Cat agree to meet Nick when they finally talk on the phone, and why doesn't she show up?

Cat is still wrestling with her self-esteem. She may still care about Nick and miss him, or she may miss how he made her feel. People often choose relationships that are similar to ones they've had early in life. Even though the relationship isn't optimal, it feels familiar and so, in some way, comfortable. Cat's not showing up is encouraging; she's making some progress.

I wish the author had made Nick a little more likable because typically the remorse and attention that alternates with the cruelty in most cases of this type of abuse are what keeps the victim involved. This may be a result of the story's being told from Nick's point of view. Perhaps if we saw Caitlin's point of view, we would see a sweeter side of Nick.

10. Nick comments that somehow writing the journal, seeing the story on paper, makes it more real. How do you explain this?

Nick realizes that journaling has the power to make things more real. How often people massage memories and truth to fit their self-images. Writing is a powerful tool in dealing with the demons that reside within. It exposes them and requires us to name and explain them; it is a healing and revealing process. This book is a natural to use with some kind of journaling exercise.

11. Why do you think that Tom forgives Nick?

Tom renews his friendship with Nick, fully cognizant that Nick did a bad thing and is responsible, but he realizes that Nick is also a victim and deserving of compassion.

8

BRIAR ROSE by JANE YOLEN

Bibliographic information: T. Doherty, 1992; 190 pages.

Themes: Holocaust, persecution of homosexuals during the Holocaust, fairy-tale adaptations, guilt, forgiveness.

Genre: Historical fiction.

Main characters: Becca, a young adult. Josef, an old man who looks back on his experience as a young man during WW II.

Tips: Readers may find the book a little slow in the beginning. Encourage them to persevere until they get to Josef's powerful narrative. Some readers may be offended by the strong language and references to homosexual sex, although the sex is not graphic. The most recent cover is strikingly beautiful. If you have both the old and new covers, ask for your group's reactions to the two.

Although a bit awkward in its contrast between present day romance and brutal history, Briar Rose would be a fine complement to Holocaust studies or the study of fairy-tale adaptations.

SYNOPSIS:

Becca grew up hearing her grandmother's version of the Sleeping Beauty story. Before she dies, her grandmother reveals to Becca that she, Gemma, is the princess of the story, which compels Becca to find out her grandmother's story of survival as a Polish Jew during the Holocaust. Becca is drawn to Poland and the man who tells his and Gemma's story and who was her prince. Through Potocki's narrative we learn about the persecution of Jews and homosexuals and of Gemma's incredible resuscitation by Potocki and subsequent escape.

DISCUSSION QUESTIONS/LEADER POINTS

1. Does the romance between Becca and Stan add to the novel?

Some readers will wish for more of the love story between Becca and Stan and find it interesting, but the romance just frames the real story, which is Potocki's.

2. Would you have liked to have had the story of Gemma's experience during the Holocaust told by a character other than Potocki? How would another narrator change the story?

Having Gemma's story told to Becca takes something away from it. We aren't directly transported into the action, although at times the story is so captivating that it's easy to forget that it's a story within a story. However, the device skillfully sets up the fairy-tale scheme.

3. Is Potocki a hero? Do his actions after he escapes from Sachsenhausen atone for his earlier lack of empathy?

It doesn't really matter what causes an awakening or what precedes it, the important thing is that it happens, as in of Potocki's change of attitude. It might be more noble to stand up for a cause that one believes is right even when it is not directly affecting one's own life, but some people need a more direct call to action. Life begins anew each moment. The formerly apathetic person becomes a hero.

4. What does Potocki's homosexuality add to the story? Why do you think that the Jews, homosexuals, and Gypsies were among those singled out for persecution?

This may be the first time that readers learn about the pink stars worn by homosexuals. Most teens will have read other novels or histories of the Holocaust, but few address the homosexual experience.

The Jews were disliked for their success in business. Hitler perceived them as taking away what rightfully belonged to the Aryans. Homophobia sometimes indicates a fear of being unmanly. If Hitler was afraid of being unmanly, he may have so aggressively sought power to counteract his insecurity. The Gypsies were often perceived as thieves and had associations with the supernatural. What groups arouse suspicion today?

5. Why do you think that the second group of partisans was more successful than the first?

The first group of partisans may have had death wishes because they all had lost people close to them, and they are devastated by the losses. Bent on vengeance, they are unable to think with more reason than passion. How does grief or anger affect judgment?

6. Father Stushu says that he cannot forgive the people of Chelmno, that he can love them but not forgive them. Are they forgivable?

The people of Chelmno were unfortunate in having atrocities brought right into their backyards. They were faced with a moral dilemma and acted, or didn't act, out of fear. Remind readers that the Nazis had a habit of keeping people obedient by threatening them with the lives of their families and friends. On the other hand, many people risked everything to fight the Nazis. What is it that makes some people stand up for what it right at great personal risk? In not being able to forgive them, the priest may be inferring that people can't know forgiveness unless they forgive themselves. The tolerance of evil by the people of Chelmno may preclude them from forgiving themselves.

7. Why is this Becca's journey instead of Eve's?

Holocaust survivors were more interested in assimilating and forgetting than laying a burden on their children, and they probably made great efforts to keep the horror from their children. Eve was likely to have been discouraged from asking about her mother's experiences if she was curious. By Becca's time, the Holocaust is studied in history class. Knowing that her grandmother is a survivor, yet a survivor who never talks about her experience, naturally makes Becca curious.

8. How well does Gemma's story fit into the Briar Rose story? What symbolic images strengthen the relationship?

Yolen fits the Briar Rose story very well into this novel. The mist that puts everyone to sleep is the gas. The briars are prison barbed wire. The prince's kiss is Josef administering mouth-to-mouth resuscitation. The curse is the Nazi scourge. Need we say that Hitler was the evil fairy?

9

DUNK by DAVID LUBAR

Bibliographic information: Clarion, 2002; 249 pages.

Themes: Independence, adults' negative impressions of teens, reactions to serious illness, the power of humor.

Genre: Realistic fiction.

Main character: Eleventh-grader Chad.

Tips: Teens will relate to Chad's insecurity in pursuing his first romance and asserting his independence. Anyone who's been misunderstood will also sympathize with Chad. A good choice for boys, Chad's straightforward, humorous narrative will appeal to girls, too.

SYNOPSIS:

One evening at the beginning of summer, amidst the carnival-like world of a New Jersey boardwalk town, Chad becomes captivated by a dunk-tank Bozo. He is certain that he could dish out the barbs to attract marks to try their luck at dunking him. His life is rife with enough frustrations to make him want to strike back: a father who deserted him; a mom who works too much; run-ins with the police who've labeled him a troublemaker; a girl he wants to date who's swept away by his rival; and a best friend who may be dying of a mysterious illness. The dunk-tank Bozo he admires turns out to be a boarder in his own house with whom he has had several unpleasant encounters. Under the Bozo's tutelage, Chad learns a lot about humor and its ability to heal and hurt and reaches his goal of becoming a dunk-tank Bozo.

DISCUSSION QUESTIONS/LEADER POINTS

1. Do you agree with Chad that where he lives is one of the "coolest places on the planet?" Why or why not?

Chad appears to have remained unjaded living in a place most people go for vacation. The setting has great teen appeal, but some might see drawbacks. One review calls the setting "tawdry."

2. What's your reaction to the way the police treat Chad? Do you think an adult perception of teens as troublemakers is a common problem?

Not only is Chad mistrusted by the police, he's also wrongly accused of stealing by a shopkeeper, sneered at by his teacher, and hated by his best friend's mother. The issue of adults' negative perceptions of teens is a very big can of worms that comes up fairly often when you work with teens. Hours could be spent discussing this issue alone. Does expecting negative behavior create it?

3. Why does Chad want to be a Bozo? Would you like to give it a try? Why or why not?

4. After his fight with Malcolm, Chad realizes that he has a choice and decides to fight back instead of rolling over and dying. How does Malcolm help him reach this realization? How does it help him to deal with Jason's illness?

Chad's denial of Jason's illness is a common reaction to the mortality of someone close. Chad learns to take responsibility for meeting life's challenges without feeling victimized and that the first step in this is accepting whatever life dishes out. Malcolm adroitly shows Chad that feeling sorry for himself and allowing himself to feel like a victim is a no-win attitude, and it is a choice. If only we could all be as good a student as Chad is.

5. When Malcolm offers to tutor Chad on being a Bozo, he says, "It's a job nobody is going to appreciate. Yeah, people will laugh when they walk by and maybe notice how clever you are. Even so, they'll think you're nothing but a loser who can't find anything better to do. ... Maybe one person in a million will hear and actually understand what it takes to do the job" (p. 185). Why isn't Chad deterred? What ultimately makes the choice to work for something most satisfying?

Chad makes his choice to do something no one may appreciate because it fills some deep need. Chad wonders why Corey wants to design Web sites, why Ellie likes biology, why someone is compelled to practice something for hours (p. 200). Jason suggests it's something one's good at. This is a good point to start a discussion about why it's important to consider callings such as these when thinking about the future, how it feels when you're doing something that moves you, and it is to what extent important it is to be practical. The issue of satisfaction in career choice is a point to consider. How is a "calling" different from a career choice?

6. Is it fair for Chad's mother to forbid him from working? Should he have talked to her about his job before she found out?

It's never fair for parents to make assumptions about the lives of their children based on what they wished had been different in their own lives, but it happens too frequently. The understanding and tolerance that teens have when talking about such issues are impressive. Teens are grateful for their parents' wanting them to have better lives than they had, and at the same time they're determined not to allow themselves to get too far from their own needs to please their parents. What things does a parent have the right to forbid? How does a kid balance the right to privacy and independent decision-making with the responsibility to inform a parent of these decisions? Lubar presents a healthy and realistic reaction in Chad's determination to work while he admires his mother's determination that he won't. This story is a great opportunity for teens to see the distinction.

7. Why does Jason's mom hate Chad?

Besides being just another adult who misunderstands Chad, Jason's mother has a need to blame someone because of her feelings of helplessness in the face of Jason's illness. She's awfully stubborn, though, and mostly just a foil. Should the author have fleshed her out more? Would it have been more realistic for Chad to have had a more positive effect on her?

8. Should Malcolm have made the phone call about the party? Should he have thought more about the repercussions that would affect Chad?

Malcolm does act impulsively when he calls the police about the party, but his intentions are the best, and he obviously cares about Chad.

9. How does Chad help Malcolm?

Malcolm is a wonderfully complex character. He bristles with his own anger. He makes mistakes; he doesn't speak up as he should when Chad's accused of stealing. He comes to blows with Chad. He is only a few steps from despair. Chad makes Malcolm care once again for another fragile human being who has the ability to die; it's something he needs to do if he's going to recover from his grief. Chad also gives him confidence in his ability to teach, helps him face his hospital demon, and values his craft.

10. When Chad's in the tank, Malcolm advises him to stop being Chad. When Malcolm admits his apprehension about teaching, Chad reminds him that it's another role. Is acting a valid way to get through daunting circumstances?

After taking a couple of acting courses in college, I quickly came to the conclusion that acting can benefit anyone, and I've used it countless times in job interviews, when giving presentations, any time when my confidence is challenged. Picture Deborah Kerr as Anna from the King and I, whistling a happy tune to convince herself she's not afraid.

11. A sign above a shop entrance says, "We have whatever you want" (p. 133), which causes Chad to think not only about what he wants immediately, but also about the future. He realizes that he is clueless. How and why do his experiences during the summer change his feelings about the future?

At the end of the book, Chad's plans for the future are still uncertain, but he is at peace with the uncertainty. He's had the experience of reaching a goal well, and met misfortune actively and responsibly. Whatever lies ahead, he knows he is equal to it.

10

FEED by M. T. ANDERSON

Bibliographic information: Candlewick, 2002; 236 pages.

Themes: Corporate power, the influence of advertising, consumerism, social consciousness, identity.

Genre: Science fiction.

Main characters: Titus and Violet, both 16.

Tips: Strong language and situations recommend this book for older teens. Questions of global responsibility and the dangers of consumerism will make some teens uncomfortable.

SYNOPSIS:

In this dystopian novel, "feeds," computers implanted in the brains of most of earth's people, control all life functions and anticipate all information needs and emotional desires. All of this information is continually supplemented with advertising. Feeds continually bombard their hosts with information. When a group of teens hook up to party on the moon and a hacker attacks their feeds, major parts of their feeds are temporarily disabled while doctors try to assess the damage. One member of the group, Violet, has permanent damage and her feed begins to shut down. Titus was into dating Violet for a couple of months, but now she's dragging him into this "eternal thing," and she's always finding disturbing bits of information that most people ignore. Titus resists Violet's influence, but slowly begins to look for little broken pieces of information beyond the advertisements and trivia of his feed. He finds that the world is on the brink of war, rioting has broken out in malls, and the earth is dead; he then chooses truth over the feed.

DISCUSSION QUESTIONS/LEADER POINTS

1. In Titus's world, corporations control everything. Do you think corporations could become this powerful? Why or why not?

Depending on how politically savvy your group is, you might talk about how corporations influence politics with campaign contributions and more subtle pressure. Ask your group if they think that the environment is sometimes sacrificed when corporations move operations to countries with less restrictive policies and cheaper labor. Do they exploit workers? Do they create economic imbalance in the world?

2. While shopping on the moon, Titus knows he wants to buy some things, but doesn't know what they are. He and his friends walk around for a while till "everything seemed kind of sad and boring so we couldn't tell anymore what we wanted" (p.24). What makes people just want to buy things sometimes when there is nothing they need?

The way we are bombarded with advertising, and the messages that advertising gives us, that stuff will make us cool, happy, and fulfilled, are hard to resist. The aim of advertising is to make us feel unsatisfied, that we need something. Shopping is often used as a comfort, but it's a false comfort so after the buzz wears off it leaves one empty. It's easy to understand why Titus and his friends can't tell what they want.

3. When Titus is in the hospital with the major part of his feed down, he observes a picture of a boat on the wall. He finds it uninteresting and wonders why anyone would paint a picture like that. What does this reveal about Titus?

Without the feed telling him what he's looking at and suggesting what it means and what related things he could purchase, the picture of the boat is meaningless to Titus. He has no associations of his own to reflect on. Furthermore, those with the feed have lost the ability to appreciate simplicity and quiet.

4. At the beginning of their relationship, Violet says to Titus, "Keep thinking. You can hear our brains rattling inside us like little Russian dolls" (p.75). How are their brains like little Russian dolls?

Violet's Russian doll analogy shows that their brains, their ability to think for themselves, is locked deep inside and covered over by layers created by the feed.

5. When Titus feels dumb, his parents buy him an upcar of his own. Is this a good solution? Why or why not? Is it wise to use *things* to make people feel better? Why or why not?

Titus's parents buy him an upcar because they don't know how else to distract him from his sadness. People aren't encouraged to feel and talk about their feelings. Their solutions are to distract themselves. That doesn't honor his feelings, so they are never satisfyingly resolved.

6. Do the feeds make people dumb? Are there things today that make people dumb?

Titus shows by the end of the book that he is not dumb; he is just unaccustomed to thinking. Maybe things don't make people dumb, but the mindlessness of some of the things people occupy themselves with is noteworthy. TV, video games, and computer surfing don't often sharpen critical-thinking skills.

7. When the president calls the minister of the Global Alliance a big shithead, the PR team tries to spin it to mean that his head is fertile ground, ready for new ideas. Can you think of contemporary examples of how blunders are spun? Recall President Bush's term "Operation Infinite Justice," which morphed into "Operation Enduring Freedom."

Examples of political spin abound. In the case of Operation Infinite Justice somebody must have realized that the term infinite justice was infinitely arrogant. Freedom is a much more positive identification. Who wouldn't support freedom?

8. As Titus flies to Violet's house, he passes communities called Fox Glen, Caleby Farm Estates, Waterview Park, and Creville Heights. Why are these names ironic? Do you see similarities in the names of contemporary communities?

The kinds of community names in the book are just as common today and just as ironic. Creville Heights is at the bottom of the heap. There are no foxes in Fox Glen, and it's not a glen. There's no view of water at Waterview Park and it's not a park. Caleby Farm Estates are not farm-like. Ask your group what's attractive about the images the names imply. Why do they appeal to us?

9. When Violet says words Loga and Calista don't understand they make fun of her. Why do you think they do this? Do you know anyone who uses words and talks about things most teens don't? How is that person treated?

Teens are sure to know kids who don't fit in because their backgrounds are different. Maybe their families don't have a TV or they're home-schooled. Somehow they are just a little bit outside of the mainstream. Why do some kids make fun of people who are different? Is there something threatening about these people?

10. Titus says that Violet is scary sometimes, like "you're watching us instead of being us" (p. 134). Why is Violet scary?

Violet makes people uncomfortable because she's bringing up injustices and problems that no one is addressing. Take a page from the newspapers and point out the juxtaposition of articles about war and famine and half-page advertisements for cosmetics, clothes, or electronics. What's easier to look at? There's a game show that showers contestants in cooked spaghetti noodles at the same time children are starving in Africa. Do you want to watch the fun or think about starving children?

11. When lesions become chic, Quendy has her body cut with artificial lesions to look good to Link. Do women currently do any similarly destructive things to appear attractive?

Women have always suffered pressure to look good. Refer to the heroin-chic models; the rampant eating disorders affecting American women; plastic surgery, including breast implants that almost always leave women with no feeling in their breasts and are a barrier to self-examination.

12. On page 174 Violet describes what she thinks of when she thinks of really living, saying that it's like the opening credits of sitcoms. Do you think of things in this way sometimes?

Like the images that Violet describes, images of what lovers do fill our movies, music videos, TV shows, and books. Do these images reflect reality or an ideal? Do we come to expect life to be like these images, and are we disappointed if it's not?

13. When Violet begins to lose her memories, she sends them to Titus and says that someday she may ask him to tell them to her. Why is it so frightening to lose one's memories? Who are we without our memories?

Losing our memories is akin to dying. Violet's desire to have her memories kept by someone is similar to the desire to leave something behind as a legacy—children, a book, a building. Ask readers if they can think of other examples. Why are people compelled to leave something behind?

14. What keeps Titus from opening Violet's memories? Why does he change his mind?

Titus is overwhelmed by Violet and the trust of her memories. She lives to explore the depth of feelings while he is used to living on the surface. But like Pandora's box, once it's opened, there's no turning back. Innocence is lost.

15. Is there any hopefulness in this story?

It is hopeful that at least a couple of people have woken up and are trying to resist the feed, but it may be too late; the planet is dead and on the brink of war.

16. What is the author's trying to tell us?

Anderson has presented a bleak picture of what happens when society is controlled by consumerism and corporate greed. The dangers he suggests are present in more subtle forms today. He is warning us of where some of the paths we've begun to walk can lead.

11

THE GOSPEL ACCORDING TO LARRY
by JANET TASHJIAN

Bibilographic information: Henry Holt, 2001; 192 pages.

Themes: Consumerism, simplicity, advertising, global responsibility, family loyalty, celebrity

Genre: Realistic fiction.

Main character: Josh Swensen, 17, a.k.a. Larry.

Tips: Tashjian provides the best kind of book for discussion, full of questions about ethics and values that invite us to question our very way of life. You might want to set aside more than an hour for this book. Some readers may think the story within a story is real, especially after visiting the Web site (www.gospelaccordingtolarry.com). Even some of the respondents on the Web site's message board aren't sure if the book is a work of fiction. Someone thought we would have heard about Larry on the news if he were real, or we would have known about Larryfest; after all this is a world where we know when the president gets a colonoscopy. Meanwhile, assuming the Web site will be up for a while, which is likely with the buzz of a sequel, it is worthwhile checking the forum for what visitors are talking about. The book has sparked some interesting and passionate online discussions.

SYNOPSIS:

When Josh anonymously launches a culture-bashing, anticonsumerism Web site, his alter ego, Larry, becomes a cult figure. His popularity peaks at Larryfest, a free concert organized by activist-musician Bono. Meanwhile, an obsessive fan exposes Larry's identity, causing his life to become a three-ring circus and his best friend and stepfather to feel betrayed. Josh thinks that Larry's celebrity may offer him an opportunity to spread his message, but he finds that the media is more interested in what breakfast cereal he prefers. Continually hounded by the press and by fans, Josh decides to stage his suicide and goes into hiding. Following a vision quest, Josh decides to write his story and give his manuscript to popular young adult novelist Janet Tashjian.

DISCUSSION QUESTIONS/LEADER POINTS

1. In her introduction, the author says that some readers suggested that Josh suffers from bipolar disorder, or ADHD, or has a Messiah complex. What do you think of Josh's emotional health?

Readers may argue about whether Josh is mentally healthy. His concerns will be very foreign to some readers. He is at the age when schizophrenia often first appears. He thinks of Larry as a separate entity; he says so during the scene when Beth says goodbye to his mother at the cemetery. The author draws parallels between Josh and Jesus that go beyond a messianic mentality: similar name, the use of gospels, his altruistic motivation, his betrayal by one of his followers, his death and resurrection. Be sensitive to the group's level of comfort with these comparisons.

2. Is Larry's anonymity necessary?

Larry's anonymity is essential to the popularity of his Web site. While many people are interested in his message, his anonymity is an attraction, especially when he begins posting photos of his possessions and folks begin trying to discover his identity. Is his anonymity a sign of immaturity, of not standing behind his views? Would he have gotten as much notoriety if it were known that he was a 17 year old?

3. Is Larry an alarmist, or is advertising really so pervasive? Did you ever consider brands on your clothes as free advertising, that you're consenting to be a walking advertisement when you wear them? If more teens thought about this, would they x out or remove brand names?

Advertising is such a part of their lives that, while teens may agree that it is pervasive, they probably won't view it as particularly harmful. They may even note that some big corporations do philanthropic work to balance making megabucks. If they go there, ask about tobacco companies. Is philanthropy less impressive if the company sells a known harmful substance?

Most teens don't think about being walking advertisements. Why would you buy a shirt at the Gap that didn't say Gap? Exactly. Why buy an overpriced T-shirt sold by a company that outsources overseas for cheap labor and less rigid environmental laws? Can you really feel good about using products that exploit others in another part of the world?

4. Josh has 75 possessions. If he acquires something new, he gives up something. How would it be to have 75 possessions? Do we accumulate things unconsciously?

It would be hard to find an American who doesn't have more than he or she needs. While teens are big consumers, the older generation is probably more interested in downsizing. This is a good debate to have with teen-adult groups. What about the responsibilities that go with stuff? The more stuff you have, the more you have to take care of. Consider the example of a car. You have to keep it clean, you have to maintain it, you worry about dents and scratches. It might be worth it, but you have to agree that it adds a lot of worry and responsibility.

5. Is the prank that Josh played on his counselor consistent with his altruistic personality? Why do you think the author put in this scene? Do you have to be nice all the time to be a positive influence?

Josh's prank in getting his school counselor to wait for a nonexistent blind date is cruel and out of character, but shows his humanity, as does Sermon 113, in which he seems unforgiving of people who are fair-weather friends. Even Jesus ranted occasionally.

6. What do you think of Josh's method of communicating with his late mother by asking questions and having them answered by passersby? Did you ever get an answer in this way?

Most everyone will have had an experience in which they were looking for an answer and seemed to receive it from an unlikely source. Some readers may find Josh's method dangerous and irresponsible, but it is a great example of how faith works. Josh appreciates the guidance of what he calls the Universe. He trusts it and it seems to guide him.

7. Is Larry making the world a better place?

Some of the issues that Larry takes to task are overwhelming, but individuals are able to effect change in small ways. Maybe the lesson of the book is the unexpected escalation of effects that can result from a single cause. Being kind to someone may cause that person to be kind to someone else, and so on; it ripples.

8. In Sermon 113, Larry reacts to Beth's disregarding their plans when Todd becomes free. He says he is sick of welcoming people back into the fold. Does Larry expect too much from people?

Here is a place where Josh's humanity looms large. His Achilles heel is Beth. He wants her, and he hurts when she drops him to be with Todd, who is obviously not good enough for her. Larry forgives Beth. He's just venting. He does expect too much from people, though. What he preaches would require people to give up comfort and distraction, stuff they think they need. That's scary for most people. Consume is a lot of what people do.

9. In Sermon 137, Larry writes, "Our STUFF lives better than most of the people in the world do." Do we have a responsibility to those people? What can we do? Is Peter right when he says the people making American goods in foreign countries are lucky to have those jobs?

You have to be sensitive to your group's comfort level when talking about whether we have the right to be comfortable in our skins when we have so much compared to people in the Third World. Some people are reluctant to think about that, possibly because it doesn't seem like there's much we can do about it. I think it's natural for people to want to believe that American companies operating in foreign countries can benefit the people of those countries by raising their standard of living as long as working conditions are humane and the environment is protected. What about Americans losing jobs because corporations are taking the jobs where labor is cheaper?

10. If a real, live Larry came along, would he have as much influence as he does in the book? Is there anyone like him?

Maybe Bono is trying hard, but he seems disingenuous when it costs so much to see him in concert, and he obviously lives a life of luxury. He does, however, raise money for good causes. Teens will be able to name other celebrities who do charitable work and are political.

11. Why does betagold want to expose Larry? Is she right in saying that he's a coward and doesn't stand behind his words by remaining anonymous?

Theorizing about betagold's motivation will lead to an examination of media and celebrity. The public has a "right-to-know" attitude fostered by the media. Do we always have a right to know? Recall the paparazzi hunting down and endangering celebrities. Betagold probably foresees that she will realize some fame and financial reward by being the person who exposes Larry.

Ironically, when Josh becomes famous, people are more interested in what he eats for breakfast than in his message. Think about what we know about celebrities. Why do we want to know mundane details? Can fame hurt one's credibility? Did Josh foresee the negative effects of outing himself?

12. Is Josh right to condemn Peter for the work that he does attracting teens to alcohol and cigarettes, and obscuring the truth about workers' conditions? What about Peter's contention that his work puts a lot of food on people's plates?

Some readers will unconditionally condemn Josh for going into Peter's briefcase because it is a breach of trust. They may think that the act obscures any perceived greater good that Josh is working for. However, the idealists in the group will believe that the ends are more important than the means. Does Josh have the right to go as far as he does, endangering Peter's job? Is it reasonable to expect people to choose to only work for ethical companies? Is it okay just to take care of a few?

13. In Sermon 163 Larry criticizes our interest in celebrities. Why do you suppose people are so interested in celebrities? Should we be more thoughtful about why people gain our admiration? How do we know the celebrities we "admire" are admirable?

14. How would an antistuff campaign be received at your school?

15. Could a Larryfest really happen imagine?

Imagine.

16. Should Josh have told Beth about his alter ego? If so, when?

Teens will no doubt think that Josh absolutely should have revealed himself to Beth early on. They may find it hard to believe that she doesn't guess Larry's identity, particularly when he posts pictures of his stuff, which, by the way, is how betagold ultimately recognizes Larry — by the necklace he wears to Larryfest and posts on his web site. Beth may chose to ignore some clues because the knowledge of Josh's alternate identity may change their friendship, just like she never expresses the desire that she and Josh become more than friends when she has been interested in that. Their fear of expressing their romantic feelings for each other is a reaction teens will easily relate to.

17. What is Larry's next move?

While we await the sequel, one hopes that Josh will let Peter and Beth know that he is still alive. How will they react? Ask whether Josh has any hope of returning to normal life for him once he outs himself (again).

12

GUTS: THE TRUE STORIES BEHIND HATCHET AND THE BRIAN BOOKS
by GARY PAULSEN

Bibilographic information: Delacorte, 2001; 148 pages.

Themes: Wilderness survival, hunting, nature, alcholism.

Genre: Biography.

Main character: Paulsen at different times during his life.

Tips: This may be a hard sell to girls, but, if persuaded, they will find that Paulsen's spare, riveting narrative capture's their interest. Experiences out of the realm of urban and suburban readers become fascinating in his hands.

It would be interesting to tie in other books that offer life lessons learned from nature (Henry David Thoreau's *Walden*, Annie Dillard's *Pilgrims at Tinker Creek*, Rachel Carson's *A Sense of Wonder*, or something on Taoism.)

SYNOPSIS:

Paulsen writes about his wilderness adventures that inspired some of his fiction books, including *Hatchet*. Paulsen's unflinching views of life inform readers of the harshness, thrills, and character-building aspects of nature. Whether it's hauling a 200-pound deer home on a bicycle, enduring a moose attack, or eating raw turtle eggs, Paulsen fully engages his readers and, at times, leaves them breathless.

DISCUSSION QUESTIONS/LEADER POINTS

1. What do you think is the most difficult or frightening challenge Paulsen faced?

2. What lessons did Paulsen learn about life from his experiences in the wilderness?

His experiences taught him perseverance, patience, and humility; to expect the unexpected; that lack of attention can cost you your life. Ask readers what things they have learned from nature. Like Paulsen, I find being in nature healing. There is nothing that soothes me as much as nature. Everywhere there is evidence of balance and interrelatedness. Ask readers whether our society has a healthy respect or reverence for nature. What are the consequences of being alienated from the natural world? Paulsen describes a shocking example with the story of a toddler who is killed by a buck deer while his mother prepares to photograph him feeding the deer candy.

3. What's the most surprising thing you learned from the book?

4. How does the book make the wilderness appealing (or not)?

5. Paulsen is obviously a skilled outdoorsman, yet he writes in detail about his blunders, for example, he repeatedly fails to shoot a grouse with arrows; when he approaches the bird it takes off in his face, and he admits that he almost wet himself. What do you think is the author's purpose in reporting his blunders?

By relating his blunders, Paulsen reveals his humility and humanity; we know he is an expert outdoorsman but we never feel patronized. We are made to realize that he didn't become an expert overnight. Also, it shows his respect for nature and his attitude of living in accord with, but never being the master of nature.

6. Is it more admirable to hunt only if necessary, or only for what you'll eat, rather than for sheer sport? Why or why not? What about culling? Are there other solutions for overpopulation?

7. How does the negligence of Paulsen's parents shape his life?

Having grown up in a grossly dysfunctional home, Paulsen never sentimentalizes his beginnings. Perhaps his parents' neglect led him to become a risk taker just to feel alive. It certainly made him self-reliant. His story is a good example of viewing adversity as character building and exploring the mystery of what makes one person sink and another rise above his circumstances.

8. Paulsen writes, "As hunger increases the diet widens" (p.121). Which unconventional "foods" eaten by the author would you try and which would you eat only if you were starving?

9. Why does Paulsen feel such a sense of accomplishment for having started a fire with a hatchet and a stone? How does an accomplishment like this measure against our usual accomplishments?

The challenge of producing fire by natural means is great. One can relate to early times when each fire took effort and was protected. Ask readers if they have seen the movie *Cast Away* in which Tom Hanks conveys the desperation and joy of making fire. When something is as easy as turning on a switch, we lose appreciation for the mystery.

10. Is Paulsen a thrill seeker, an adrenaline junkie? Do you think he would be happy in another profession?

Paulsen seems to be a fiercely independent person. He would no doubt have a hard time taking orders. Also, he needs the flexibility to get back to nature when he needs to. It's fortunate that his writing compliments his other interests so well.

13

HOLE IN MY LIFE
by JACK GANTOS

Bibliographic information: Farrar, Straus, and Giroux, 2002; 200 pages.

Themes: Prison, drugs, writing, redemption.

Genre: Biography.

Main character: Jack Gantos, 19.

Tips: The author makes no bones about having enjoyed taking drugs, which may offend some readers or their parents. The age of the protagonist, strong language, and descriptions of prison life may make the book more suitable for older readers.

SYNOPSIS:

Trying to earn money for college, Jack agrees to help sail a boat full of hashish from St. Croix to New York. After his partners are busted and give federal agents Jack's name, Jack turns himself in and faces a sentence of up to six years in prison. Jack is paroled 15 months later, after having been accepted into college. The other part of the story is the evolution of his writing life, from keeping journals about books he read to chronicling prison life to entering college.

DISCUSSION QUESTIONS/LEADER POINTS

1. Jack says the true test of character is how well a person makes decisions during difficult times (p.8). Why do you agree or disagree?

Difficult times have a way of burning through superficiality and reaching one's core values. I'm reminded of the passengers who took over the airplane on 9/11 and crashed it in Pennsylvania.

2. What do you think of how Jack handles his freedom when he lives in the motel and attends school in Florida? What would it take for your parents to allow you to do this?

At first this seemed shocking to me, but it's not much different from the experience lots of teens have when they go to college, they just have lots more support. Lots of people go a little wild partying when they first leave home, but Jack has more responsibilities than the average college student.

3. Jack's school friends are nervous about visiting him in the motel because they perceive it as a high-crime area. How do our perceptions affect our experience of new places? Have you ever come to feel comfortable in a place you first thought might be dangerous?

My own example is that my mother would have perceived my neighborhood to be dangerous simply because it's integrated. I have a friend who lived in well-maintained, upper-class suburban neighborhood, and most of the houses on the street had been robbed.

4. What kind of a role model is Jack's father?

While Jack's father may not be the most stable provider and disregards the law on at least two occasions (allowing Jack to make the box for a drug dealer and wrecking Jack's car for insurance money), he does love Jack and is able to tell him so when he visits him in prison. Jack must have had some grounding to have been so driven to redeem himself and reach his goal.

5. In high school, Jack is not allowed to take writing because his grades are low. What are your thoughts about this practice by the school?

Unfortunately, the numbers of students in most schools prevent them from treating students as individuals. Sometimes rules should be guides instead of unalterable mandates. If Jack had gotten into the writing class, he may have received more encouragement and met people willing to help him get into college. He would have missed a very rich experience, however. College meant much more to him after prison than it would have had he not been there.

6. When Jack is asked to make a box with a false bottom, his father explains that Rik is a drug dealer. Should Jack have refused to make the box? Would you?

You can't put your head in the sand once you know the truth. Then it becomes a conscious choice to act in a way that enables a law or ethic to be broken. We do have responsibility for these things; we are fooling ourselves if we think we don't. What about a lawyer who defends a guilty person? Is that ethical? Is it ethical to drive a car that's more harmful to the environment simply because you like its looks?

7. When Jack tries to find Lucas who had bought some of the hash, he learns that he's awaiting sentencing. His wife asks Jack if he ever thought of what would happen to the people who bought the dope. What responsibility do we have in anticipating how our actions affect others?

It may be argued that as the buyer, Lucas should be aware that he is involved in illegal acts, but shouldn't Jack be responsible for making the hash available? Does he have a duty not to tempt the weak? Are we required to try to protect others from themselves? Is Jack as responsible as the actual dealers?

8. What's your reaction to how Jack's father gets money to buy his plane ticket to be at Jack's trial?

Jack's father performs a blatantly dishonest act in crashing Jack's car to get the insurance money. Without the money, he might not have gotten to Jack's trial. Has he performed a victimless crime? Do the ends justify the means?

9. Did Jack get a fair sentence? Explain.

We know that Jack's a good kid on the inside, and we know that he does turn his life around, but the law doesn't consider individuals much. He may have been young and foolish, but he was fully cognizant that he was breaking the law and should have been prepared for the consequences of being caught. Should first time offenders be treated with lenience? Be sent to a "junior". prison? If Jack had not gotten some of the breaks he did get (sleeping in the hospital, getting out early to attend college), could prison have made Jack a criminal? Why or why not?

10. What are your impressions of prison life? How could it have been more rehabilitative?

The ease with which inmates can get drugs and prey on other prisoners doesn't make it the healthiest environment for contemplation. Performing useful work and required journaling would benefit some prisoners. I've read that meditation and diet has had positive effects on prisoners. More careful supervision might cut down on use of drugs and abuse by fellow prisoners

11. How does Jack cope in prison?

Jack tries to project a "nonthreating yet dangerous appearance" (p.164). He's lucky in landing a job as an X-ray technician, which keeps him safe from rape. His constant writing helped him process his experiences and grow as a writer.

12. When Jack reads his chart he finds that he's been labeled as "uncooperative and unwilling to tell the truth." The psychiatrist has labeled him a "situational sociopath" who is unable to honestly describe himself (p.177-8). How did he come to get these labels?

We cannot be objective observers of others. Our perceptions are filtered through our own experiences in addition to assumptions we make based on the facts we know about someone. If we know that someone has committed a crime would we be less trusting of his word? Should we be?

14

JUST ELLA
by MARGARET PETERSON HADDIX

Bibliographic information: Simon and Schuster, 1999; 185 pages.

Themes: Feminism, life work, finding satisfaction in a romantic relationship, fairy-tale adaptations.

Genre: Fantasy.

Main character: Ella Brown, 15.

Tips: The book reads more like historical fiction than fantasy. Haddix provides realistic explanations for the magical elements of the original Cinderella story, and they are products of Ella's resourcefulness. A good choice for those looking for a story of a "shero."

SYNOPSIS:

The ball has ended, the enigmatic woman who lost the glass slipper has been found, and she's living in the castle in preparation for her marriage to Prince Charming. It seems that Ella has everything she ever dreamed of, but she finds the life of a princess tedious and realizes that Charming is a shallow bore. Why can't he be more like her tutor, who is smart and socially conscious? When she informs Charm of her decision not to marry him, she lands in the dungeon; it seems one doesn't say no to the royals. Ever feisty and resourceful, Ella escapes and follows her wiser, more cautious heart.

DISCUSSION QUESTIONS/LEADER POINTS

1. Is there an advantage to the hardships Ella has endured growing up?

Ella's background makes it hard for her to be waited on and to be idle; she's able to act. It also makes her resourceful because she has had no one to depend on but herself. She knows how to survive, and, deprived of luxuries, she's had to find joy in simple, deeper things. It's also made her strong physically and emotionally.

2. In what ways is beauty a hindrance or advantage to Ella?

Sometimes girls who are pretty aren't taken seriously or are even perceived as dumb (e.g., the dumb blond). It might be harder to attract someone who appreciates your other attributes if you're pretty. It could also scare some potential suitors away. Ella and Charm are solely attracted to each other's looks. They don't talk much at the ball. They really don't have any basis for a sustaining relationship. Ask readers what they think of love at first sight? There are some examples of love at first sight that endured, and everyone would like to believe that it's possible to recognize a kindred spirit very quickly. Everyone has had the experience of meeting someone who seemed immediately familiar and that they felt they knew better than they possibly could have. These cases are based on more than just looks, though, and Ella's wasn't.

3. In what ways is her lack of beauty a hindrance or advantage to Mary?

Because Mary is not attractive, she seems almost invisible and is able to move freely around the castle without attracting attention. It's unlikely for her to be in a position where a suitor is only interested in her looks.

4. Why do you think Ella is so confused about whether she's in love?

It's easy to see why Ella's confused. She seems to have had her dreams come true. Her story is very romantic. Who wouldn't envy her marrying a handsome prince and going from rags to riches? But all of those things are superficial. When it comes to what really makes one happy, Ella finds her situation lacking. Ask readers if they've had a crush on someone who turned out to be different from what they at first perceived.

5. Ella believes that she has three choices in life: to hire out as a servant, to marry, or to become a tutor (p. 76). Women have many more choices these days. Is marriage as much of a goal as it once was? Should it be? What's the most important thing to consider when choosing what to do with one's life?

Ella realizes that it's important for her to have a useful life. She balks at the fact that the prince doesn't care about feeding his hungry subjects and appreciates Jed's efforts to provide for the war refugees. While marriage may be desirable, it shouldn't be the same kind of goal as a career; women should choose their careers without considering marriage as inevitable. Ask readers what things they consider when thinking about their life plans. How important is a feeling of usefulness or of contributing to society when making choices?

6. Could Ella have been smarter about gaining her freedom? What advice would you give to her?

She could have been deceptive, but seems unable to be so. Are there times when being true to yourself should be compromised — say in the case of saving your life?

7. Manners dictate life at court to the point where they could endanger life. Ella's quick response may have saved Lord Reston's life. Can you think of contemporary examples in which attention to manners may have negative results?

Women often put up with things like sexual innuendo or sexist labels because of manners. If they protest, they risk being labeled bitch.

Another example of when we may disregard our natural instinct in helping someone stretches from manners to liability; these days some people might hesitate to administer lifesaving procedures for fear of being sued if things go wrong.

8. Jed says, "People would rather believe in fairy godmothers than think that you take charge of your own destiny." What does he mean? Is this true?

If it were so easy to take charge of your own destiny, many more people would be fit, thin, and rich. When someone succeeds, it's easier to believe that they got all the breaks than to believe that with hard work you could do the same. It's probably the fear of failure that keeps some people from even trying. You have to take a risk and work hard to realize your dreams.

9. What did you think of how the author handles the magical elements of the tale?

Ella's resourcefulness wins her the glass slippers. Her deadline is also believably handled in a way that would make it possible for wild rumors to surface. Haddix did a good job of making the story realistic and hinting at how some elements could have been embellished by retelling the story. Straining realism, however, Ella seemed very modern and at one point says that she feels like an automaton (p 119). Ask readers if they detected any other anachronisms.

10. After Ella escapes from the dungeon and returns to Lucille's house, she chooses six of her father's book's to take with her. What do you think of her choices? What books would you take with you?

Ella's choices are practical and will serve her well. This is a fun question, but you'll want to keep track of the time you spend with it.

11. What lesson(s) does Ella learn from her experiences?

Ella learns that what you think you want may not be all that it seems. She learns to be more cautious with her heart. She learns that she needs to feel useful to be happy.

12. Do you think that Ella will marry Jed?

Some readers may feel cheated that Ella and Jed don't have a romantic moment, but we're given hope that their love will grow in a realistic and strong way as they work together and as Ella pursues her own dreams for herself. Here's a reminder that when someone truly loves you, he wants you to realize your potential.

15

THE KILLER'S COUSIN
by NANCY WERLIN

Bibliographic information: Delacorte, 1998; 129 pages.
Themes: Guilt, blame, emotional problems, murder.

Genre: Mystery

Main character: David Yaffe, 17.

Tips: This is a very well crafted mystery with interesting characters, intriguing sub-plots, suspense, and satisfying twists and turns. Strong language and references to sex may put off some readers, as will the ghost.

SYNOPSIS:

Seventeen-year-old David Yaffe, recently acquitted of murdering his girlfriend, moves into the home of his aunt and uncle in Massachusetts to finish his senior year in anonymity. The family is still recovering from the suicide of teenaged Kathy five years earlier. The relationship between David's aunt and uncle is strained, and David begins to believe that his antagonistic 11-year-old cousin, Lily, is very troubled. Living in the attic where his cousin Kathy died, David begins feeling her presence and realizes that she is trying to tell him something.

DISCUSSION QUESTIONS/LEADER POINTS

1. Does David deserve to feel as guilty as he does about Emily's death?

While it's natural for David to feel some responsibility for Emily's death, he is being especially hard on himself. However, his burden might ease with time. What might allow him to stop punishing himself? He *was* wrong in resorting to throwing a punch. He almost hits Lily, also. His natural violent responses are a problem. What makes one person react physically and another not?

2. David wonders why people want to look at pictures of others who are in pain (see page 76). Why do you think that they do?

We may be drawn to viewing the pain of others as a means of reassuring ourselves and feeling lucky. It might make us feel safe. As if there were only a measured amount suffering to go around, it's almost a relief to see it being experienced by others. We may just be drawn empathetically, since we've all experienced pain and its depth. Ask readers to recall seeing pictures like Raina's. Bring photos like Dorothea Lange's faces of the Depression and ask teens how they make them feel.

3. Why does Frank choose to look so different from his peers? Does he have a positive self-concept? Courage?

Frank will, no doubt, be a favorite character of your group. Smart and unpretentious, everyone would like to enjoy the kind of comfort he has with himself. He has the courage to be different. Ask your group if shaving his head is a little too extreme. It probably has the effect of making some people think he's dangerous or racist. Is this his intention? What kind of assumptions do people make based solely on looks? What impressions do things like piercings, hairstyles and colors, tattoos, and the like give people? Do teens fully think through the consequences of making the choice to have a certain look?

4. Frank says he's shaved his head to upset people and that when people get upset, you find out who they really are. Would you agree with his statement? Why or why not?

Don't we really always try to put on a pleasant face? When someone asks how you're doing, do you always tell the truth, or do you just say, fine or great even when you're not? However, when someone is moved to anger or fear, reaction's become less calculated and you see beyond the individual's persona.

5. Why is Julia so cold to David?

Julia blames David's mother for supporting Kathy's decision to choose her own path, for suggesting Vic give back her rent money, and for marrying outside of her religion.

6. Why is it so hard for Vic and Julia to realize that Lily's in trouble?

Julia and Vic are too involved in their own dysfunction to notice Lily's unusual behavior. They haven't gotten over Kathy's death. You'll want to mention that marriages often break down after the death of a child. There is tendency to want to blame someone, and it turns out to be the spouse. Also, it's not uncommon for parents to overlook their child's problems because they don't want to admit that she's troubled. Sometimes parents focus on their child's trouble more as a reflection on themselves, which is very painful.

7. Why does Lily want to serve as a go-between for her parents? Why is she threatened when they talk to each other?

Lily feels so miserable about Kathy that having her parents or David not miserable may be intolerable. Also, she is so troubled that she may feel privileged in being in the position of go-between. She has a special role for each parent. Also, her parents' division keeps them from focusing on her, which she may feel she deserves. Like David, she has a need to punish herself.

8. How are David and Fox Mulder alike?

The references to the X-files unfortunately date the book. Most of the members of my own group weren't viewers and yours may not be either. On page 71, Werlin writes that Mulder's quest for truth would never restore his innocence, and David's innocence is also beyond restoration. Also, Mulder feels responsible for not being able to protect his sister. Similarly, David couldn't protect Emily from her brother and her accidental death.

9. Would the story have been as effective without Kathy's ghost? Did she enhance or detract from the story?

Some readers might find the supernatural element of the ghost troubling. Except for the ghost, it's a realistic story with authentic characters. What if the ghost's appearances were manifestations of David's intuition, not actual ghostly interventions? Would that have changed the story? Is it more interesting to have an actual ghost than for David to intuit Kathy's message?

10. When David rescues Lily, he tells her that she is like him. In what ways are they alike and not alike?

Lily and David are alike in not trusting themselves and not quite forgiving themselves for their deeds. They both have lost their innocence. Lily's deed did take a little planning and was done with some malice, however, and David's act was purely an immediate angry response. Does this mean David is less guilty than Lily? Lily was young enough that she couldn't have thought through the consequences of her action, so maybe that makes her less responsible than if she had done it when she was older.

11. Is it reasonable for David to want his father to know that Emily's death was an accident without having to tell him?

Teens will sympathize with David's wanting his father to know that Emily's death was an accident. Ask whether it's reasonable to expect a parent to know his child that well, or whether David was being stubborn, as if his father's knowing would grant him some magical forgiveness. Just as he initially wouldn't defend himself, it may have been part of his feeling that he deserves to suffer.

12. What is the significance or the winged figures in the eyes of Raina's drawing of David?

The girls in the eyes of Raina's picture were Emily and Lily—the girls who haunted him, but there is some argument for it being the sisters, Kathy and Lily, signifying the mystery David was on course to solve. Nancy Werlin kindly answered my e-mail and wrote that you could make a case for either, but that she thought it was Emily and Lily.

13. What is the significance of David having his own Star Market card at the end of the book?

Readers might not understand the significance of the Star Market card exchange or why people would want to be so protective of their privacy. Some might miss the rebellious fun of the exchange, but others will understand and appreciate it. The fact that David's card comes back to him, full circle, is a reflection of his completing his quest by unraveling the mystery of his cousin's death and coming to terms with his past.

16

THE KINDLING
by JENNIFER ARMSTRONG
and NANCY BUTCHER

Bibliographic information: HarperCollins, 2002; 224 pages.

Themes: Survival, culture.

Genre: Apocalyptic science fiction.

Main characters: Mommy, Hunter, Teacher, Action Figure, Teddy Bear, Baby, and Doll, whose ages range from five to fifteen.

Tips: While the premise and the damage the characters display sound like they make for dreary reading, interesting details about how the children piece together the remains of a culture, the interaction between characters, and the continuous action make this book a page turner. It is the first in a series.

SYNOPSIS:

Five years after a deadly virus has wiped out the population of the world, the only survivors, Mommy, Hunter, Teacher, Action Figure, Teddy Bear, Baby, and Doll have formed a functional, unlikely family. They assume names that represent the roles they adopt, having forgotten most of what life was like before the year of the Fire-us. One evening after a dinner of cones meant for ice cream, they hear a knock at the door. Enter Angerman with the mannequin Bad Guy in tow. Angerman is on his way to Washington, D.C., to find President, whom he believes may be one of the few adults still alive. On his heels are two wild children, and the family adopts Puppy and Kitty. When the some of the children decide to go with Angerman to Washington, Mommy must confront her agoraphobia so that the family can stay together. Their journey begins under the guidance of Teacher, who keeps The Book, a compilation of phrases gleaned from such varied sources as the Bible, magazine advertisements, newspaper headlines, and a telephone book. In The Book, Teacher records the dreams of the others and looks for answers; travelling on everything from bicycles to boats the group begins their journey. The book ends with a cliffhanger: a mysterious adult woman dressed all in white is sighted on the shore.

DISCUSSION QUESTIONS/LEADER POINTS

1. What is the significance of the name of the town (Lazarus) where the family lives for five years?

Lazarus, the biblical character, rises from the dead. The town of Lazarus in the book similarly has a second chance at life as the home of the survivors.

2. Is it conceivable that the survivors could have such vague memories? To have forgotten their own names?

It is not surprising that the children have lost memories, not uncommon for people to block out trauma. Being left to fend for themselves after having witnessed the death of everyone around them and being at the mercy of the elements and wild animals is more than enough trauma for anyone. It's why Teacher can't sleep. In sleep we can't keep memories from coming into our consciousness.

3. The characters adopt roles that are reflected by their names? Which role would you take, and why, if you were part of family of survivors?

This is sure to reflect aspects of participants' personalities. The more adventurous will choose the role of Hunter. I am attracted to the piecing together of what remains of the culture, like Teacher.

4. There are many examples of how things have become translated by the children as if through so many whispered telephone game messages. Teacher teaches the children their "Baby-sees." Kids used to go to LMNOP School. Can you think of examples of this kind of childish translation from your life?

My daughter said that she was having a Velcro class instead of Dalcroze. She says we can open the windows and let the air come in through the screams. She told me that an octopus has action cups on its legs. Everybody has at least one of these stories from his or her own history or from someone they know. It's easy to imagine how these kinds of mistakes are transformed into the family's vernacular.

5. What symptoms of trauma do the characters display?

All of the children display emotional problems. They have bad dreams. The youngest children act too young. Mommy is agoraphobic. Teacher is an insomniac. Action Figure seems to have reverted to a more primitive state of being. Angerman is most extreme, assuming his anchorman persona and reporting news at a safe distance while carrying around his strange charge, Bad Guy.

6. How do you think that Teacher decides what to include in The Book?

It's interesting to find out what gets included, what looks important to her. Ask readers how advertisements are constructed to make them seem important. It's easy to see how one might develop misconceptions based on facts that are pieced together in a different way from the original intention. Ask readers if they can think of examples of how conclusions were made about artifacts from the past that were later proven incorrect, for example'., the dinosaur Iguanadon was once thought to have a horn on its head that turned out to be a thumb.

7. Which of the children do you think has the best chance of emotional well-being and why?

It may be argued that Hunter seems the most well-adjusted, but Action Figure is the most carefree and fearless, probably because he's too young to remember much about the Fire-us. Readers might make cases for the others.

8. Why don't the others demand that Angerman leave Bad Guy behind? Why is Bad Guy so important to Angerman?

They understand that somehow Bad Guy is necessary for Angerman. Angerman needs to have someone to blame so that he can accept what has happened. Perhaps Bad Guy allows him to not feel guilty for being spared. Ask readers whether they think the survivors might feel guilt for surviving.

9. Mommy reflects on her love for the younger children. "Looking at them was sometimes the most terrifying part of the day" (p. 57). Why does she think this?

When you love people you face the risk of losing them, and their hurts become worse than your own. The world is a very dangerous place for Mommy; she can't even go outside. The chances of something bad happening to her loved ones must be a possibility she's constantly aware of.

10. Angerman persuades the others to go to Washington with him to find President. Is this good plan? Where would you go and whom would you try to find if you were in this situation?

It's probably a good plan to look for others so that their future is richer and more varied. If others are alive, they will add skills and hands to aid in the group's survival. They have to move at some point to find more resources.

11. Why does Angerman want to take Puppy and Kitten with him?

Company offers comfort and help, and, when they are weaker and younger, they can make you brave. Ask readers whether it's easier to be brave when you're taking care of someone else.

12. How is Mommy a good mother?

She's very protective. She reassures the younger children even when she doesn't believe her words. She faces her fear to rescue them and to keep the family together. Their well-being is her priority.

13. Who do you think is the woman in white?

Is she an angel? Have they died? Is she a doctor or nurse? A nun? Whatever theories readers may have, one this is certain: they'll want to read the next book in the series to find out.

17

KISSING DOORKNOBS
by TERRY SPENCER HESSER

Bibliographic information: Delacorte, 1998; 149 pages.

Themes: Obsessive-compulsive disorder.

Genre: Realistic fiction.

Main character: Tara, 14.

Tips: Reassure readers that everyone has some compulsive behaviors, it's only when your compulsiveness interferes with your free will that it becomes a problem.

SYNOPSIS:

Tormented by her compulsions, Tara struggles to appear normal to her friends and avoid the wrath of her frustrated mother. Repeatedly misdiagnosed, Tara's condition is recognized by a visitor and she begins her journey toward understanding and overcoming obsessive-compulsive disorder (OCD).

DISCUSSION QUESTIONS/LEADER POINTS

1. Why is it valuable to read about people who have behavioral disorders?

Ask teens how accommodating they would be of Tara's disorder, especially if they didn't know it was a disorder. Are they more likely to be understanding of someone's weird behavior if they are familiar with the disorder and know that she has it? Ask readers if there are people they perceive as weird who might suffer from OCD. Will the possibility make you think of or treat them differently?

2. Tara's mother implies that Tara's problems stem from her religion. What would make her think this? Are there similarities between Tara's behaviors and the beliefs and practices of a religious practitioner?

It may be possible that because Tara's mother is not religious she might wish to blame Tara's Catholic father for her disorder. There is a human tendency to want to assign blame for what one doesn't understand or doesn't have control over. Rituals are integral to religious expression, and Tara's behaviors are also ritualistic. Ask readers if they can think of similarities between rituals that they've witnessed and compulsive behavior.

3. Why is it so important for Tara's parents to figure out whether Tara's condition is their fault? Does it keep them from helping her?

As if in finding the source, they will find an answer, Tara's parents are distracted by their desire to blame. There is probably also the desire to reflect blame. Each feels guilt about the possibility of the problem being his or her fault. They fear their own imperfection or that they are responsible for damaging their child. All this ruminating is about them, and it keeps them from focusing on Tara and being persistent about getting help.

4. Is Tara's mother's growing anger a reasonable reaction to this baffling condition?

Her reaction is realistic, if not reasonable. Anger is one reaction to fear, lack of control. Anger causes Tara's mother to cavalierly admit that she has smoked marijuana, thereby fueling Tara's behavior. Later she is driven to lashing out literally and she strikes Tara. While Tara's behavior is trying, anger and violence are not justifiable. Tara's mother is an angry person who needs to learn how to manage her anger.

5. Is it plausible that Greta and Tara would be so different? Is Greta's response to Tara's disorder healthy?

Ask readers how different they are from their sibs. No reader could help but cheer when Greta humiliates the boy who molests Tara. He certainly deserves his fate, but like her mother's anger, Greta's anger manifests itself in violence, and she, too, must learn control.

6. Keesha and Kristin disagree about the model in a magazine. Kristin thinks she's beautiful, and Keesha thinks she looks starved and bruised. Which side do you think is more accurate and healthier?

The effects of the tyranny of advertising and its images of women on the female psyche is large. Unrealistic images in magazines can make girls feel unhappy with their bodies. Remind readers that only a very small percentage of women in the world can attain the "ideal" we see in media images naturally, and even then it may not be a healthy way of being. Keesha gets the cheers for feeling good about herself the way she is. There are hints that Kristin's life may lack some stability, so maybe she exerts control where she can—with her weight. Are there similarities between obsessive-compulsive disorder and eating disorders?

7. In Donna's orbit, Tara seems to relax and lose much of her obsessiveness. Why do you think that Donna has this effect on her?

It seems mysterious how Tara's problem becomes less persistent when she is with Donna. It may be a coincidence, a natural ebb, or it may be a result of Donna's infectious devil-may-care attitude. Donna is a risk taker. She does things that Tara would be afraid to do, and she has survived and not broken her mother's back.

8. Why do you think that Tara keeps being misdiagnosed?

It's disheartening and frightening to see how many times Tara is misdiagnosed. The misdiagnoses' complicate her situation and frustrates her family. It's clearly difficult to diagnose such a mysterious and unusual disorder; there are no tests to confirm its presence and the symptoms vary from person to person. Tara can't even name which of her behaviors are obsessive because she doesn't have a guide. Also, some of her obsessiveness is less problematic. For example, her mother has no idea that Tara experiences the symmetry aspect of the disorder because it isn't as obvious as some of the other manifestations.

9. Why do you think Tara feels relieved when something bad happens (e.g. when she is molested or when her mother slaps her)?

It validates her behavior, which is predicated on the belief that bad things will happen if she doesn't perform rituals to keep them at bay.

10. Uncle Joe: hero or devil?

Readers will cheer when Tara insists on buying condoms for Donna, who has just confided that she has had sex. Tara's concern over her friend makes her uncharacteristically assertive. She demands that the pharmacist (Sam's Uncle Joe) sell them condoms, which he refuses to do without parental permission. Should parental permission be required? (It's not.) Uncle Joe may think he is acting responsibly and discouraging them from having sex, but there isn't anything heroic about denying teens contraception or protection. Lack of protection doesn't ensure abstinence. It ensures the possibility of unfortunate consequences.

11. What is your reaction to Sam's relapse?

Not a Hollywood ending, Sam's relapse elicits sympathy. It is, however, a feasible occurrence when compared to *Multiple Choice* (also about OCD) by Janet Tashjian which has an incredibly easy resolution.

18

LOVE AMONG THE WALNUTS
by JEAN FERRIS

Bibliographic information: Harcourt Brace, 1998; 216 pages.

Themes: The pros and cons of isolation, how mental health is defined, the healing power of love.

Genre: Farce.

Main characters: Sandy, (male) a young adult.

Tips: Teens who enjoy books like Louis Sachar's *Holes* will enjoy this book. Pragmatists may have some trouble with it, but most will find it entertaining.

SYNOPSIS:

Tired of the rat race, multimillionaire Horatio Alger Huntington-Ackerman moves his new bride to an isolated mansion, where the closest neighbor is an exclusive psychiatric hospital. There they raise their son, Sandy, in happy seclusion from the outside world. The only break in their happiness is the monthly visits from Horatio's jealous, conniving brothers, Bart and Bernie. When the brothers try to poison the family so they can inherit the fortune, all succumb to coma (including Attila the chicken) except for Sandy and Bentley, the butler. The comatose patients are moved to the neighboring Walnut Manor where their nurse, Sunnie, is true to her name and effects change on all of the residents while Bentley (who happens to be an amateur chemist) searches for an antidote. All comes out well in the end, although Bart and Bernie continue to attempt murder. The bad are brought to justice, the patients are liberated, and love prevails.

DISCUSSION QUESTIONS/LEADER POINTS

1. Why does Horatio reject the world? Is his exile cowardly? Heroic? Selfish?

It's especially hard for teenagers to appreciate the desire to get away from the buzz of culture. They find it preposterous that someone wouldn't want to know what's going on in the world, even though they will acknowledge that even their lives get too busy sometimes. Ask if it's easier to understand someone like Horatio, who had some life experience wishing to live in isolation.

Horatio doesn't really give anything up in his exile. His companies are running themselves. He has enough money. It isn't like he's rejecting the capitalistic life; he is actually benefiting from it. So he isn't making a statement or being heroic. He just chooses what makes him happy, but choosing isolation for his son may be selfish. His desire may be noble: He wants to protect Sandy, but Sandy deserves to be informed and allowed to make a choice for himself. Ask readers whether Sandy's parents cause him harm in protecting him. What is he missing? What things is he protected from?

2. What are the pros and cons of growing up in isolation?

Boredom, no choice, and no challenge are some of the drawbacks of growing up in isolation. Absence of conflict is both a positive and negative. Conflict is necessary to develop coping skills, and, unless one remains isolated, one will certainly encounter conflict. Ask whether beliefs are stronger when they are challenged, when one is required to question them. What decisions do we make based on our reactions to culture or global issues? The biggest outrage for the teens will no doubt be the lack of exposure to culture and other people. At a time when they are trying to find their places in society, when society almost seems to define them, it's hard for teens to imagine life without it.

3. Should this be a young adult book? Why or why not?

Many adults have enjoyed and recommended this book. Since it doesn't have a teen protagonist or address teen issues, it may be classified as young adult merely because Ferris's other work is considered young adult. You could easily foray into how books are defined as age appropriate. What about books like Harry Potter, a children's book enjoyed by all ages. As a former children's librarian, I read many children's books that were more engaging and well written than many adult books. Is there a way to get beyond the limits that labels put on books?

4. Are the inmates of Walnut Manor crazy? What transforms them? Do you think real patients could be healed similarly?

Many emotional maladies could be healed with love and attention, the lack of which is why most of the Walnut Manor residents are there. Sunnie's simple ministrations transform them. Ask readers whether they believe people who are labeled "troubled" may just be unloved.

5. Do you think that a place like the Walnut Foundation would attract lots of guests? Why or why not? How would a visit to the Walnut Foundation be different from a regular vacation?

There's no doubt that most people could benefit from taking time out of their busy lives and recharging at a place like Walnut Manor by learning to play and relax and relate to others. Teens might not find a hiatus at Walnut Manor as attractive as adults. My guess is that they would rather go someplace exciting. They may not have experienced vacations as stressful. Ask whether they have, or whether they think vacations have been stressful for their parents and why.

6. Do you think that it's necessary for the residents to return to the outside world to stay healthy? Why or why not?

A consequence of living in isolation might make one intolerant, but it doesn't seem to have that effect on Sandy. His life is very narrow. Many people find that making a contribution to society makes life satisfying. Also, exposure to the variety of life is expansive and pleasurable. If we pay a price for the pleasure, most people would think it worthwhile. So, while escaping from the world for a time seems like a good way to recharge, total exile may be irresponsible. Do we have a responsibility to contribute to society?

7. What is the significance of Mousey's postcoma change of voice?

Mousey's change of voice is puzzling. If the story is to be read like a kind of fairytale, she is enchanted or cursed by the evil brothers then awakened by love, and not just restored, but also made better than before because the world has been expanded. How is she better after the enchantment? Her voice is loud enough for others to hear. It will reach beyond her small circle of family.

8. Why do you think that Jean Ferris wrote this book?

Ferris addresses the need for balance between the busyness of life and simplicity. She asks us to question what responsibility we have to be active members of society. She reminds us that love is transformational and necessary for health. She does all this in a very entertaining way. Does the humor make big questions easier to consider or does it lessen the impact?

19

THE LOVELY BONES
by ALICE SEBOLD

Bibliographic information: Little, Brown, 2002; 328 pages.

Themes: Justice, grief, guilt, vengeance, the nature of Heaven, victims of crime.

Genre: Realistic fiction with fantasy elements.

Main character: Susie Salmon, 14.

Tips: This book is for older teens. Technically, it is an adult book, but teens are asking for it. Sebold does a good job of portraying a 14 year old, and it's a high interest subject for teens. Some teens will be uncomfortable with the supernatural elements and sexual situations.

SYNOPSIS:

From her heaven, Susie Salmon observes the effects that her brutal rape and murder have on her family, friends, and her murderer. Those she loves move toward healing, and Susie pushes on the "in-between" and extracts justice.

DISCUSSION QUESTIONS/LEADER POINTS

1. Susie learns that each person's heaven is custom-made to fit his or her desires and dreams. If this were true, what would your heaven be like?

What a lovely notion of heaven Sebold gives us, although it is still limited by human longing, at least in Susie's case. One would think that part of heaven would be freedom from that. Ask your group why the author didn't portray heaven as blissful for Susie. Do those who die with unfinished business have to come to terms with their deaths to enjoy heaven fully, or is that just Susie's fondest wish.

2. Is it an accident that Susie touches Ruth as she leaves Earth? Why is Ruth a good or a bad choice?

Whether or not Ruth is Susie's choice, she is the perfect one. She seems to understand the dubious gift with which she is bestowed. It makes her a more sensitive writer. She is able to somehow appreciate her special position and bond with Ray, eventually in the most intimate way.

3. When police question Ray about Susie's death their ardor is "fueled by the guilt they read into Ray's dark skin" (p 26). Can you think of other examples in which a person's ethnicity alone has raised suspicions?

Question 3 will bring loads of examples of racial profiling; especially these days when it seems all Middle Eastern-looking people are suspect.

4. When Susie observes her mother alone in the morning, she discovers her mother for the first time as a person (p. 43). Do you understand this feeling? How do you think of your mother as a person, separate from being a mother?

Seeing parents as people is a provocative idea for teens. Often we don't see our parents as individuals till we are adults. Ask for descriptions of parents that involve their not being parents. This may be especially telling if mom doesn't work outside the home. Dad may be a lawyer, but who is Mom outside of family duty?

5. Susie observes that Lindsey suffers from "Walking Dead Syndrome," when people see the dead person and not the surviving relative (p 59). How does it affect Lindsey that people don't seem to really see *her*? How would it make you feel?

It seems to Lindsey that when people look at her, all they see is Susie. Teens will sympathize with Lindsey. We've all had feeling of invisibility; having lost a sister compounds this awful feeling for Lindsey. It helps fuel her resolution to find evidence and take an incredible risk by breaking into Harvey's house. Ask readers if they think she did this for herself or for her father.

6. Which family member is least affected by Susie's death? Why?

The point of who is least affected by Susie's death is debatable. Buckley, the youngest and most resilient family member, handles Susie's death the best, yet his life will be the one most overshadowed by it—he had less time before the event that changed everything for the family. Lindsey may have a better foundation for happiness because she had more time in a stable, secure home.

7. Because he realizes no one ever really looks the way they do in photographs, and that the photo is not Susie, Ray retires Susie's picture to one of his mother's giant volumes of Indian poetry like the flowers she's pressed that are turning to dust (p. 112) Is this a fitting place for her photo? Abigail echoes Ray's act later when she leaves Susie's picture in the airport. How are these two acts alike?

Susie is like one of those flowers pressed in Ray's mother's book, plucked in the bloom of life she remains forever as she was in memory, forever 14, although her body is turning to dust. Ray's act of putting away her photo signals that he is ready to go on with his life. When Abigail leaves Susie's photo at the airport, she, too, is moving on, albeit more tenuously.

8. The surgeon who prepares to repair Jack's knee reflects that he and Jack are alike, the same age and married with children, but yet how very different they are (p. 142). Can they ever be alike?

The surgeon's thoughts reveal his empathy in the sort of "there but for the grace of God" sentiment someone else's tragedy awakens, especially when we can see how ordinary and like us that person is. It makes us aware how fragile our fortune is, how quickly it can change, and how precious it is.

9. Abigail says she wants to be more than a mother. What does she mean by this? How does this explain her leaving?

There is evidence that Abigail never wanted to be a mother, but she accepted the role, and her leaving is motivated more by needing to define herself as someone other than a mother. If one is a mother, she can be hurt in the most devastating way, by having her child killed. It's unfortunate that she leaves her living children to try to achieve this. Ask readers if they think she's afraid to be their mother.

10. Do you think that the dead really watch us? Has anything you've experienced suggested to you that this is possible? Does the author make the notion comforting or disturbing?

We hear many stories of angelic intervention. Who pushes a child's head a millimeter to the right to avoid taking the corner of a piece of furniture in the eye? Who cradled my baby's head as it sped toward the hard bathroom floor, so that it eased down gently like slow motion? Sebold gives us a comforting image rather than a frightening one as some other authors do.

11. "Lindsey and Buckley had come to live their lives in direct proportion to what effect it would have on a fragile father" (p. 244). What does this mean, and how do you think it affects the siblings?

It must be a burden to be constantly aware of how important you are to someone, how you must protect yourself for them more than for yourself. How could this have limited Lindsey's and Buckley's lives? Is it fair of Jack? Ask readers if they think about being this important to their parents.

12. As Abigail takes her husband's hand in the hospital, Susie recalls a play she and Lindsey acted out as children. Lindsey, as the widow of a dead knight, recites, "How can I be expected to be trapped for the rest of my life by a man frozen in time?" (p. 276). Is Jack frozen in time? Will Abigail be stuck?

13. Why does Abigail describe her attitude about her mother as a "scorched earth policy" (p. 318) the wartime practice of burning everything in one's path so as to leave no resources that the enemy can use to regain strength and fight another day)?

Abigail's hesitation in committing herself to staying has to do with realizing that Jack will always be haunted, but accepting that. It may be argued that he did a better job of getting on with his life; he didn't run away. Abigail had to run away to begin to accept the events of her life, including her all or nothing "scorched earth policy" regarding her mother. It's immature to judge people solely for their unattractive qualities. Ask readers whether they've ever assumed a "scorched earth policy" toward someone else.

14. When confronted with fresh evidence connecting George Harvey to Susie's murder, Abigail doesn't want the investigation to begin again because "connecting her life to his capture and punishment spoke more about choosing to live with the enemy than about having to learn to live in the world without me" (p. 290). How do you interpret her feelings?

Abigail has come to terms with the absence of her daughter; she doesn't want to dwell on Harvey's presence in the world. Is this a healthier attitude than wanting vengeance?

15. What's your reaction to Susie's inhabiting Ruth's body and making love with Ray?

The weakest part of the book was Susie's possession of Ruth's body. It seemed to take the book to a less realistic realm. Does it bring peace to Susie? How would you feel if you were Ray or Ruth? Would you feel used? It is certainly a gift on Ruth's part. What do you think the future will hold for Ray and Ruth?

16. What are the lovely bones?

On page 320, Susie says the lovely bones are the connections her death created, and she finds peace in the fact that her life resulted in these lovely bones. Why do you think she uses the image of bones?

17. What's your reaction to the way George Harvey is killed?

Harvey's death is very satisfying, although some readers may want him to suffer more. Didn't he suffer all of his strange life? This question may draw you back into a discussion of whether the dead intervene in our world.

20

MARTYN PIG
by KEVIN BROOKS

Bibliographic Information: Scholastic, 2002; 230 pages.

Themes: Alcoholism, family dysfunction, acceptance, judgment, crime.

Genre: Mystery

Main character: Teenager Martyn Pig.

Tips: Philosophical issues don't slow the pace of this fine mystery. Teens will enjoy the plot twists and turns and will relate to Martyn's awkward crush on Alex and how vulnerable it makes him. Martyn is an offbeat, captivating character. He is accepting of what life brings his way and doesn't feel sorry for himself. He lives very much in his head, and the reader has a vicarious, front-row seat. Some teens are bound to find Martyn unrealistic, but there are few who won't be drawn into the story.

SYNOPSIS:

Darkly humorous, Martyn Pig is the story of a teen jaded by neglect—an absent mother and an abusive, alcoholic father. During an argument Martyn, accidentally causes his father's death and is stunned into inaction. He confides in his neighbor, a slightly older teen with whom he is infatuated. He persuades Alex to help him dispose of his father's body. Meanwhile, Alex's untrusting boyfriend bugs Alex's purse, learns of the death and the plan to dispose of the body, and tries to blackmail Martyn. The plot thickens with a visit from Martyn's aunt, whom Martyn and Alex manage to convince that Martyn's father is alive. There's an inheritance up for grabs, an edgy scene when the teens dump the body, and another death and a double double-crossing. This is a gripping mystery with an offbeat voice.

DISCUSSION QUESTIONS/LEADER POINTS

1. After his father's death, is Martyn's situation really as desperate as he thinks it is? What do you think he should do?

Martyn is probably stunned by his lack of feeling as much by as his father's death. He might feel guilty that he doesn't care. He might think that the police will realize that he doesn't care. Do you think Martyn is afraid of being accused of his father's murder or of not caring? Are both offenses punishable? After some time has elapsed, he's convinced his hesitation is incriminating.

2. Is Martyn responsible for his father's death? Why or why not?

Martyn is a typical child of an irresponsible adult. He feels responsible and is made responsible for things that aren't his responsibility. His father was a horror. Martyn probably was relieved he was dead. He may have wished he were dead. His guilt over those feelings makes him feel responsible. His father was responsible for his own death because he drank too much and became antagonistic, contentious, and unsteady.

3. Does the author make what Martyn and Alex do with the body believable?

The decision to dispose of his father's body and the disposal are absurd, but the reader is right there on that white-knuckle ride through the blizzard. Also, absurd and comical are the lengths to which Alex and Martyn go in order to deceive his aunt into believing that her brother is alive. If not totally believable, these incidents are highly entertaining and good excerpts for booktalking.

4. Martyn tells Alex that badness is a relative thing (p. 75). Is Martyn correct in his assessment that a thing is wrong only if you think it's wrong or if you're caught by others who think it's wrong?

Martyn's philosophical musings provide much fodder for discussion. Is badness relative? Can our judgments be completely objective? Is lying always wrong, for example. What if you lie to save someone's life? Teens will think of many examples of how bad thing can be justified for a greater good.

5. How do you explain Martyn's encounter with his father on the beach? Was his father really there?

Is the encounter on the beach an act of forgiveness? Does his father actually appear? Martyn may be dreaming. It's a very common occurrence for people to encounter the recently deceased in dreams and be given some kind of advice or reassuring message. Ask your group if they know of examples.

6. Martyn says, "Home is home, I suppose. No matter how much you hate it, you still need it. You need whatever you're used to. You need security" (p. 114). Do you agree with him? and How does this belief color his life?

Martyn's belief that one needs what one's used to illustrates his acceptance of intolerable circumstances. Thinking his situation is intolerable would only add to his suffering. The only security he's ever known, albeit questionable security, is in his home. Why would he assume anything's better when he has no examples of something better?

7. After considering records, books, and a luxury item, Martyn concludes that there's nothing he'd choose to have with him if he were stranded on a desert island. How does this conclusion reflect his state of mind? What would you take?

Martyn's choice not to take anything with him if he were stranded is another example of his acceptance of his situation. Being deprived of basic needs has made him stoical; what relief would luxuries bring?

8. When Martyn was younger, he used to try to imagine what is was like to be dead, "a total absence of everything" (p. 149). Does this practice reflect feelings of hopelessness, a wish to escape reality, philosophical curiosity, or a natural talent for Zen meditation? Have you ever done this?

Martyn seems to question the very nature of reality. Why does he think this way, and is he insightful or disturbed? Martyn's practice of trying to imagine what it would be like to experience a total absence of everything is similar to a meditation technique, getting at what is beyond the thoughts. The practice probably reflects all of the above.

9. Martyn is very introspective and philosophical. He wonders why people so aggressively clean away snow, why mail carriers whistle, what happens when one loses oneself in sleep? Are these common thoughts that most people just don't articulate, or is he unusual?

Why do people so seriously concern themselves with trivialities? This can be a fun topic. Why *do* people shovel snow when it's unnecessary? Why do people water their lawns so they're green? Who cares? Why do people weed so aggressively? Why do people edge their lawns? Why do people dress fake geese and display them in their yards? Maybe in some cases there are city ordinances requiring, for example, shoveling snow, or maybe the fear of being sued motivates some people. Sometimes people do some of the above because they enjoy them, but often that is not the reason.

10. Which character acts most deplorably?

The most deplorable character is a matter of opinion. Is it Alex for leading Martyn on and killing her boyfriend? Is it her mother for helping helping carry out the scheme? Is it Alex's boyfriend for trying to blackmail Martyn? Or is it Martyn's drunken, abusive father?

11. At what point did you suspect that Alex is double-crossing Martyn? Why is it so easy for Alex to fool Martyn?

Toughened by a hard life, Martyn is conversely innocent in the ways of the heart. He has a very big crush on Alex and dreams that she will come to care for him in the same way. He's so lovestruck that he overlooks clues to her real motives, though the reader begins to suspect she is not the girl Martyn believes she is.

12. Why does Alex write to Martin? Do you think that they'll see each other again? Should he be angry with her?

Alex's letter nicely completes the circle of events. It finishes the story that Martyn will write or has written. There is really no point in Martyn's being angry, but it would certainly be understandable if he were. Here is yet another example of his acceptance. What make's him so accepting?

13. Is Martyn better off with his aunt?

Martin is marginally better off with his aunt, though he is still missing love and attention. We assume she doesn't malign or hit him.

14. What is the significance of the up-curve arrow on the last page?

The arrow points upward, which seems a hopeful course, but it also curves, which implies that the course is not straight. The arrow may also represent guiding forces that exist outside of Martyn. He has been swept along. If followed, the curve will make a circle, like the story. On Martyn the cover, the exit sign is on the outside, and Simon is still going around.

21

MIND'S EYE
by PAUL FLEISCHMAN

Bibliographic information: Holt, 1999; 108 pages.

Themes: Reaction to disability, use of imagination, escapism.

Genre: Play.

Main characters: Courtney, 16, and Elva, 80.

Tips: Some teens will especially enjoy the imaginary trips and appreciate the creativity involved. It would be an interesting assignment to translate a guidebook into a narrative. Courtney's total self-absorption and seeming absence of redeeming qualities make her unlikable and unrealistic. However, but the book raises some interesting points for discussion and the format is appealing and makes for quick reading.

SYNOPSIS:

Courtney is a 16-year-old with a severed spinal cord who finds herself interned indefinitely in a convalescent home. Her roommates are May, an Alzheimer's patient, and Elva, a retired schoolteacher who is nearly blind. Courtney's friends have all but deserted her. She has no family. The TV doesn't work. Elva teaches her how to live in her mind, a journey she begins with a 1910 *Baedeker's Guide to Italy*. The world of Courtney's mind's eye becomes more real than her bed and broken body.

DISCUSSION QUESTIONS/LEADER POINTS

1. What are the advantages and disadvantages of the format (dialogue) Fleischman uses for this novel?

The format allows the characters to speak for themselves and minimizes background information and description. We don't know why Courtney is as bitter as she is, although we know that her parents are gone and she has no other family to care for her. We don't learn the details of her accident. We don't know much about her school life except for what we can imagine from the conversations with her friend, Denise. Denise's references to drinking and partying might make one guess that Courtney's injury resulted from driving while drunk or riding with a drunk driver. Ask readers how this knowledge would affect their perception of Courtney?

2. Elva says that Courtney has been given a "golden opportunity" because she will be forced to develop a "mental life" (p. 7). What is your reaction to this statement?

Readers may find Elva's comment about a "golden opportunity" to be insensitive, although viewing unfortunate experiences as opportunities certainly makes for a more positive point of view. It's true that people don't memorize poetry like they did in the past or read classics. So maybe teens today have fewer reserves stored in their minds. Ask your group how well they'd fare with only their thoughts for entertainment?

3. Does Fleischman inspire the reader to care about Courtney? Do you find her lack of friends or significants likely?

Courtney is a difficult character to like. It's hard to imagine a teenager as alone as she is. One might surmise that she probably wasn't a good friend even before her accident, that the accident intensified an already bitter personality. Her interaction with Denise indicates that she likely drove away her other friends, too, after the accident. Her intentional cruelty to Elva in adding disturbing elements to their "trips" illustrates her meanness.

4. What advice would you give to Courtney?

Teens may be tempted to tell Courtney to work with what she's got left and try to achieve a more independent life, but at some point Courtney decides not to fight. How can you inspire fight in someone who doesn't seem to have it?

5. Do you agree with Elva that "a good loving childhood fills you up?" Why or not?

Teens will agree that a good and loving childhood fills one up, and it's easy to see why Courtney is empty. Ask how it fills one up.

6. Elva criticizes television. Are books a better escape? Why or why not? Would Courtney's existence be made better or worse by TV?

Readers will readily acknowledge that Courtney's existence would have been made more tolerable by having a TV. TV doesn't require one to interpret, so it's more passive than reading and doesn't involve imagination the way books do or exposure to language and new vocabulary. On the other hand, it's not all bad and would have provided a welcome, occasional diversion. Also it might have kept Courtney interested in the outside world, which may have motivated her to work on trying to re-enter it.

7. Is dwelling in one's imagination a healthy way to live? Why or why not?

In Courtney's case, living in her mind becomes pathological. For Elva, it was a pleasant pastime at the end of a full life. For Courtney, who probably wasn't emotionally healthy before her accident, it is a total escape and it's hard to ascertain whether it's healthier than addiction to TV or not. Courtney has given up on life and won't even try to become functional.

8. Discuss the transformation that Courtney undergoes as a result of her journeys of imagination. Is she on the path of healing or further withdrawal?

Courtney's fantasy life has become more real than reality. She has no motivation for participating in reality. She seems headed for madness.

9. What do you think of the book cover?

I thought the cover picture was intriguing, but the teens in my group didn't like it. One teen said it looks like Courtney is dead and buried underground.

22

MULTIPLE CHOICE
by JANET TASHJIAN

Bibliographic information: Holt, 1999; 186 pages.

Themes: Obsessive-compulsive disorder, perfectionism, responsibility, self-imposed limits, anagrams.

Genre: Realistic fiction.

Main character: Monica, 14.

Tips: Some background on, obsessive-compulsive-disorder (OCD) will enhance your discussion and your group will probably be curious. A more realistic and informative novel on the subject is Terry Spencer Hesser's *Kissing Doorknobs*, (Discussion Guide 17) Reassure your group that everyone has a touch of obsessiveness; it's only pathological when it rules your life. It's tempting to do something anagram-related with this discussion. I considered doing anagrams of the groups' names on cards and asking them find theirs.

SYNOPSIS:

Driven by her compulsions and perfectionism, Monica is a prisoner of her mind until she devises a way to break out. Her love for word games leads to her to create a game in which drawing one of four Scrabble tiles will determine whether she does something normal, silly, mean, or sacrificial. Monica suddenly seems free and spontaneous, but when her game requires her to write a slur about her best friend on a school bathroom wall, she loses her friend; and when her game requires her to lock preschooler Justin in his room for five minutes, he jumps out the window. Justin escapes injury except for a scratched eye, but Monica is finally forced to take responsibility for her actions and seek help for her obsessive-compulsiveness.

DISCUSSION QUESTIONS/LEADER POINTS

1. When Monica begins playing Multiple Choice she is able to do and say things she wasn't able to before and finds that, for the most part, the consequences

aren't devastating. Have you ever done something totally out of character? What were the results?

Our thoughts keep us from doing things that sometimes we wish we could do, and there's really nothing else keeping us from doing them except fear of embarrassment or failure. Monica's fears are, of course, more extreme than usual. How do you know when your fears are reasonable?

2. Playing the game makes Monica feel daring and spontaneous instead of timid. What are the advantages or disadvantages of being spontaneous? Daring? Timid?

Monica needs to allow herself some genuine spontaneity framed by her values, not dictated by a game. Spontaneity opens the door to the unexpected and asserts a "can do" attitude. Even forcing yourself to be spontaneous can be beneficial. Being daring, testing oneself, gives one a sense of accomplishment and confidence. Timidity assumes uncertainty and maybe even shame. Ask readers how it makes them feel to think of themselves described by each adjective.

3. Monica's obsessiveness hinders her creativity; do you think that creativity is important to one's happiness? Health? Success?

Creativity seems to help Monica. There is literature that points to the healing effects of creativity. Since we are creative by nature, it may be unhealthy not to express creativity, and it may even cause physical or emotional problems. Ask your group how they feel while they are engaged in creative activity. How do they feel afterwards?

4. What lesson can be learned from Justin's reaction to his fallen scoop of ice cream?

Justin, like all children, is much more in tune with the present moment. Free of expectations, he is able to enjoy what happens. If the ice cream falls, it makes an interesting sight. Most children probably would have expressed disappointment at losing their ice cream, but Justin is more easygoing than some kids. Ask readers why they think he has such a healthy attitude.

5. Monica says that she's "trapped and suffocated by all the rules governing [her] life." What kinds of rules govern our lives and who makes them? Who makes Monica's rules?

Our parents, teachers, and society enforce some rules on us. Other limits we place on ourselves out of fear or beliefs about what we should or can't do. Ask your group for examples of things they've kept themselves from doing and why.

6. Monica creates her multiple choices, although previously she wasn't able to give herself these choices. Do you think people normally limit their choices and stick to what's comfortable? Is there a benefit in doing something out of the ordinary?

When faced with a challenging new situation or activity, most of us have had good and memorable experiences—even the times of our lives, but it's not so easy to choose to do something outside your comfort zone. For example, changing jobs is difficult when you don't have to, even if you know that you'll benefit from the change. It's more comfortable to protect the status quo, but more rewarding to shake things up. Trying new things allows one to test and discover new aspects of oneself. Ask for examples of when readers tried something new and daunting and how it made them feel afterward.

7. Should Lynn hold Monica responsible for writing the slur on the bathroom wall?

Although readers will be sympathetic toward Monica's affliction, most will hold her responsible for writing the slur against Lynn on the bathroom wall. Should that experience of losing her friend have made enough of an impact on her for her to seek help? The scene in which Monica allows herself to lock Justin in his room is hard to read. It shows just how disturbed Monica is. Does a disorder absolve someone of responsibility?

8. How do you think Monica's parents could have been more supportive?

Monica's parents don't realize the magnitude of Monica's problem and probably don't want to. They are so relieved that she seems to be more normal that they fail to notice her bizarre behavior.

9. How do you feel about Monica? Is she a likable, sympathetic character?

Monica's irresponsibility is hard to overlook, but she is clearly bewildered by what she seems required to do. Mostly Monica's foibles are benign and humorous. Her talent with anagrams is interesting.

10. Is the resolution (Monica beginning to work with Darcy) believable?

It's unrealistic that Darcy would be forgiving and understanding enough to work with Monica, or even that she should, though it's convenient. She's too close to the situation. Also, Monica's guilt might hinder their professional relationship.

23

MY HEARTBEAT
by GARRET FREYMAN-WEYR

Bibliographic information: Houghton Mifflin, 2002; 154 pages.

Themes: Family expectations, homo/bisexuality, friendship, finding inner guidance.

Genre: Realistic fiction.

Main character: Ellen, 14.

Tips: Sexual situations make this a book for more mature teens.

SYNOPSIS:

Ellen adores her brother Link and has a crush on his best friend, James. When she enters the same high school, one of her classmates wonders if Link and James are a couple. When Ellen nonchalantly asks, she doesn't get a clear answer and sets into motion unexpected reactions. Link begins avoiding James and starts dating Polly. James and Ellen become closer and eventually have a sexual relationship, although James admits that he's slept with men. Link trades "maths for freaks" for piano and abstains from taking exams. Ellen discovers running and art and begins to find balance between parental expectations and her own heartbeat.

DISCUSSION QUESTIONS/LEADER POINTS

1. Ellen's father says, "Geeky people often have that which is most valuable in life ... a mind with its own heartbeat" (p. 10). What does he mean? Do you agree? Why or why not?

Geeks, as the kids who don't fit in, may already be listening to their own heartbeats, especially if they are geeks who feel good about themselves. Popularity and the compromises one might make to be in a certain group can divert energy away from developing one's talents and interests and better preparing for life after high school.

2. James' and Link's fathers both have trouble accepting that their sons might be gay. Why do you think it's easier for the mothers?

Homosexuality seems to threaten the macho ideal, a fact that doesn't affect women. Women might be more accepting of the dual nature of people. It may also be argued that mothers are more accepting of their children, that the bond is stronger because of having carried them. Or it may be that the mothers in this book are smart people and know better than to think it's shameful (to paraphrase Ellen).

3. Why does Link get so angry with James?

Link is obviously not ready to accept that he is at least confused about his sexuality. He's probably angry that he can never quite meet his father's expectations in this and other ways. The feelings he has for James make him uncomfortable and scared. Anger is often preferable to fear. How do you think life would change if someone who is gay were to come out?

4. Does Ellen's father have Link's and her best interests at heart? What makes you think that he does or he does not?

Ellen's father does want what's best for his children, but he makes the mistake of believing he knows exactly what that is. It's impossible for anyone to absolutely know what's best for another. Parents often want to guarantee that their children don't miss their own lost opportunities without considering that those opportunities may not be desirable to the children. Ellen's father isn't empathizing with his children.

5. When James asks Link what makes _him_ gay and not Link, Link says, "You've slept with people" (p. 42). Does the purely physical act of sex determine one's sexual orientation? If not, what does? Is James gay?

Unrepressed people know whom they're attracted to. If someone consistently is attracted to members of his own sex, it's safe to assume that he's gay even if he doesn't act on his feelings. To say that having sex is the defining characteristic is just like saying one has to have heterosexual sex before one is heterosexual. Also, many people have same sex experiences, but aren't really gay. One of the great things about this book is that it's not just a book about homosexuality; it's also about bisexuality, which hasn't been addressed as much. Readers are offered an opportunity for talking about whether James is gay or bisexual and the shortcomings and inaccuracies of labels.

6. Does Ellen betray Link in any way by having a love affair with James? If so, how? If not,why not?

This is akin to the "is it okay to date your best friend's ex" question, which is a matter of opinion and situation.

7. What do you make of Ellen's father's laborious task of reading a three-volume German novel about "a life just out of reach?" What does it say about his heartbeat?

There is a lot of humor and irony in Ellen's father's choice of books to read. He seems much more interested (and misguided) in challenging himself to complete a joyless, laborious task than to listen to his heartbeat. He forgets that joy has much to do with what makes one's heart beat.

8. Why does Link hide the fact that he's quit "maths for freaks" and begun to study piano?

In their family, Ellen and Link have learned the response of silence, of bottling up feelings. While Link is first ready to explore the guidance of his heartbeat, it's another step to out it. Readers can only hope his first steps foreshadow viewing himself with complete honesty and fearlessness. How is silence dishonest? What's implied by not speaking up? Can you be defiantly silent?

9. About being gay, Ellen says, "Only people who don't know better still think it's shameful or wrong to be gay, but not people we know. Not smart people" (p. 52). Is she naïve to think this? What are the characteristics of geographic locations where homosexuality is acceptable?

Ellen is idealistic in her comments about acceptance of homosexuality. Her father, who's intelligent (but lacks emotional intelligence), thinks being gay is wrong at least for his son. Even smart people have blinders about some issues. It's interesting to note that areas where gays are accepted are usually close to areas rich in educational and cultural resources. What does that tell us?

10. What's your reaction to Link's father giving him an allowance for Polly?

Paying Link to date Polly is a desperate and pathetic act. Link's father is essentially paying Link to betray himself and to keep from telling the truth.

11. Why do you think that Link's shrink suggests that he tutor third graders instead of run?

As a runner who finds running a good way to get things in perspective and solve problems, I am puzzled why a therapist would advise Link to replace running with tutoring, especially when physical activity is a stress reliever, not to mention its physical benefits. Maybe the author is addressing Link's habit of isolating himself; running isn't a social activity. Helping others is a way to bring the focus outward instead of inward, and it makes you feel good.

12. Does Ellen find her heartbeat? In what?

Ellen is a wonderfully mature and self-possessed character. She isn't unrealistic about her relationship with James and is able to accept it for its positive, affirming aspects. She discovers a love of running and art. She does begin to recognize the sound of her heartbeat and to act on what she hears, as do the other two teen characters in this smart and subtle novel.

24

MY LIFE AND DEATH
BY ALEXANDRA CANARSIE
by SUSAN HEYBOER O'KEEFE,

Bibliographic information: Peachtree, 2002; 217 pages.

Themes Divorce, suicide, self-esteem, moving.

Genre: Mystery.

Main character Alexandra (Allie) Canarsie, 15.

Tips: Allie is a wonderfully quirky character—fresh, funny, and abrasive with an imagination that tends toward the extreme. The combination of mystery and humor make this page-turner fun to read.

SYNOPSIS:

Every time Allie's mother is sure she's going to be fired or Allie's rebellious behavior at school becomes a problem, they move. After the tenth move in six years, Allie doesn't hold much hope for her new surroundings, her mother's hometown. She finds an oasis in the cool greenness of the town's cemetery and finds herself compelled to attend the funerals of strangers. Her aunt and mother wonder if she's working out her feelings for the father who deserted her when he divorced her mother. Allie feels kinship for a 15-year-old boy whose funeral she attends. Like her, Jimmy had a talent for math and would have been in her class. After meeting his best friend, Dennis, she becomes convinced that Jimmy was murdered and is determined to find proof.

DISCUSSION QUESTIONS/LEADER POINTS

1. Why do you think Allie feels compelled to attend funerals? Is she acting out feelings about her father, as her aunt suggests, or do you think there are other reasons?

When Allie first stumbles into Evergreen cemetery, it seems ironically lush and green with life. It's a haven from the hot, dusty trailer park. Rather than it being related to feelings about her father, when Allie stumbles on the funeral, she is more attracted to being weird and doing something that would annoy her mother. The idea of being a mystery woman also appeals to her.

2. Why do you think that Allie's mother always thinks she's going to be fired?

Allie's mother has never forgiven herself for blowing her chance at college. She was the first in her family to get there, and when she became pregnant with Allie, she quit. Also, her marriage failed; her husband left her. She likely has labeled herself as a failure. She feels inferior because she didn't finish college.

3. How are Allie and her mother alike?

They both fear failure and rejection. Allie reacts to her fear by being abrasive and deliberately weird. Her mother quits her jobs and moves.

4. Do you think that Jimmy and Allie would have been friends if he hadn't died? Why does Allie think that they were so alike they may as well have been "separated at birth?"

Because they are the same age, both have divorced parents, and they both are math whizzes, Allie assumes that she and Jimmy are so alike as to have been "separated at birth." In reality, Allie knows very little about Jimmy. How well do we really know even the people closest to us? For example, Dennis was Jimmy's best friend, but he never realized the depth of Jimmy's depression. Jimmy's reaction to Allie probably would have been closer to Dennis's first reaction, which was to steer clear of a troublemaker.

5. Is Wheatley too good to be true?

One reviewer criticized the book for the portrayal of Wheatley as too good, but having had a teacher whom O'Keefe could have based him on, I obviously didn't. There are dedicated teachers who strive to reach difficult students.

6. Is Allie responsible for Wheatley's ending up in the hospital? For provoking Creighton to the car and bat incidents?

We really can't be responsible for others. Wheatley knew that Allie was impetuous. He made the choice to go along with her. Living can be perilous; the alternative is to be safe and boring.

Allie goaded Creighton, but that doesn't excuse the car incident or the bat. Dennis realized that Creighton was a volatile character and warned Allie not to antagonize him. Allie did go too far, and she was wrong about Creighton's involvement in Jimmy's death, but Creighton's potential for violence would have surfaced eventually. When does antagonism justify retaliation, and what kind of retaliation would have been more appropriate?

7. Should Allie's mother have told her the truth about her father sooner? At all?

The conventional wisdom is that one should never criticize a divorced partner to the children. In Allie's case though, it would have saved her from romanticizing her father and missing that unrealistic version of him. As long as she thinks he's wonderful, she can't reconcile the fact that he has no contact with her. Her mother was no doubt acting with Allie's best interests in mind, but knowing the truth would have given Allie resolution. Allie's hesitation to contact her father at the end implies that she is nearing resolution and realizing her romantic version of her father is inaccurate.

8. Do you think that Allie will contact her father? Why or why not?

Allie will probably think about the fact that she hasn't heard from her father for six years more clearly now that she doesn't idolize him and will not set herself up for a potentially hurtful reunion. Ask readers if they could imagine her using her investigative talents and tracking him down anonymously in a sequel.

9. Should Dennis have told Allie what he knew about Jimmy's death? Why or why not?

Maybe Dennis felt that telling Allie that he believed that Jimmy committed suicide would have been a betrayal. The public version called his death an accident because some people consider suicide shameful; it would have tarnished Jimmy's image. Dennis also probably hoped to be proven wrong or at least to have some information to assuage his own guilt for fighting with Jimmy right before his death.

10. Did Allie do the right thing in telling Mr. Muller she hadn't found anything about him in Jimmy's diary? Why or why not?

Allie performs an act of kindness in destroying Jimmy's journal and not revealing its contents to Mr. Muller. She realizes that Mr. Muller has suffered profoundly already.

11. How do you think that Allie will be different after all she's experienced?

Predictions about Allie will be interesting. I don't think that she'll become a model student, but she might make some friends. She and her mom may stick around this time. Ask whether readers think that Allie and Dennis will get together. Will Allie find another mystery to investigate?

25

THE NEW YOU
by KATHLEEN LEVERICH

Bibliographic information: Greenwillow, 1998; 108 pages.

Themes: Moving, identity, self-acceptance.

Genre: Realistic fiction with a time slip.

Main characters: Abby, 13. Abby, Thais, and Celeste as 20-somethings

Tips: The book poses some intriguing questions about the nature of identity and is a good jumping off point for discussion of a subject so close to the hearts of many teens. Teachers may find it worthwhile to recreate Mr. Mayjis' Laboratory of Ideas in their classrooms.

SYNOPSIS:

When Abby's father marries and they move to the city, Abby leaves behind everything familiar, everything that defined her. She finds that she doesn't know who she is in her new environment, and, therefore, she can't find a way to make friends and fit in. On an evening when she is coming down with the flu, she has a supernatural experience: she finds a listing for "The New You" under "Identities" in the phone-book and impulsively makes the journey to the address. Once there she finds three young women who inadvertently nurture her and give her spirit a boost. Later it seems the visit was a delirious dream brought on by her illness, but Abby discov-ers that she has glimpsed her future.

DISCUSSION QUESTIONS/LEADER POINTS

1. Why does Abby lose her identity? Have you ever felt this way? What was the cause?

Abby's loss of identity is temporary and a result of a uncertainty she feels after her move. Ask readers whether they think that Abby would have recovered without her visit to the future. Teens who have experienced a move will relate to Abby's feeling of isolation, although maybe not to the extent Abby does. Ask if one of the positive things about moving away from a place where people have always known you is that sometimes people who know you well don't allow you to change. For exam-ple, they always think of you as being afraid of something even after you've con-quered your fear, or they always remember some embarrassing thing you did years before. So there are some bonuses in making a clean start.

2. How would you approach fitting in at a new school? What allows us to "fit in"?

Abby keeps herself apart from others at first. She doesn't elaborate when someone asks her a question. Perhaps it's appropriate to feel a period of mourning for her old life. Maybe at the time when it's so important to make efforts to fit it, she feels least like doing it because she's not through experiencing feelings of loss. When she becomes open to fitting in and making new friends, Abby doesn't have a problem. Asking questions is a good way to get to know other people and to get to know your way around a new place. Ask readers what other strategies they can think of to break the ice.

3. Would you reinvent yourself if you could? How?

4. What is identity? How much do surroundings define a person?

Asking teens how they define themselves will no doubt lead to an interesting dis-cussion. They will easily think of all kinds of labels: student, cheerleader, daughter, friend. Ask them who they would be if they were the only person in the world. If they don't think of themselves in relationship to others, would they be more likely to call themselves different names like poet, dancer, dreamer, gardener? Which names that we call ourselves define us in relationship to others and which don't? Abby has an opportunity to redefine herself because no one at her new school remembers her. Who would we be without memories?

5. Celeste describes the experience of seeing herself in the mirror at the salon and, not recognizing herself for a moment, sees herself as others see her. How do we see ourselves differently from how others see us?

Most people have had the experience of accidentally seeing their reflections and for a moment not recognizing themselves. It is definitely disorienting and may give them the same feeling in their stomachs as riding over a dip in the road—temporary suspension. Regarding our reflection without recognizing ourselves reminds us that we can't see ourselves as others see us, that our feelings color our perceptions. Ask how readers feel when they have a pimple. They probably think it's all someone else sees when they look at them, but we know that's not true. Teens often question their attractiveness. Ask if they have ever had the experience of getting to know someone and later thinking that the person is more (or less) attractive than their initial impression. Almost everyone has had this experience.

6. Why does Abby feel better after she tells her class her dream?

Abby makes herself vulnerable by revealing something about herself. Her openness creates the opportunity to let others in as she lets out something of herself. She is finally sharing something with her new classmates. Isn't there always a give and take in establishing relationships? You have to give a little of yourself to get something back.

7. If you could visit your future, what would you like to learn? What things about yourself today would you not have anticipated five years ago?

Many teens experience situational shyness. Everyone wants to be comfortable in challenging situations, but that takes experience. Maybe having a glimpse of the future would be reassuring because you would know that whatever problems seem big now will work themselves out; nothing lasts forever. Everyone will have at least one aspect of her life she wouldn't have anticipated five years earlier. You can make plans, but you can't know about all the things that can alter them. Of course, someone will wonder how you'd feel if you found out something bad happened. Then, would you have the chance to alter the future like Scrooge? Or would the preview doom you to that future?

8. Thais and Celeste indicate that their future careers will be as Abby has seen them. Do you think it's likely for someone to be that focused at that age?

Most teens are still considering plans for their future's. Most will have areas of interest they believe they will pursue, but will admit the possibility of diversion. Everyone will know of someone who went off to college and changed majors a few times. So the author may have stretched credulity a bit to have Celeste and Thais so directed at the age of 13.

9. Does the author make believable the fact that Abby doesn't recognize her future self?

The fact that Abby as Gail had a different hairstyle and highlights, in addition to being older, won't be enough for some readers to explain why Abby doesn't recognize her future self, although her mindset alone might have kept her from realizing she was seeing herself. She never would have expected to encounter her future self; her mind doesn't entertain the possibility.

26

NIGHT FLYING
by RITA MURPHY

Bibliographic information: Dell Laurel Leaf, 2000; 129 pages.

Themes: Independence, controlling behavior, challenging rules, the beauty of rituals.

Genre: Realistic fantasy.

Main character: Georgia Hansen, 15.

Tips: Murphy has created a book with an intriguing premise—a family tradition of women flyers, and some food for thought about rules and rituals, secrets, power, and fear. The first line of the book is a real attention-grabber, and the details of the initiation ceremony and descriptions of flying are quite engaging. Characterizations are slight, however; so don't count on character studies. Some teens might find the rituals and flying too closely related to witchcraft or the occult.

SYNOPSIS:

As Georgia Hansen nears her sixteenth birthday, she prepares for her initiation ceremony and her first solo flight. All of the Hansen women have the ability to fly, but strict rules govern the use of their gift. When her estranged Aunt Carmen visits, Georgia learns some secrets about her past and begins to question some of her grandmother's rules.

DISCUSSION QUESTIONS/LEADER POINTS

1. What makes Georgia and her family follow rules? What reasons do we have for following rules? When is it wise to challenge rules?

One hopes readers will realize that many rules are followed out of fear, and that what makes sense for one generation may not necessarily make sense for those following. Georgia has proven that eating meat doesn't affect the ability to fly. It doesn't make sense that keeping the Hansen name or not having a man in the house will affect it either. These rules seem like superstitions. However, some rules are followed out of respect for tradition — more of an expression of honor or gratitude, like the initiation ceremony itself. Some rules, like only flying at night, are just sensible. Readers will be able to think of examples of rules that fall into these categories. Rules that limit others and keep them from developing their talents and interests should be challenged. Why should the best flyer in the family be forbidden to fly?

2. Why is Georgia's grandmother so rigid? Do we learn enough about her to explain her severity or why she rejects men?

We learn that Myra's father was a sort of absent-minded professor/inventor, and her mother was left to manage practical matters. Her mother may well have spoken negatively about men. We might guess that Myra's sister Charlotte, who was lost, may have been his favorite by the way he carries on once she is missing. His behavior may have increased Myra's disregard for men. There is no detail about Myra's lovers, no hint of mistreatment. The book would be richer if we had more background about the events that may have caused Myra's rigidity. As it is, much is left for the reader to guess.

3. Can you think of examples of initiation ceremonies that would compare to that of the Hansen women? What benefit do these rituals serve? Would you like to have an initiation ceremony, and what would it mark and involve?

Two initiation ceremonies for girls that teens might be familiar with are the Jewish bat mitzvah and the Latino quinceanera. They may also know examples of family traditions to mark one's coming of age. For example, I know a family who gives a girl a Celtic ring to mark her first menstrual cycle, and they celebrate with a mother-daughter lunch and shopping date. There has been speculation that initiations serve an important psychological function. It would certainly seem appropriate and affirming to celebrate the passage from childhood to young adulthood.

4. Why is it necessary for Georgia to believe that Maeve is her mother? How does Myra use secrets?

5. Why does Myra convince Maeve that she's frail? What kind of limitations is put on those who are considered frail?

Perhaps Myra feared that if Georgia knew the truth about Carmen, she might have tried to contact her or even have left to be with her. It's unfair of Myra to charge Maeve with the responsibility of raising Georgia, and even unfair that she would make Maeve believe in her own frailty. To subvert a child's power is countrary to what a parent's goal should be. Myra has an incredible need for control. Since Maeve is the strongest flyer, she probably fears her. Myra uses secrets as a means of control. If all of the cards were on the table, she wouldn't have a hand to play. Ask teens if they can think of other examples of people using secrets used to control others.

6. Do you feel sympathy for Myra? Why or why not? What would make you care for her more?

The character of Myra is so lacking in any redeeming quality that you have to feel sorry for her. She has a miserable existence and operates from a base of fear. She must exert constant vigilance to keep the world under her control. It's hard to get a sense that she can ever relax and enjoy anything. Readers might wish that the author had given her a modicum of joy. As she is, she is nothing but an evil stepmother archetype. Remind those who would condemn her that she exists to allow the other characters an opportunity to assert themselves in a big way.

7. Did you guess the true nature of Carmen's and Mr. Gowen's relationships to Georgia? If so what made you guess?

I missed any reference to Mr. Gowen's age and wondered if he was Georgia's father. His devotion to Georgia made it seem very likely that he was more than just the family handyman. He was also one of the most developed characters. Ask readers if they felt that it was hard to get a sense of some of the characters. Did they wish for more development? Meanwhile, it was no surprise that Carmen turns out to be Georgia's mother.

8. Did Murphy make the women's ability to fly believable? Why or why not? What would you do if you had the ability to fly?

The details of flying are one of the most enjoyable parts of the book. It's curious that the flyer's arms got tired, and reminiscent of the old joke (I just flew in from _____ and boy do my arms hurt). Ask readers if they have ever dreamed of flying and what it felt like.

9. Georgia recalls reading a story about a goose with an injured wing that was kept company by three other geese until healed in the spring. Then the geese went their separate ways (p. 85-86). What's the significance of this story? How does it relate to the Hansens?

The geese represent a healthy functioning relationship. For them to symbolize the Hansen women would require the women to develop their independence from Myra. Georgia has begun this process, and we have the sense that she will continue to grow more independent. She begins to recognize her power when she flies on her own. It enables her to make a decision about the horse. She claims her power when she tells the truth about having flown solo. It would have preserved the status quo to have lied and may have been kind to Myra, but it would have hurt Georgia and squelched the family's opportunity for healthy change.

10. Did you think that Georgia would tell the truth about her first solo flight? Why or why not? What gives her the courage? Would it have been better if she hadn't told the truth?

Georgia's telling the truth is consistent with her character. It may have been kind to Myra if she had lied and preserved the status quo, but it would not have been the healthy thing to do. When is it wise to lie to protect someone?

11. How do you think that things will change in the Hansen house as a result of Georgia standing up to her grandmother?

Maeve will no doubt continue to fly and discover her own strength. One wishes Carmen would hang around. We don't get a sense of what her life in California is like or whether there is something drawing her back. Suki and Eva will likely enjoy more freedom. My guess is that Myra will try to ignore the changes, but a more democratic house will result.

27

19 VARIETIES OF GAZELLE: POEMS OF THE MIDDLE EAST by NAOMI SHIHAB NYE

Bibliographic information: Greenwillow, 2002; 141 pages.

Themes: War, displacement, family.

Genre: Poetry.

Main character: Nye as witness.

Tips: Poetry presents unique and ample sources of discussion. Not only can you discuss the story of each poem and the theme of the collection, but also the mechanics: rhythm, irony, metaphors. Nye's book in particular conveys the tragedy of the Middle East. The Palestinian perspective may be one with which readers aren't as familiar. For a simple, balanced version of the Arab Israeli conflict, see the National Public Radio Web site (www.npr.org/news/ specials/mideast/history). What Nye does brilliantly is to give identity to the tragedies; the identity she applies is that of human being, not of Arab or Israeli.

SYNOPSIS:

Nye writes about the experience of her family as Arab immigrants to the United States and of visiting the Middle East, describing the details of daily life and celebrations of culture and family in a place touched intimately by war on a daily basis.

DISCUSSION QUESTIONS/LEADER POINTS

1. In the introduction, the druggist who observed Nye's father at his soda fountain called him dreamy. Nye writes that that's how immigrants look because they have "other worlds in their minds" (p. xiii). What does she mean?

On page 79 she writes that people in exile are waiting for something to fit again that is bigger than their own clothes. In that she implies that home is as intimate as clothes. How much a part of you is home? If you were relocated to a very different environment, the desert perhaps, would you be filled with longing for your home? How would you feel if you knew you could never return?

2. Nye writes that after 9/11, people found solace in poetry because it slows us down and cherishes small details, and that large disasters erase those details (p. xvi). Do you agree? Why or why not?

Then, again, perhaps large disasters make small things dearer, and since poetry honors those small details maybe that's why people find solace in it. Poetry breaks things down into bits that may be easier to swallow when there's a large disaster. Terrorism dehumanizes its victims; it doesn't want to see the teddy bear or the family pictures.

3. Why can't Nye tell Flinn what took place on the day of his release from prison (9/11)?

A world he has so looked forward to rejoining isn't the same world he left. His time for celebration comes on a day of mourning. Perhaps Nye wanted him to enjoy his happiness as long as possible. Perhaps she just didn't want to be the bearer of bad news.

4. Many of the poems present extreme contrasts: one day a town is touched by war and the next a man is stacking pita, a table of people is toasting each other and laughing. What do you think she's trying to communicate by doing this?

The contrast shows the double-edged nature of life and the dogged way the human spirit rises again and goes on. The pendulum swings from complexity to simplicity, bitterness to sweetness.

5. The Arab proverb advises that when a stranger comes to your door, feed him

for three days before you ask his name because by then you will like him enough that you won't care. What does this mean?

If you are unaware that someone is your enemy, is he? After three days, someone has a past, a family, a heart. You realize that he is like you, desires the same things — happiness and safety. How can you take up arms against him now.

6. In the poem "Passing the Refugee Camp" (p. 32), Nye asks how the soldiers are able to know the sweetness inside oranges but forget so many other things. Why is this ironic?

Sweetness isn't something that comes to mind when you think of a soldier, a trained killer. Yet there it is, that thing inside him that can know sweetness. Where does it go when he fires his weapon?

7. Read aloud the wonderfully rhythmic "Visit" (p. 58). How does the rhythm enhance the mood of the piece?

This sounds like Poe's "The Raven" to me — menacing. It has an essence of fear. Ask your group for volunteers to read it differently. Can they?

8. Nye describes many details that transcend cultures such as children falling asleep at parties and lonely grandparents complaining that no one visits them (p. 73). why in media and everyday life are we so often given examples of how people are different rather than how we are alike?

Over and over Nye puts an identity to war. We don't often empathize with people dodging snipers as they pick fruit from their trees, people living with war in their backyards, but she makes us do that. If we believe that people are immoral or evil, it's easier to make war against them. If we think about the people who are just like us, perhaps diplomacy would be more stubbornly pursued.

9. In "A Definite Shore" (p. 103), life is reduced to one wish, for a flat highway. Have you ever had this experience, asking the universe for just one wish? What was your wish? How soon before you had another wish?

Nye invites us to laugh at ourselves with this one. As a former teen, I especially remember bargaining with the universe or my parents. If this boy will call, if I can just go to this party, if I can get my ears pierced, I will never ask for anything again, but then you do. Almost immediately. Do we ever feel entirely satisfied? How is it when you feel like there's nothing else in the world you could need or want? Describe the scene when you felt this way.

10. "Staying Close"(p. 109) is chock-full of interesting metaphors and similes. How do these devices describe things more precisely or beautifully or succinctly than the way we usually say things?

We know snow is rare in this place because the lemons are surprised. They wear caps and they have feelings — how much more interesting this is than saying that there is snow on the lemons. A lid on a pot rises or opens its mouth. Which image is richer? Seams bring things together like talk and words become stitches — how much lovelier this is than saying that our conversation made us feel close to one another. The man has deep-set eyes and bushy brows or his eyes are like furry animals curled into their lairs for winter — they are warm eyes.

11. "Ducks" (p. 110) presents an émigré living in the U.S. who has had no contact

with her family in Basra for a year, so that she doesn't know who is alive. Why is it worse not knowing than knowing? The ducks are building a nest, but can she?

Not knowing is worse because one is left suspended. The knowledge will make a difference in how she conceptualizes the rest of her life.

12. "'Let's change places,' the teenagers said. 'For a week, I'll be you and you be me.' Knowing if they did, they could never fight again" (p. 118). Why is this true? Why can't adults figure this out? Is this a naïve point of view? Is it always possible to find a compromise that two sides will agree on? Does that justify war?

Let the teens speak, but be careful it doesn't turn into an adults bad, teens good diatribe.

13. In her dedication, Nye quotes her father, who says the Muslim, Christian, and Jewish religions all have the same first commandment but don't take it seriously. How can this be so?

Maybe this ties in with the idea of dehumanizing the enemy. Extremists believe that their way is the right way and the only way. Somehow they twist their belief into something that justifies eradicating the others. Or they make exceptions. It's okay to kill in self-defense or in war? Who makes these distinctions? Are there amendments to the commandments?

14. In her "Postscript," Nye wishes that she had said nothing. What do you think she may have said?

This is about being misquoted or quoted out of context. The Arab-Israeli conflict is such a loaded issue; many people have strong feelings about it. Ask readers whether they recall a time when they felt similarly. What happened?

28

OVERBOARD
by ELIZABETH FAMA

Bibiliographic information: Cricket Books, 2002; 158 pages.

Themes: Survival.

Genre: Realistic fiction.

Main character: Emily Slake, 14.

Tips: Teens will be sympathetic to Emily's feelings of being disregarded by her parents. The exotic locale and the gripping survival narrative will hold their interest.

SYNOPSIS:

Feeling she is taken for granted by her parents, who are humanitarian doctors in Sumatra, Emily impulsively decides to visit her uncle on the nearby island of Weh.

She boards an overloaded ferry and gives her life jacket to a child when the boat begins to sink. This is the story of Emily's harrowing 16 hours in the sea and her struggle to save a nine-year-old Sumatran boy.

DISCUSSION QUESTIONS/LEADER POINTS

1. How do the choices of Emily's parents affect her? Are they being as responsible to her as they should be?

Although they are doing admirable work, James and Olivia do take Emily for granted. She apparently had no input into the decision to go to Sumatra, and she doesn't even have a real bed. They are insensitive to how Rabina's death affects Emily and her need to be consoled that it wasn't her fault for misplacing the phone.

2. How well has Emily adjusted to living in Sumatra? How well do you think you would do?

Emily has trouble with the climate, ringworm, and being so obviously a foreigner. She must be lonely. Most teens would be horrified at the prospect of leaving civilization as they know it.

3. Why does Emily give away her life vest? Would you?

Emily is probably used to doing the mannerly thing, and she probably doesn't realize that it's her last chance to have a vest. It's a natural instinct to care for the weaker and younger, and it's what most people would do. Ask readers whether they would have given their vest to an adult.

4. What is your response to how people reacted when the ferry sank, pushing away strangers, trying to save themselves? Is Fama's portrayal realistic? How could some of the confusion and fear be assuaged?

Sadly, Fama's description is realistic. Perhaps some people are less spiritually evolved than others. The most primitive actions center on self-preservation. Higher level concerns place the welfare of others in a more important place. If a leader had arisen from the group, they could have been organized so that everyone had a turn at the raft to rest according to his or her needs.

5. Why is it so hard for Emily to let the drowning woman choose to drown?

Emily has grown up with the example of her parents, whose work is to save lives. Also, it's her instinct to stay alive and she assumes it is everyone else's, also. Later, when she sees another woman crying over the lifeless bodies of a child and man, she realizes that some things may be worse than dying. Readers might cite Emily's lack of religious background as a factor, in her continued fighting for life while the drowning woman's faith may have made it easier for her to accept her fate.

6. When Emily and Isman share the tomato, Isman tells Emily that his father has told him that nothing in the world is ours, that everything is "on loan from God" (p. 108). How would your life be different if you believed that?

A person operating from that point of reference would be much less preoccupied with accumulating things than the average American. Also, one would be in a continuous state of gratitude, from which springs joy. Ask readers how their lives might change if they expressed thanks for their blessings more frequently. Would it make them more conscious?

7. Emily notes that even a sleep-deprived person thinks more clearly at dawn. Why do you think this is?

Dawn is a time of awakening and natural instincts would still tell us so, even if we hadn't gotten any sleep. Anyone who has ever driven through the night will have experienced dawn's energizing effect.

8. When Emily and Isman get pulled into a whirlpool, they escape by swimming with the current and are helped by the rhythm of Isman's chanting. How is this a metaphor for living?

Where do expressions like "go with the flow" come from? Ancient Taoist thought advises practitioners to work with the natural order of things rather than against it. Ask readers whether they've had the experience of fighting against the current, trying to do something that didn't come naturally. What does it feel like? Ask readers what experiences bring them a feeling of harmony. Nature is endowed with rhythms, from the flap of a wing to the repetitive refrain of the seasons. Isman's rhythmic chanting is an expression of our natural rhythm working with the rhythm of nature.

9. When the man with two "floaties" approaches, Emily becomes very cautious of upsetting a balance, a truce each had made with the ocean (p. 128). What does she mean? What do you think the man said to Isman?

Emily has witnessed some very inhumane behavior since the sinking of the ferry. It wouldn't be surprising if she's untrusting. The man may have asked Isman to remain with him and offered to share his extra floaty. Having a companion would be appealing in their situation, someone to keep watch while the other rests, someone to help pass the time with conversation. Ask readers if they can think of other benefits of having a companion.

10. Emily keeps Isman alive. What does he do for her?

Isman keeps Emily alive as well. Often it's easier to find strength when someone else depends on you. Why is this? Why does Emily feel such an awesome responsibility for Isman? Is there something intensely bonding about sharing a catastrophe? Why do some people risk their lives to save others? Why don't others? What is stronger than fear?

29

PHILOSOPHY ROCKS
by STEPHEN LAW

Bibliographic information: Hyperion, 2000; 214 pages.

Themes: The big questions.

Genre: Nonfiction.

Tips: For the intrepid, inquiring mind. Some teens will find some of these questions disconcerting or even frightening, but for those who wonder about these ideas, a discussion will be a welcome adventure, and the opportunity to talk with like-minded individuals will be a relief.

SYNOPSIS:

Law describes very basic philosophical questions and theories in simple terms and with examples that teens will relate to. The questions addressed include the following: Who am I? What is real? How do I know the world isn't virtual? Should I eat meat? Can I jump in the same river twice? Where do right and wrong come from? What is the mind? Does God exist?

DISCUSSION QUESTIONS/LEADER POINTS

1. What do you think of Plato's idea of perfect forms? Where do you think that the knowledge of things like justice and beauty come from? Can imperfection be perfect?

Are we born with knowledge, or it is learned from parents and society? If we are born with knowledge, does it come from past lives, a shared unconscious, knowledge of God? The Japanese have a term used for the perfection of the imperfect, *wabi-sabi*. It's a Zen belief that imperfection adds to the beauty or perfection of something. What do you think?

Beauty, especially, is very subjective, and teens will easily see how it's changed over time and is interpreted differently by different cultures. Don't universal ideas require making judgments, and aren't judgments individual?

2. Do you think that there is a Shadowland? Describe things that have made you suspect that there is.

Ask readers what they think about supposed coincidences that lead them to exactly what they need at the moment. Ask if they've ever experienced the universe's or God's sense of humor. Do they ever feel that what concerns so many people is meaningless?

When we dream, doesn't that world seem as real as the waking world? Is our dream life a valid experience? What about people who have experienced different states of consciousness. Are those states real?

3. What makes us who we are? If you lost your memory would you be the same person? If you had a new body, would you be the same person? What part of you is unchanging?

We seem to hold onto our identity fiercely. If we lost our memories, it would be like dying. I know a woman who had encephalitis and lost her memory. When she recovered, she no longer knew her husband or her children. She was a blank slate. Do you think as time went on she displayed the same likes and dislikes and talents that she had before her illness? She did not. Was she the same person?

Suppose that when we die, we simply lose our memories, and the combination of atoms of which each of us is made gets mixed up again, and what is "I" begins as something or someone else. Nothing dies; it just changes. Does that make death less scary, Or does it make it scarier? If we could be assured a continuation of consciousness, is death less scary? What if it is a continuation of consciousness with no memory?

4. Does Ockham's theory that the simplest of two equally plausible theories is probably true convince you that the world is, or is not, virtual?

I think that this is like the language problem with the river not being the same twice. What's simplest is really a matter of opinion. I certainly find the idea of being a brain in a vat simpler than the complex reality we usually experience. Ask readers if they can think of other examples of the simplest explanation being the most unlikely.

5. If you can't step into the same river twice, can you every repeat anything exactly?

Even if changes are very subtle, nothing can be repeated. Similarly, some people would say that only the present moment exists. What do you think of this idea? If that's true, do we truly experience the present moment or are we most often making plans for the future or reviewing what happened in the past?

6. Which of the ideas discussed in this book make you uncomfortable and why?

Here's a chance to see if anyone's really uncomfortable and to remind them that these are all just theories.

7. What arguments for not eating meat did you find most persuasive and why?

As a fan of the humane treatment of animals, I find the treatment of meat animals very disturbing. Are we intended to be masters or trustees of our world and its creatures? How about the fact that it takes more resources to raise meat animals than to raise grains that could feed more people?

8. The author presents different theories of where morality comes from. What do you think? Can you think of an absolute right or wrong?

Readers will assert that morality is learned from parents and society. Are there absolutes that we know innately? Not to kill and eat each other, for example? Or is that okay if you're starving like the Andes survivors and one of your party is dead? If readers are familiar with Robert A. Heinlein's *Stranger in a Strange Land*, they will recall that the aliens honored the lives of loved ones by eating them when they died. So is the taboo on eating our own cultural? When cows eat cows they get mad cow disease. Is that significant?

9. How about an absolute right? Is the golden rule an absolute right?

10. Did reading this book change your mind about anything? What?

11. Do you think that the mind and brain are separate? Why or why not? How about the mind and body?

The fact that there is no way to record or register someone's private thoughts is a persuasive argument for believing that the mind and brain are separate. Out-of-body experiences, those who have been revived after death, and even dream states suggest that the mind is separate from the body.

12. How would you reconcile a belief in God and the existence of evil?

The idea of a god who is personified as an old man with a long white beard who sits in judgment of the world or acts as a puppeteer is an immature relationship to the infinite. Love and goodness exist; if one believes in God, don't they come from God? Is it irreconcilable to think that God can allow evil and care? The presence of evil brings response of its opposite. Isn't it naïve to think that God would share our own judgments? If God is everything and God must be if he/she made everything, why do we insist on excluding the parts of God we don't like. Why would God intervene if (s)he's given us free will? We seem to want to believe that our thoughts and actions don't have consequences.

13. What might be the meaning of our lives?

This is the answerless question that religions and people strive to answer. One answer is the kabbalistic view that God's self-awareness manifested itself in sparks that fell upon the world and live in each of us, and our purpose is to realize that spark of God in ourselves and in each other. It's one I like because it is a hopeful and joyful way to live.

30

THE RAG AND BONE SHOP
by ROBERT CORMIER

Bibliographic information: Delacorte, 2001: 154 pages.

Themes: Criminal interrogation, persuasiveness, prisoner abuse, self-doubt, shame, and guilt.

Genre: Realistic fiction.

Main character: Jason, 12, and Trent, a seasoned, professional interrogator.

Tips: Although Jason is 12, this book is not appropriate for younger readers. The subtleties of Trent's manipulation, his insinuation of sexual motive, and the brutal treatment of Jason are not for the meek. It's a grim, but gripping and provocative, story and an excellent choice for discussion.

SYNOPSIS:

When seven-year-old Alicia Bartlett is found dead, Jason becomes the prime suspect. He was the last person to see her alive. Jason may be a little slow, but he knows he'd never hurt his friend Alicia. The trouble is that this expert interrogator, Trent, has confused him so that he barely knows what he's saying. Bent on a confession, that's just what Trent gets as he tries to ignore his doubts about Jason's guilt. When Alicia's brother confesses, Trent's career is ruined, and Jason, broken, believes himself capable of murder.

DISCUSSION QUESTIONS/LEADER POINTS

1. Why doesn't Rebecca report what Bobo did? What should a girl do in this situation? What options might she have? What would you do?

Misplaced shame is especially common among girls and women. When I was in junior high (back when they called it junior high) a boy pulled up my skirt one day. Because I'd had a fight with my mother about the skirt being too short, I felt like it was somehow my fault, as if wearing a short skirt made me deserving of the stunt. I never told, and I never wore the skirt again. Maybe this is similar to what Rebecca feels—like somehow she caused the assault, or maybe she's just embarrassed. It would be hard for a girl that age to tell an administrator, especially a male administrator, that a boy had tweaked her breast. Also, society puts a lot of pressure on girls to be nice. Girls who stand up for themselves are sometimes viewed as bitchy or unfeminine. Ask readers if they can think of other times when girls and women may put up with unpleasantness to be "nice."

Rebecca might have talked to a female teacher with whom she felt more comfortable and confess that she doesn't want to talk to an administrator.

2. What's the connection Jason describes between hitting Bobo and not crying anymore?

When Jason shoves Bobo, he empowers himself. He doesn't accept his role as victim anymore. Would there have been a better way that Jason could have empowered himself? Does his use of physical violence foreshadow the end of the book?

3. When Jason doesn't try to stop the tears, no tears will come, and he says that that's worse than crying (p. 39). Why?

Although Jason's self-assertion may be a better response than being continually victimized, his determination to never cry is unhealthy. As he finds out on page 39, it is worse when tears don't come because tears are cathartic, and crying is sometimes the most appropriate response.

4. Read Yeats' poem "The Circus Animals' Desertion," which is the source of the title. On page 123, Trent says, "We now go down to where the ladders start." What does he mean?

I believe that Trent's comment about where the ladders start refers to Jason's heart. Now Trent is going for the jugular, going for the heart. Now his line of questioning gets crueler and accusatory. Why did Cormier call this book *The Rag and Bone Shop?*

5. Is Jason especially vulnerable, or do you think Trent could also have made a stronger, smarter person confess?

Trent's heart is a rag and bone shop. He's squandered his love on emblems and missed the real thing. He's lost a loving partner because he values power and position more than caring for or about other people. He has lost his humanity in his desire for false idols and has been robbed of his capacity for empathy. His inhumanity allows him to brutalize Jason and make a rag and bone shop of his heart as well.

6. Do you think this could really happen? Would Jason's confession have held up in court?

Trent's actions are especially cruel because Jason is a child and is even more vulnerable because he's not bright. In reality, this kind of interrogation should never be allowed, and the confession should not be admissible in court. There may be interrogators as sly and driven as Trent, however, and Cormier deftly illustrates how one could twist words and utterly confuse his victim.

7. Why does Trent go so far? Does he believe that Jason is innocent?

Trent seems to reach the point of no return. He struggles to convince himself to ignore his doubts about Jason's guilt, but once his momentum is at top speed, he can't put on the brakes. Does he ignore his doubts? He may be motivated by the prospect of advancing his career, having the senator's favor.

8. How are Trent's actions a betrayal?

Trent betrays his professional duty to uphold the law, and he betrays a humanitarian law in his treatment of Jason. He violates Jason's rights as a citizen and a person. What ethical rules apply to adults' treatment of children?

9. What convinces Jason that he could be a murderer? Do all of us have the capacity to be murderers?

If one believes we're all made of the same stuff, we must all have every potential in our hearts. It's our values and beliefs, conscience, grace, or karma that keeps us in check. When what we believe is broken down and we are given to question the nature of reality, as Jason does, it's incredibly painful and frightening. Jason has lost his sense of self. He's seen his shadow side and concludes that the only way to quell the pain is to act on it.

10. How does Trent makes Jason feel guilty?

Trent insinuates that Jason's interest in Alicia is perverse, that there is something wrong with him for enjoying her company. He makes him feel guilty for his sexual curiosity in looking at explicit pictures. Why is it easy to feel shameful about what one does in private?

11. Why do you think that Brad killed Alicia?

Ask readers if this question nagged them. Brad isn't portrayed as a particularly evil character; in fact, we don't learn a great deal about him, but we do learn that he has a secret that Alicia probably threatened to tell. What secret could be bad enough that Brad would kill to keep Alicia quiet?

12. Will Jason kill Bobo?

Jason is so utterly broken, I wondered if he might kill himself and was surprised when he went after Bobo. It wouldn't be surprising if Jason confronts Bobo, then kills himself. Ask if any readers think Jason has a chance of healing. How could he heal?

13. Lottie tells Trent, "You are what you do." Is this true? What is Trent? If you define yourself this way, what are you?

Trent specializes in breaking people down and is broken down himself. It seems this might be another way of saying you get what you give. Ask readers for examples from their experience.

31

THE SECRET SACRAMENT
by SHERRYL JORDAN

Bibliographic information: HarperCollins, 2000; 338 pages.

Themes: Respect for other cultures, forced relocation, living in concert with nature versus nature for man's exploitation, guilt, sacrificial redemption, courage.

Genre: Fantasy.

Main character: Gabriel from boyhood through young manhood.

Tips: Similarities with well-known, historic clashes between opportunistic cultures and indigenous ones (Similar to Maori, Aboriginal, Native American cultures) make this fantasy accessible to readers reluctant to dip into the fantasy genre. Plenty of action holds readers' interest.

SYNOPSIS:

Overhearing a brutal attack on a Shinali woman and not coming to her aid colors the rest of Gabriel's life. As a result, he chooses to go against the wishes of his father and his uncles and becomes a healer. Gifted at his vocation, he is accepted as a student at the prestigious Citadel, where he progresses at an unprecedented rate. He wins the favor of the empress when he realizes his talent for interpreting dreams, but makes an enemy of her chief adviser. His naiveté in dealing with the empress and her adviser cause him to make himself an enemy of the state. Meanwhile, the tentative peace treaty between the Shinali and the Navoran peoples is threatened, and it seems that Gabriel is to fulfill a prophecy in which the Navoran Empire falls and brings a time of cleansing and peace.

DISCUSSION QUESTIONS/LEADER POINTS

1. What similarities are there between the Shinali and Navoran and real cultures?

The Shinali culture is reminiscent of that of Native Americans, Maori, or Aborigines (performance of rituals, reverence for nature, alternative healing methods). All of these cultures were disrespected and overcome by a less peaceful, more technically advanced culture that took their prime land to exploit for profit and relegated them to a specific area and limited their rights. Why do you suppose some peoples assume superiority over others?

2. When the empress declares Gabriel her interpreter of dreams, he remembers his mother's words: "There are times to run, and times to stand firm. You'll learn the difference" (p. 215). Was there a better decision Gabriel could have made at this point?

Gabriel's youth and immaturity cause him to make some unfortunate choices, especially in dealing with the empress and Jaganath. He is idealistic and won't compromise himself. Perhaps he should have stayed off Shinali land from the start, but once he meets Ashila and spends time with her people, there is no way he could have promised not to see them again. You may want to talk about the instant chemistry between Gabriel and Ashila and ask whether readers believe in love at first sight. How would they explain such an immediate, strong bond between people? Gabriel and Ashila are both dedicated healers; perhaps it is this bond that they recognize, mutual values and ideals.

3. How could Gabriel have defended himself when Jaganath twisted his dream interpretation? Is he stubborn in his righteousness?

Gabriel may be stubborn. Although it's unlikely that Gabriel could have defended himself, it doesn't occur to him to even try. It almost seems as if he believes that he has "right" on his side and so will prevail. Ask readers if this idea is naïve or idealistic. Is it smart? Is it sometimes better to be deceptive to achieve a greater good?

4. What's the significance of Gabriel's practice of running? Did it seem out of place (anachronistic) in this more primitive time period?

Gabriel's reaction to danger is to run (until his decision to stay with the Shinali). This is mirrored by his practice of running for exercise. The group I discussed this book with did think it was a strangely modern hobby for Gabriel. Remind them that running was appreciated by the ancient Greeks, the first Olympians.

5. How did Gabriel's guilt over not helping the Shanali woman affect his life? Is guilt ever a positive motivator?

Gabriel's guilt probably turned him toward a service vocation. He has become the very person he would have had to be to help the Shinali woman of his childhood. That he is so gifted at healing is fortunate, or, as some people believe, maybe the experiences of our lives fit our gifts. Maybe each life is challenged by the things that can bring about that life's greatest potential. What does your group think? What if Albert Einstein were born into the Osborne family?

6. What do you think of the Shinali way of dealing with guilt?

Guilt is such a negative, crippling emotion. The idea of having a ritual to exorcise grief would be beneficial for those who are unable to forgive themselves. Like the Catholic practice of confession, or reconciliation, the act of surrendering grief or sin is essential to emotional health.

7. Why do you think that Tarkwan decides to move his people? Is it the best decision?

While it is unfortunate that Tarkwan's decision cost his group their freedom, the Shinali would have been slaughtered if they had held their ground, although that is certainly what they would have done without Gabriel's influence. Already Gabriel is effecting the change of the prophecy. Ask the readers whether it is preferable to die with honor as a warrior or to live in subservience.

8. Do you agree with Gabriel that "The river and the sky aren't worth dying for. No things are worth dying for" (p. 307). Is his attitude toward the Shinali condescending?

Initially Gabriel thinks that the Navoran are superior to the Shinali, but he changes his mind, and in the end finds their ideals worth dying for. Ask your group if they can think of other examples of cultural ignorance causing people to make wrong assumptions. What about slavery? Hitler? Missionaries?

9. Is Gabriel's sacrifice necessary? Does he make a good Christ figure? Why or why not?

Just as in other situations, he doesn't dig in his heels to fight, but runs (this time metaphorically). One might ask whether he doesn't have a higher responsibility to remain alive and use his gift? Doesn't he have a responsibility to Ashila and his baby? Is it necessary for him to infect himself to persuade the guards? The guards believe that *everyone* in the fort has the plague; Gabriel could have exchanged blood with someone else who wasn't actually infected to prove his point. One teen in my group thought maybe he infected himself so that he could carry the plague back to the Navoran, but this seems to be counter to his healer's ethic.

10. The book ends with the words, "the beginning." Is the end satisfying? Why or why not? Do you think that the author had the end of the story in mind before she got there? How does this affect the story?

The final words seem oddly less hopeful than intended. Some readers won't understand that the prophecy is about to be realized. Does it leave readers wanting for a sequel? In general, the last quarter of the book seems a little forced.

11. Are there elements of the story that seem unbelievable?

It seems unlikely that a skilled healer like Gabriel would fail to notice Ashila's symptoms of pregnancy. I wondered whether the guards wouldn't notice Gabriel's blonde roots since he wasn't able to touch up his dyed hair.

12. How does the cover affect your feelings about the book?

Everyone in my group thought that the cover art was confusing. The teens disliked the feminine look of Gabriel, even though I pointed out that we couldn't hold different cultures to our American twentyfirst-century standards of masculinity or attractiveness.

13. What's the significance of the title?

Gabriel's exchange of blood with Tarkwan can be understood as a sacrament, but it isn't really a secret. It was confusing that the rite of grieving is called the seventh sacrament. One teen in my group thought that the author had made a mistake and used seventh when she meant secret or vice versa. Or, maybe the title refers to when Gabriel releases his secret in the Shinali way.

32

SHATTERING GLASS
by GAIL GILES

Bibliographic information: Roaring Brook Press, 2002; 215 pages.

Themes: Popularity, bullying, controlling behavior, parental expectations, incest.

Genre: Realistic fiction.

Main characters: Young Steward, the narrator; Rob Haynes, the alpha male; Simon Glass, the nerd; all high school seniors.

Tips: Strong language and violence would recommend this book for older teens. A teen stopped by my desk one day and said, "I'm reading *Shattering Glass*. I can't put it down." With a recommendation like that, I had to read it. Another teen who had read it said that it was so depressing she couldn't finish it. It's a realistic scenario, but one you hope would never happen. It an excellent book to use for discussing the power of peer groups and the power of a charismatic leader.

SYNOPSIS:

Charismatic Rob Haynes easily takes over the top spot in his new school, surrounding himself with a group of popular boys who unwittingly become his lieutenants. When Rob decides to flaunt his power by making the class nerd popular, that's exactly what he and his group do, but Simon Glass isn't a patsy. He's smart and manipulative, and his new found popularity allows him to wield some power of his own, leading to a bloody, shattering climax that leaves one boy dead and one boy's future radically altered.

DISCUSSION QUESTIONS/LEADER POINTS

1. Why is Rob so powerful? Why does he go so far with Lance? Is what happened with Rob's father an adequate explanation for his actions?

What makes someone charismatic? It's certainly part looks, part confidence and directedness. Unfortunately Rob uses his charisma to control others. His total loss of control in what his father has done to him makes him want to have complete control of others. His father has broken his trust. Maybe he wants to destroy someone else the way he feels he was destroyed. Maybe he was always cruel. The extremes he goes to with Lance foreshadow his breaking point with Simon.

2. Each chapter begins with a quote from someone in the present, reflecting on the incident five years earlier. How does this technique affect the reader's interest?

The quotes from the present interspersed with the story build tension and propel the reader along to the climax. We keep getting teased with hints as we try to figure out exactly what happened.

3. Ronna tells Young that people think he's a good guy just because he never says no. Is this a fair assessment of Young? Is he a good guy?

The question of whether Young is a good guy is most compelling. He is totally a follower, even when it comes to losing his girlfriend on command. Young may become a good guy, but he hasn't yet asserted himself.

4. Should Ronna have been more forgiving of Young for breaking up with her so that Simon could take her to the Favorites' Dance and increase his popularity? Should he have revealed Rob's secret to her?

Ronna may have been more understanding if Young had told her why he felt so devoted to Rob; she may have even gone along with it. It most certainly would have made her feel better. Young is dishonest and doesn't treat Ronna like a person with feelings. She's right to give him the boot. How can you trust a person who can't steer his own course?

5. Ronna says that what happened is "all about fathers" (p. 112). Do you agree? What are your reasons?

Each boy in the story is affected by the expectations and mistakes of his father. The main characters react to the influence of their fathers by proving themselves in a variety of ways: Rob reacts by taking charge; Young by displaying utter compliance; Bob by appearing strong and brave, Coop by honing sports skills.

6. Young says, "Once I knew Rob's secret and I knew, _knew_ what it does to a person—then I needed to patch a hole in him like he'd done for me." How does Young know about Rob's experience? How are their experiences with their fathers similar?

Both Rob and Young suffer a loss of self-directedness because their fathers have taken it from them. They react in very different ways—Rob becomes controlling and Young becomes a doormat. When Young learns Rob's secrets, he is especially vulnerable because he empathizes

7. Is Coop innocent?

Coop took advantage of Simon's fixing his test. There's no question that Coop cheated, but that crime pales in comparison to others, like Simon's manipulation of Lance's records not to mention Rob's conniving and cruelty.

8. Why won't Young testify against the others? Does he deserve the punishment he gets?

Young's guilt for what happened, probably his guilt for never standing up for himself, keeps him from testifying against the others. He wants to be punished. He's beginning to realize that he's allowed someone to control him all of his life, and he's had a shocking lesson in what can happen when you allow that.

9. Young says, "The parole board asked how I felt that Rob's been free all these years I've been in prison. I told them, We're all imprisoned in different ways" (p. 173). How is Rob imprisoned?

As for Rob being free, in a karmic sense, he never was. Only someone who is suffering can do what he has done. Some teens will balk at his having gotten out of serving time, but Young is right in understanding that Rob is imprisoned in his own way. Young's understanding at least spares him the demon of wishing for revenge.

33

SIGHTS
by SUSANNA VANCE

Bibliographic information: Delacorte 2001; 215 pages.

Themes: Child abuse, self-image, popularity, rape, the gift of prophecy.

Genre: Magical realism.

Main character: Baby Girl, 13.

Tips: Some readers may have problems with the genre because elements of the story seem "too far fetched." Teens, however, will relate to Baby Girl's insecurity about her looks and feelings about being an outsider.

SYNOPSIS:

Baby Girl and her mother leave her drunken and abusive father one middle of the night in the early 1960s. They drive until their money runs low, settling in the small town of Cot, where "the boys are athletes and the girls are apricots." Baby Girl, who begins high school in cliquish, small town Cot, finds fitting in difficult. Her glamorous mother has a somewhat easier time, opening a custom formal wear business to which Baby Girl contributes by giving a reading of the future with each fitting. Yes, Baby Girl can see the future, but that doesn't always guide her to wise decisions. When she teams up with a couple of other outsiders and finds friendship, music, and love, she learns to appreciate her assets. Offbeat characters, including Baby Girl's father, who is hell-bent on killing her, make for a raucous read that is at turns deeply touching and hilarious. The ending is shocking and all too satisfying for reality, but it's the way you'd want things to be. Baby girl's father reappears and attempts once more to kill her, but Baby Girl and her friend Selda thwart him, so that he accidentally kills himself. If readers can transcend the desire for realism, they will find a humorous story with strong, resourceful, and endearing characters who easily elicit empathy and admiration.

DISCUSSION QUESTIONS/LEADER POINTS

1. Would you like to have the sight like Baby Girl? Why or why not?

2. If you were offered a forecast of the future, what would you want to know?

While it's tempting to wish you knew specific information about the future, interpretation may be difficult, as Baby Girl learns. Also, there's a danger of your prophecy becoming self-fulfilling. Is it more likely that what we expect will happen? Some people believe that we attract what we expect, that we can manifest our destiny.

3. Does Baby Girl handle her sight responsibly? Are there things she should not have revealed?

Baby Girl tries to be responsible about using her sight, but those to whom she gives her glimpses do not, so maybe it would be better if she kept her sights to herself.

4. Selda's ultrafeminine room seems to be a contradiction of her persona. Why do you think she has such a feminine room?

Selda may wish to downplay her femininity after having been raped. Or maybe her romance-writing mother designed it. Either way, the room's femininity is unexpected given Selda's looks and personality. Like the anomaly of her mother's writing sexually explicit romances, things aren't always what they seem. Are there other examples of things not being what they seem in the book?

5. Why do you think Selda peeps?

The book's title implies that sights are important, and they are important not only to Baby Girl but also to Selda (her peeping). Selda gets her information the hard way, looking in windows at night, in contrast to Baby Girl, who can call up her sight at any time. Another question might be whose sight is more valuable? Who has the bigger picture? If Selda knows what's going on around town all of the time, does that protect her? Was there a time when she was surprised and got hurt?

6. Is it reasonable for Baby Girl to be upset with Dempster for being at the diner with Mary Lou?

Dempster is an outgoing, affectionate boy. Teens may sympathize with Baby Girl's insecurity. When you open your heart, you take the chance of having it broken. However, if you hide your heart away or reject love as Baby Girl does in response to her fear when she sees Dempster with Mary Lou, you keep yourself from experiencing love.

7. What does Baby Girl learn about love?

She learns that her boyfriend is a person whose needs and talents she must allow and respect, although they don't always coincide with her own. She also learns that love can hurt, but it's probably worth it. Baby Girl and Dempster's breakup hurts their ability to make music together. When Selda comments that Baby Girl isn't the only one whose feelings get hurt, Baby Girl realizes that she can have the love she wants, but she has to accept Dempster the way he is and take her chances. We must caution ourselves when we have the desire to control another's behavior because, after all, we fall in love because of who the person is. Love shouldn't limit. Ask readers if expectations of one party ever had a negative impact on one of their relationships?

8. What things help Baby Girl with her self-image/body image?

Baby Girl is able to appreciate her physical strength and her hard athletic body. Was the image of an athletic female less desirable 40 years ago? How about now? Even the Williams sisters are criticized for being large, and they're goddesses! Baby Girl's sight into her own future reveals that perceptions of success and attractiveness can be especially skewed during the teen years.

9. What is your favorite scene?

With so much absurd humor in this book, recounting favorite scenes is a natural stimulus for talk. There are also moments of great tenderness. Ask readers whether they think the humor diminishes the tenderness.

10. What do you think of the Cot High School motto, "Where the boys are athletes and the girls are apricots?"

The importance of looks in popularity, body image, and the cultural stereotypes of girls in the late '50s and early '60s and the discouragement of athleticism in girls will no doubt serve as lively discussion topics. Although we are lucky enough to live in a time when athletic women are celebrated, many media images make teens feel even more insecure about their appearance. Cozy is the nicest girl in town, and even though she suffers the effects of polio, the beautiful, but heartless, Carline pales in comparison. Ask readers what an apricot is. A pretty, sweet fruit? Something to be devoured?

34

SILENT TO THE BONE
by E. L. KONIGSBURG

Bibliographic information: Atheneum, 2000; 261 pages.

Themes: Aside from a study of shame, *Silent to the Bone* is a moving story of friendship and how real friendship blossoms in the face of adversity. Other themes include family expectations, family blending, divorce, and forgiveness.

Genre: Mystery.

Main characters: Branwell and Connor, both 13.

Tips: While this book is written on a level that is accessible to tweens, the issues are deep and provoke mature speculation. The mystery and character are engaging and will hold the interest of all ages.

SYNOPSIS:

When Branwell finds his baby sister, Nikki, unconscious and calls 911, he discovers that he is unable to speak. The family au pair reports that Bran has dropped and shaken the baby. His inability to speak continues during his stay at the Clarion County Juvenile Behavioral Center, while his sister lies unresponsive in the hospital. Connor, Bran's best friend since nursery school, finds a way to communicate with him and unravels the mystery of what really happened on the day Nikki was hurt.

DISCUSSION QUESTIONS/LEADER POINTS

1. Why is Connor a good narrator and the best person to figure out what really happened?

Branwell's confusion and shame over how he feels about Vivian, the au pair, makes Connor a sympathetic narrator, especially when Vivian focuses her charm on him. The friendship between the boys guarantees Connor's loyalty and motivates him to do all he can. Also, he knows Bran well enough never to doubt him.

2. Why does Bran first choose Margaret in his attempt to communicate about what happened?

Margaret understands how Bran felt when his father remarried because she had had a similar experience with her own father—although hers was more complicated because her father left her mother for another woman. Bran probably realizes that Margaret would understand the delicacy of the situation. Also, he probably recognizes her tenacity and ability to get things done.

3. What do you make of Bran's inability to ask for what he wants? For example, he wants his father and Tina to use his design for the birth announcement, and he wants to hold Nikki when he first meets her.

Branwell's father and stepmother should have been more considerate about Bran's feelings and should have taken extra care to make him feel like an important member of the new family. Tina has never taken any pains to try to bond with Bran, and his father seems oblivious to the fact that Bran needs extra attention while adjusting to the change in his family circumstances. Sending him to the Ancestors when Nikki was born must have seemed like they wanted to him out of the way, certainly not like they wanted him to be part of the special event. It may be hard for some readers to accept this kind of neglect from people who are as intelligent as Bran's father and stepmother. Ask readers whether they think that falling in love can impair judgment or make people self-involved.

4. Is it fair of Margaret to hold a grudge against her father?

Margaret is certainly entitled to her feelings of betrayal, but one might expect her to deal with them in a more mature way, allowing for a better relationship between her father and herself. Some people never escape the habit of acting on old hurts. We are allowed a glimpse of Margaret's maturation as she and her father come to a touching, subtle truce in working together to help Bran. Ask readers for their impressions of the difference between forgetting and forgiving?

5. How would you attempt to communicate with Bran? Can you think of a better method than the one Connor comes up with?

The method of communication that Connor devises is interesting and accelerates the tension in solving the mystery, but we don't know why Bran can't write. Somehow his being able to communicate in such a limited way as blinking his eyes is appropriate, though. It's not just that he can't speak, he can't allow himself to communicate with ease because he's ashamed. He imagines that it is because he didn't speak when he should have that Nikki's life is in danger.

6. Vivian is clearly an unsympathetic character. Does the author make her unbelievably heartless?

Narcissistic Vivian is unsuited to a profession in childcare because she has no real interest in it. Ask readers whether Bran's parents should have been more attentive in assessing her suitability. Were they too trusting of the agency that employed her?

7. Several times Connor thinks that if you don't say anything, you can't say anything wrong (p. 90, p. 123). Is this true? Can silence be incriminating?

When Connor says that if you don't say anything, you can't say something wrong, he is right in the sense that it protects someone whom you might hurt or incriminate. However, in Bran's case, it makes him appear to be as guilty as he feels. Ask readers if they can think of other examples of someone's silence being incriminating.

8. Except for her lie to get at the truth when she says she had switched her silverware drawer, Margaret believes that there are two reasons people lie: out of fear or to protect someone (which may fall under fear as well). Do you agree? Why or why not?

Some other reasons people lie include lying to make one look better somehow, lying for personal gain, lying to entrap someone (like Margaret).

9. Is Branwell choosing not to speak or has he lost the ability?

Most readers will understand that Branwell is absolutely unable to speak, although not physically. How much can our mental state affect our health and capabilities? Ask for two volunteers and instruct one to think of a moment of personal sadness. Instruct the other to think of a time of great happiness. Ask them to raise their arms to shoulder height and to resist you when you push down on their arms. This experiment should demonstrate the power of emotions over the body.

10. On page 126, Margaret talks about the gift of love being adversely affected by lack of maintenance and by aging. Do you think this is true?

Young people often have some magical beliefs about love, They think, for example, that Bran shouldn't have had to ask to hold the baby or explain what he meant by sharing his design for the birth announcement, but that his father should have just known his wishes. While Bran's father is sadly out of touch, it is common for people to want the object of their love to know and anticipate their needs, and that's not a good way to get what one needs. Love takes lots of communication, a.k.a. maintenance. By not being clear about what you want, you set yourself up for disappointment.

11. Why isn't Vivian afraid that Bran will tell the truth about her?

Vivian has confidence in her charm. She is aware that Bran has a crush on her and undoubtedly realizes the shaming effect seeing her in the bath has on him. Meanwhile, he is so taken with her that he is happy to help out with changing Nikki and doesn't see clearly that Vivian is neglecting her duties. It is not uncommon to make excuses for unattractive behavior in someone you're enamored with. Ask readers if they can think of times when they have done this.

12. As you read the book, did you think that Nikki would recover? Why or why not?

Whether one thinks that Nikki will recover depends on whether one sees that proverbial glass as half empty or half full. Most readers will vacillate back and forth as they read. It certainly would be a different story if Nikki hadn't recovered and would make for an interesting writing assignment or further discussion point.

13. Will Connor and Branwell be lifelong friends?

The history and affection between Connor and Branwell could only be strengthened by the events of the book. Touchingly, Connor says that if Bran recovers, he'll never mind him standing too close again. The temporary estrangement of the friends is caused by Bran's uncomfortable feelings for Vivian. Ask readers whether they've had the experience of a crush altering a close friendship.

35

THE SISTERHOOD OF THE TRAVELING PANTS
by ANN BRASHARES

Bibliographic information: Delacorte, 2001; 294 pages.

Themes: Friendship, death and dying, mental illness, divorce, blended families, competitiveness, and shyness.

Genre: Realism with a magical element.

Main characters: Carmen, Tibby, Lena, and Bridget, all 15.

Tips: Definitely a "girl" book with strong, independent characters and provocative issues. A good choice for mother-daughter discussions. Give your group the background on the inspiration for the magical pants; read the interview at www.bookbrowse.com.

SYNOPSIS:

Born within weeks of each other, Carmen, Tibby, Lena, and Bridget share a very special friendship. While their mothers, who met in an aerobics class for expectant mothers, have grown apart, the girls have remained close. They especially look forward to spending summers together; so when they are faced with their first summer apart they come up with a unique way of staying in touch. Carmen has purchased a pair of jeans from a thrift store. While they look like ordinary pants, they are magical, fitting each proportionately different girl like a glove and make each look fabulous. The friends decide to share the pants, mailing them to each other twice during the summer. They find that the magic of the pants extends to the experiences that they have while wearing them. The summer of pants becomes a summer of self-discovery for each girl.

DISCUSSION QUESTIONS/LEADER POINTS

1. The sisterhood establishes rules governing the traveling pants (p. 24). How would your set of rules differ?

The rules and the magical nature of the pants are a clever device to capture the interest of the audience. The more practical reader may have trouble with the rule about not washing the pants. The taboo on using the word "phat" will likely date the book, as will the cover art. The pants depicted on the cover looked cooler when the book was first published.

2. Which character do you relate to the most? Why?

There is some aspect of the characters that most readers will relate to. Some will recognize Carmen's anger, Tibby's cynicism, Bridget's competitiveness, or Lena's shyness at least some of the time. Ask readers how the girls' different personalities enhance their friendship. Is it believable for such different personalities to be friends? Childhood friends often stay close despite their differences, whereas the adult mothers, who's only commonality was that they were taking prenatal aerobics together and expected babies during the same month, drifted apart. Most people have had a long-time friend whom were they to meet today they might not develop as close of a friendship with.

3. What should Carmen's father have done to make it easier for Carmen to accept his fiance and her family?

It's hard to imagine anyone insensitive enough to think that the best time to tell a daughter about his new family is when she arrive's at his house for a long visit. Carmen had no reason to think she would be doing anything but spending the summer alone with her father until that point. No wonder she feels hostile. While divorced parents need to be careful about prematurely introducing potential partners to their children, Carmen should have been told as soon as her father began considering marriage that there was someone in his life. Several telephone conversations and some time spent together alone would have eased the shock.

4. What is the significance in Carmen's breaking the window?

In a very literal way, Carmen is demanding to be seen. No one seems to notice her absence; the family goes on functioning without her and seemingly without a care for her. Justifiably, Carmen feels invisible and is nursing a big case of attitude, but she is healthily unrestrained in expressing her feelings, and she takes responsibility for her expression.

5. Is Lena's beauty more of a liability than an asset for her? Why or why not?

Shy people prefer to blend in with the scenery. Someone as beautiful as Lena would have trouble doing so, so her looks may have been an unwelcome gift to her. Ask your group whether there are other drawbacks to being exceptionally attractive, for example, are boys less secure about approaching exceptionally attractive girls?

6. Why is it so hard for Lena to be forthcoming about what really happened when Kostos stumbled upon her at the pond?

Lena fails to quickly correct the misinterpretation of her disheveled appearance and her statement that "Kostos is not a nice boy." This may be a result of her shyness and her initial state of shock at being seen naked; it feels as though Kostos has done something wrong in seeing her naked. Language is another difficulty, since she can't understand enough Greek to know what the others were saying. Eventually, Lena does set the story straight and apologizes to Kostos. In doing that, she faces and overcomes some of her demons. Most teens will empathize with the difficulty of her apology, and, if time permits, they may want to share stories of when they felt similarly.

7. When discussing Eric with Bridget (p. 105), Deana says, "Getting in trouble is kind of the point, isn't it?" Is it? Why does Bridget pursue Eric regardless of the rules?

Some teens may find Bridget to be an unbelievable character because of her single-mindedness in pursuing Eric. You may need to inform your group that promiscuity or sexual activity is not an uncommon response to the loss of someone close.

Bridget misses the physical closeness that a mother often expresses, and so she is drawn to look for it elsewhere. Her need is, indeed, "as big as the stars," and cannot to be filled. Bridget is also extremely competitive as evidenced by her inability to be a team player at times. Bridget's behavior might possibly be symptomatic of bipolar disorder—the book hints that her mother may have suffered from this disease and it may have caused her to take her own life. After Bridget loses her virginity, she hits bottom and spends days sleeping. This could be seen as the downward side of bipolar disease, but also could be seen as the result of her disappointment at allowing a challenge to take her that far and her still feeling the emptiness inside. Bridget engenders a lot of sympathy. She needs more than her friends to become healthy. It's unlikely that readers will blame Eric for not resisting Bee more; he was human, after all, and she was very persuasive.

8. What do the quotes preceding each chapter add to the book?

The quotes are unnecessary, but nicely frame the chapters. Many teens love quotes and collect their favorites. Ask what favorites readers have from the book and why they think that the author chose them.

9. Is it believable for Tibby's parents to have changed so much, that is from activists to yuppies?

Everyone knows someone who's had a "second family," usually with a second spouse. Like Tibby, the much older siblings are frequently expected to care for their younger ones, but Tibby's parents expect too much. They rely on Tibby for childcare while they pursue their careers. Their values have shifted from idealistic to materialistic, and readers may find it unusual for people to have changed as drastically as Tibby's parents have. Ask readers whether they think that their shift is reflective of maturity or resignation. None of the adults in the story is well developed and they are mostly inconsequential to the story.

10. How does Tibby change as a result of working on her "suckumentary"? How does Bailey change her?

While Bridget's story may be the most disturbing, Tibby's story elicits the most heartfelt reaction. Some readers will admit to shedding a few tears. If you use this book with a mother-daughter group, ask whether reactions are generationally different. When considering Bailey, mothers will tend to think about what it was like to lose a child rather than a friend.

Tibby starts out as a very cynical character with a lot of attitude. She envisions her suckumentary as an exposé of pathetic people, but when Bailey makes her carry out her plans for making the film, she finds compassion and appreciation for those she once thought to be pathetic. She is required to look beneath the surface and find the basic desires, hopes, and fears that we all share. Her friendship with Bailey, which begins because she feels sorry for the dying girl, leads Tibby to realize that one can't make assumptions about people based on age, although Bailey isn't a typical 12-year old. Bailey and Tibby really are kindred spirits. Bailey is brutally honest, but that may be because she is aware that she doesn't have much time left and wants to make sure she isn't wasting it by playing games. The source of Tibby's honesty is bravado. In befriending and losing Bailey, Tibby undergoes the greatest transformation of the four; she softens.

You may want to ask whether readers think that Bailey's parents are wise in allowing her to act like an ordinary child, and how they would want to live at the end of their lives.

11. How would the experiences the girls have during the summer been different if they'd been together?

All of the girls experience extraordinary events during the summer of the pants. All of them grow in ways that require them to be alone. Having one or all of her friends with her would have influenced Bridget especially, but may have just delayed an inevitable crash. Ask readers whether having friends with them in new situations can limit their experiences. Are they less likely to make new friends or discover things on their own if they are with old friends? Are they more likely to grow if they are on their own?

12. Eric tells Bridget how he feels about her and the future, "but it wasn't what she needed. Her need was as big as the stars, and he was down there on the beach, so quiet she could hardly hear him." What is Bee's need?

It's easy to guess where Bridget's need comes from; the loss of her mother, who probably suffered from mental illness and may have been distant or inconsistent in her treatment of Bridget, would leave a big hole. Ask readers what they think might help Bridget to heal..

13. Why is Carmen a good narrator to begin and end the book?

Carmen is absolutely guileless in expressing her feelings, whether they are admirable or not. Teens will enjoy this honestly and relate to her thoughts.

14. What implausibilities do you find in the book besides the magical nature of the pants to fit each girl perfectly?

Even in great haste, it's inconceivable that someone could put her jeans on inside out. Other stretches of credibility were that Lena could purchase airline tickets by herself and travel freely at her age. Also, when Carmen asks Paul what happened to his girlfriend, he asks if she means "Skeletor," although he couldn't have known that that was the term Carmen used when he thought of her.

36

SKELETON MAN
by JOSEPH BRUCHAC

Bibliographic information: HarperCollins, 2001; 114 pages.

Themes: Native American folklore, self-reliance, guidance from dreams, kidnapping.

Genre: Horror.

Main character: Molly, a sixth grader.

Tips: In this twist on the popular fairy-tale adaptations, Bruchac adapts a Mohawk myth about a man so lazy he eats his own flesh and then his relatives rather than hunt and changes it to a contemporary horror story. The myth, as Bruchac transfers it into a contemporary story is wholly improbable, but eerily captivating. It doesn't quite work, but yet it does: the characters aren't drawn well enough to be real, but still, the reader is drawn in.

Molly's dream life is fascinating. Her spirit guide leads her to find courage and cleverness and become a warrior. The archetypal quality of the story strikes a chord that allows the reader to suspend belief and enjoy a good yarn. This gripping page-turner would be a useful accompaniment to the study of the horror genre or Native American mythology. Compare to Edgar Allan Poe.

SYNOPSIS:

One night Molly goes to bed expecting for her parents to return home, but they don't. Days later a social worker appears, and the next thing Molly knows she is entrusted to her great uncle of whom she has had no knowledge. This uncle has the ability to seem human when he needs to, though Molly suspects he is not. He doesn't eat, is skeletally thin, and has the ability to move supernaturally. He locks Molly in her room at night, spies on her with cameras, and has a secret in a locked shed in the back yard. Through her dreams and memories of the Mohawk myth of the skeleton man she receives the guidance that allows her to escape and save her parents.

DISCUSSION QUESTIONS/LEADER POINTS

1. What is the Mohawk story supposed to tell us?

The uncle in the story takes laziness to the extreme. Perhaps the myth is saying that to be human is to have to work, to hunt, to strive. When the uncle breaks the taboo against eating human flesh, he fully becomes a monster.

The uncle's hunger could also represent insatiable desire which can also be the cause of losing one's humanity. A third possibility is that he simply represents a manifestation of evil, similar to a devil.

2. Molly waits several days for her parents to return. What would you have done?

It's unlikely that the average girl would wait as long as Molly does, but a common element in horror is the protagonist acting in ways counter to common sense. The reader wants to shout, "don't open that door," or "call the police," but the protagonist continues on her course of flirting with disaster.

3. What do you think motivates the Skeleton Man?

Is the Skeleton Man a psychotic maniac or a symbol of human desire gone awry? In Tibetan Buddhism, there is a being called the Hungry Ghost, whose desires burn a hole through his being, leaving him ever empty and insatiable. Like the uncle, his hunger eats him up.

4. Have you ever received guidance in a dream like Molly does?

Do dreams allow us to tap into inner resources and latent talents, or are they just syntheses of sensual input we encounter in our waking lives? Are there different kinds of dreams? The book provides an opportunity for presenting and discussing various theories of dream interpretation. Cite examples of composers and writers receiving ideas in their dreams, for example, Robert Louis Stevenson's "Dr. Jekyll and Mr. Hyde" or Hector Berlioz's *Symphonie Fantastique*.

5. Does the story seem realistic? Why or why not?

Readers will probably acknowledge the unlikely ease with which Molly is turned over to her "uncle." Surely a rigorous investigation would have occurred in our world, but this is the world of horror—a Twilight Zone where we suspend belief to be titillated by the stuff of nightmares.

6. What details make the story especially creepy?

The wonderfully detailed descriptions of the uncle are deliciously creepy. Bruchac successfully sets up the reader to expect a skeletal hand to reach out at every turn, especially when Molly finds her parents and spends an agonizing amount of time with them. The chase is horrific, as is Molly's victory over the Skeleton Man.

7. Was Bruchac successful in making the myth of the skeleton man a contemporary story? Are there any details you would have added?

If Bruchac had wanted this to be a more realistic story, he would have added a motivation for the kidnappings. Why doesn't he make the story realistic? Compare this story with an urban legend and you'll find the same sketchy details, unlikely elements, and raw horror. Is it Bruchac's intention to stay true to the mythological nature of the story?

8. Is the end satisfying? Does it bother you that we don't learn the Skeleton Man's goal or that his remains aren't found?

Some readers will be bothered that parts of the story are unresolved and will be left asking why. Ask what a more satisfying ending would have been.

37

THE STAIRCASE

by ANN RINALDI

Bibliographic information: Harcourt, 2000; 230 pages.

Themes: The overlap of religion and superstition, the rights of parents to make decisions for their children, respect for the wishes of others, the development of a legend, historical fiction about the Santa Fe Trail and the Chapel of Loretto.

Genre: Historical fiction.

Main character: Lizzy Enders, 13.

Tips: The story is based on the legend of the mysterious staircase that graces the Chapel of Loretto in Santa Fe. Information on and pictures of the staircase are a natural accompaniment to discussion of this book. The staircase is an architectural wonder and a major tourist attraction. Also look for information on the Santa Fe Trail so your group can see the trek that Lizzy and her family made.

Some readers may be uncomfortable with comparisons between superstition and religion or the miraculous elements of the story.

SYNOPSIS:

After her mother dies on the Santa Fe Trail, Lizzy's father leaves the Methodist teen with the Sisters of Loretto and the Bishop's grandniece, Elinora, who commences to torment and ostracize Lizzy. The strangeness of Catholicism and its many rules add to her general unhappiness, but support comes from a truly kind sister, the resident crazy woman, and, surprisingly, the bishop. Lizzy manages to have the bishop hire a wandering carpenter to build a staircase to the choir loft in the chapel. The carpenter completes the work in an astonishingly short period of time using just a hammer, a T-square, and a saw, then disappears without claiming his pay. The wood used is unidentifiable. After rescuing Elinora from a madman looking for his baby, whom the sisters are protecting, Elinora and Lizzy become allies. In the end, Lizzy is welcomed to her father's ranch with Elinora and the baby in tow.

DISCUSSION QUESTIONS/LEADER POINTS

1. Should Lizzy's father have talked to her about staying at the convent? Do parents have the right to make what they think are the best decisions for their children without consulting them?

While Lizzy's father no doubt thinks that Lizzy will be better provided for with the sisters of Loretto than with him, he acts cowardly in not discussing it with her. It spares him the heartache of saying goodbye and seeing her reaction, but it may be argued that it would have been easier for Lizzy if he had spoken to her. At least he could have explained why he believes she'll be better off there, which she may interpret as an act of love. This incident coupled with the lack of warmth in his letter to Lizzy indicates that he probably has trouble showing emotion. How can you tell that someone loves you if that person has trouble expressing emotions?

Teens will no doubt have strong opinions about a parent's right to make decisions regarding his child without consulting her. Ask if the age of the child makes a difference.

2. Sister Roberta doesn't follow all of the rules; is she a good nun? When is it okay to break rules?

Sr. Roberta allows her heart to guide her rather than following rules for their own sake. Strict practitioners would say her disregard for rules is sinful, but the good she does is undeniable. When is it okay to break rules?

3. Elinora believes that Dolores can cure a headache by passing an an egg across someone's forehead and cure a serious illness by hitting the shadow of the afflicted with a broom. Can you see some similarities between these beliefs and some of the beliefs of the sisters?

4. Does this book give a fair picture of Catholicism?

As Elinora and Lizzy are about to visit Dolores, the witch, the carpenter warns them that the only real kind of magic is the goodness of the heart (p. 78). Readers will find many examples of the blurry lines between religion and superstition in this book. You'll want to be prepared for discussing how Catholicism has changed over the years. Some things that may seem superstitious are practiced out of a sense of tradition. Maybe some things are meant to be understood metaphorically rather than literally. Ask if your group can think of examples.

5. Is Mrs. Lacey justified in blaming herself for her son's death? Is she wrong in believing that an act of goodness makes up for a poor choice?

It is human nature to imagine that one could have prevented the death of a loved one, but we can't predict the outcome of our choices with real accuracy because there are always other variables that arise in addition to the unpredictable nature of the other human being involved. Many traditions do believe that there is a balance in the world between good and bad, and so, keeping balance in mind, one can atone for wrongdoing by doing good.

6. What would you have done with Abeyto's note for Elinora if you were Lizzie? Is Lizzie's concern for Elinora genuine?

7. Is Mother Magdalena correct in punishing Lizzy and revealing her as the informant when she receives the note intended for Elinora? What do you think that she should have done? When is it acceptable to be a tattletale?

Lizzy is remarkably modern and mature in some ways, but teens will probably think she's naïve in giving Mother Magdalene Abeyto's note for Elinora. She probably acts out of real concern for Elinora, but it's not her responsibility. Mother Magdalene makes Lizza responsible for her choice to tattle. She is punished for being out without permission and then exposed as an informant, which is crueler. Do you think that is Mother's intention? Perhaps Lizzy should have disposed of the note, not involving Mother Magdalene, but still preventing Elinora from meeting Abeyto. How would this have changed the story?

8. Does Elinora have a true calling? How do you think someone would know that she has a calling?

Elinora is no doubt using her "calling" to get special recognition and privileges. Her meanness reveals that she has no understanding of what it is to be called to a life of humility and service. Perhaps a true calling wouldn't be paraded before others.

9. Is Elinora's change of heart after Lizzy "saves her life" believable? What kinds of events alter us profoundly enough to make us do a complete about-face?

Some readers will find Elinora's transformation from Lizzy's enemy to devotee when Lizzy saves her life unconvincing and the happily ever after ending in which Lizzy goes to live with her father along with Elena's baby and Elinora surprising. While having one's life threatened is an adequate catalyst for reexamining one's attitude, Elinora's about-face is complete, and we aren't given a glimpse of her thoughts. One wonders if some of the old rivalry will surface.

10. Should Mrs. Lacey's wishes not to be baptized in the Catholic Church have been respected? Why or why not?

One of the most intriguing questions is whether Mrs. Lacey's wishes not to be baptized should have been respected. The bishop believes he is saving her from damnation and it is his duty. The real issue is whether he has the right to allow her to be damned (in his opinion). Since her decision affects no one but herself, should it override what someone else believes is right? Ask your group if it's similar to the choice to end your life if you're suffering from a fatal illness.

11. How do people use interpretations of religion to justify their actions?

Elinora uses religious reasons to get the other girls to be cruel to Lizzy. Readers will have no trouble thinking of examples of this phenomenon. Consider so called holy wars.

12. There is irony in the fact that the prayers of the convent are answered, but they fail to recognize it. Have you heard the expression be careful what you wish for, you might get it? Do you think that we sometimes receive our wishes or the answer to our prayers and don't realize it? Can you think of examples?

13. Is the staircase a miracle? What is a miracle?

A miracle may be defined as something that has no rational explanation, but it may be argued that that doesn't mean an explanation won't ever be found. Ask readers if they can think of things that were once considered miraculous that have since been explained (e.g., the Northern Lights, eclipses, rainbows, seasons).

14. How could the legend have become embellished over time?

It's easy to imagine that the mystery of the staircase took on more legendary proportions over time. For example, the number of carpenter's tools and the amount of time it took him to build may have shrunk in the retelling. Talk about how stories become legends. Use an urban legend to illustrate the point.

38

STARGIRL
by JERRY SPINELLI

Bibliographic information: Knopf, 2000; 186 pages.

Themes: Popularity, peer pressure, individuality.

Genre: Realistic fiction/fable.

Main characters: Leo and Stargirl, both 16.

Tips: This is a great discussion book for both boys and girls. Some readers might be uncomfortable with the more philosophical questions, so be sensitive to comfort levels. Issues of individuality and popularity are topics teens will welcome discussing.

SYNOPSIS:

Stargirl Carraway is unlike anyone Mica High students have ever met. Is she for real? Is she an alien? How else to explain someone who is so completely unaffected by the styles and acceptance of her peers? Spinelli skillfully explores the question of what a student who has no ego would encounter in an average American high school. The results are disturbing and provocative. Stargirl unwittingly enchants students, but when her nondualistic point of view leads her to cheer for opposing teams and unabashedly express compassion for the other school's injured star player during basketball playoffs, the tide turns.

Stargirl is told from the point of view of "Average Joe" Leo, who ultimately falls in love with Stargirl and literally has the time of his life. When the entire school shuns the lovers, Leo succumbs to the pressure and cuts his ties to Stargirl, but his regrets only grow over the years. The end of the book finds Leo reminiscing about Stargirl, and the reader learns that her legacy lives on at Mica High.

DISCUSSION QUESTIONS/LEADER POINTS

1. About Stargirl, Archie says, "She is, I think, who we really are. Or were" (p. 32). What does he mean? Do you agree?

Teens will readily acknowledge that their actions are dictated by popular culture and by their peers. The desire to fit in is overwhelming even though, as Archie suggests, popular culture doesn't necessarily reflect human nature or human nature at its best. Ask readers how society would be different if most of the people were like Stargirl. Would they prefer it? Why or why not? What things have made us less like Stargirl?

2. Leo is surprised to find that Stargirl's parents appear ordinary. Do you think that they are? How would you explain Stargirl's unique way of being?

Appearances can be deceiving. If Leo observed her parents every day, he might detect some irregularities. What other influences may have affected Stargirl? We know that she has been home-schooled, but that doesn't mean she hasn't had influential teachers in addition to her parents. Maybe she has had other Archies in her life. Ask readers who's had a big influence on them other than their parents.

3. Because of Stargirl's influence, students at Mica High begin to express their individuality. It seems that conformity is a reaction to the fear of being different, but when individuality is appreciated, a new collective identity emerges — a new camaraderie. How do you explain this paradox?

When people aren't held to standards that may not reflect their true natures, they emerge as freer, richer, and more interesting people. They are free to discover their own potentials. Are there things that you like to do that you don't do because your peers would think they were strange or childish? For example, schools seem to root out those with a gift for art by the time students enter high school. Those who are not particularly gifted aren't encouraged to practice art after childhood; yet everyone can find joy and satisfaction in creating art. The second part of the question addresses the human need to form groups. Ask readers whether being a group of individuals can become as rigid as being a member of any other group and eventually rob people of the very thing (individuality) that made them part of the group.

Do all groups start out with a few people breaking away from the pack to express their individuality?

4. Was Stargirl wrong to attend the Grisdale funeral? To give a bike to Danny Pike?

Stargirl takes seriously the sentiment that we are all one, part of one big family. In Buddhist terms, we should honor everyone because in one of many past lives that person was our mother. Jesus said that, "Inasmuch as ye have done it unto one of the least of these my brethren, ye have done it unto me"(Matthew 25:40). So, she sees that the Grisdale family and Danny Pike are part of her family. Isn't this the example that all great teachers of all faiths have taught?

5. Stargirl cheers for everyone. Do you think that her lack of identification with just one team, her identification with the whole human race is naïve or enlightened?

It may be argued that Stargirl's innocence is unbelievable. Even though she's been home-schooled and doesn't watch TV, it would be hard not to be familiar with the norms of popular culture. However, she may be viewed as someone who is more spiritually evolved than most people, or enlightened. If people in your school acted like Mother Teresa or the Mohandas Gandhi, wouldn't they be perceived as naïve? Mother Teresa believed that in living a life of service she was aligned with God. Mohandas Gandhi believed that nonviolence was mightier than any weapon. Were these two naïve? Can you think of others whose vision might be viewed as either naïve or enlightened?

6. What good ideas does Stargirl have? Could you or your school borrow some of her ideas to make life better?

What if your school formed a Sunshine Club that practiced random acts of kindness? What kinds of projects could you do? What could be more thrilling than giving someone in need what the person needs, or giving someone an unexpected gift? How does it feel when a gift comes unexpectedly? Have you ever surprised someone anonymously? How did it feel? How would an atmosphere of giving and receiving affect your school?

7. When she takes him to her enchanted place, Stargirl instructs Leo to do nothing. Have you ever done nothing? What does it feels like?

People rarely take the time to do nothing, to stop at any time during their busy day to be completely aware of the present moment—the shadows on the pavement, the birdsong, the breeze against their cheeks, their feet connecting with the ground, their breath. Then look at the miracle you live—the perfection of how your body works. Wiggle your fingers. Look at the tiny flowers among the grass. Look at the amazing sky. One day I was at a crowded park and I saw a rainbow, the brightest, most complete rainbow I've ever seen. There were only two of us who noticed it. It was a very strange feeling to be surrounded by people who were unaware of the extravagance the sky was displaying.

8. Leo says, "I never saw her look in the mirror, never heard her complain. All of her feelings, all of her attentions flowed outward. She had no ego" (p. 53). How would life be different if you had no ego?

Make a list. You wouldn't worry about how you looked. You wouldn't do things solely to make yourself feel like a good person. What would motivate you? Love of life? The joy of service or learning or expressing creativity? Ask for examples of things readers enjoy that are not motivated by ego. You will no doubt be able to find that some of the example's actually do involve the ego.

9. Archie instructs Leo to choose whose affection he values more, Stargirl's or the rest of school's. What would you have done in Leo's place? Is he sorry for his decision?

It takes a very strong person to stand up against his peers and to give up so much for one person. This is especially hard at Leo's age. He loves Stargirl, but he's too young to change his life for her. His decision is tragic though. He acts counter to his heart, and he will never enjoy his former innocence. At the end of the book we get a sense that he does have some regrets.

10. Leo balks when Stargirl leaves an anonymous gift of an African violet on a doorstep. Is it important to know where a gift comes from? Why or why not?

11. Stargirl has chosen her name. Some people believe that your name helps to shape who you are. Could you change your name, and how would you go about selecting a new name?

12. When Leo tries to convince Stargirl to be more like other people, he tells her that she's not connected (p. 136-137). Is Stargirl not connected or is she more connected than most people?

Thank goodness that Stargirl realizes fairly quickly that trying to be what you're not for someone else is like wearing shoes that are too small. You can keep them on for a while, but unless you choose to live in pain, you'll throw them off. Stargirl is connected with something bigger than the students at Mica High School. When Leo accuses her of not being connected, he's talking about a very narrow slice of life. How does it feel when you think that in 20 years you won't even remember some of the people you want to impress now. Does it make some things seem less important? How?

13. Why is it painful for Leo to watch the Ukee Dooks, Stargirl, and Dori play on and on for no one? Are his feelings about Stargirl or himself?

His feelings seem to be about Stargirl; he's embarrassed for her, but they are really about himself. *She* is not embarrassed. *She* doesn't care whether she has an audience. She enjoys making music and sharing it with the Okee Dooks. If Leo's love were pure, he'd be happy to see her joy.

14. On the night of the prom Stargirl wins over the class once again. Why does this happen?

People instinctively recognize truth and beauty and respond. Stargirl is a pure person who wears her heart on her sleeve, and she knows how to have fun. When people let go of their inhibitions, they are free to have fun. Why don't adults skip? Can anyone deny that skipping is fun?

15. Do you think that Stargirl and Leo will meet again? If they do, what are their chances for staying together?

We are given hope that their second meeting is a possibility because of the tie. Being more mature and not at the mercy of peer pressure, Leo has a much better chance of being able to accept Stargirl as an adult.

39

STONER AND SPAZ
by RON KOERTGE

Bibliographic infomration: Candlewick Press, 2002; 169 pages.

Themes: Disabilities, addiction, self-perception, self-acceptance.

Genre: Realistic fiction.

Main characters: Ben Bancroft and Colleen Minou, both 16.

Tips: Strong language and sexual situations may make this more suitable for mature readers. *Stoner and Spaz* is a little gem of a book guaranteed to open a dialogue about perceptions of disabilities. It has quirky, interesting characters, a wacky romance, and an honest, humorous narrator.

SYNOPSIS:

A victim of cerebral palsy, Ben is the resident "spaz" of his high school. Since his mother disappeared, movies have become his escape and his passion. One day at the Rialto Theater, notorious stoner Colleen latches onto Ben and an unusual friendship, which ultimately becomes a romance, ensues. Despite their differences and the disapproval of his grandmother, they are good for each other. Colleen leads Ben to loosen up and think of himself beyond his physical challenges, and Ben persuades Colleen to stay sober (albeit briefly). His relationship with Colleen and with a caring neighbor who introduces him to filmmaking are catalysts for Ben's growing appreciation of his abilities.

DISCUSSION QUESTIONS/LEADER POINTS

1. Ben says that he's "just the resident spaz, invisible as the sign that says no running, and the one nobody pays any attention to" (p. 23). Why do people treat disabled people as if they were invisible? Does Ben make himself invisible?

Some people worry that looking at a disabled person might be construed as staring and rude, but Ben expects to be treated as if he's invisible and presents that attitude to the world. When he begins to approach people, they respond. When he films Stephanie, she admits that she ironically assumed that Ben thought he was better than everyone else because he wears expensive clothes and keeps to himself.

2. Colleen chastises Ben for talking to her mother because her mother says that Ben is the nicest guy who ever called. Colleen says that she doesn't want nice guys calling and that she's a total bitch. (p. 26) Why does Colleen want to be a bitch?

Acting tough may make Colleen think she is. If her skin is thick, she's less likely to be hurt. Also, if she's a bitch, she's unapproachable; the incident with her mother's boyfriend may have made it desirable for her to be unapproachable. Because Colleen's mother chose to believe her boyfriend and put Colleen at risk, Colleen probably has feelings of worthlessness that led to her substance abuse. Because her mother didn't protect her, maybe she thinks it's not worth protecting herself so she allows herself to be in a position where she will do anything. Colleen knows that she will let Ben down, so she tries to keep him from getting too close.

3. What are the similarities and differences in Ben's addiction to movies and Colleen's addiction to drugs?

Both Ben and Colleen use their addictions to escape from painful situations. Obviously, Colleen's addiction is harmful; not only does she put herself in dangerous situations, but she also compromises her health. On the other hand, Ben's interest in movies has a positive outcome in allowing him to realize his abilities in making a film. His obsession may have kept him from being more social, though.

4. Is Colleen disabled?

Colleen is more disabled than Ben. Her addiction keeps her from living a real life and will possibly cut her life short. Her future looks bleak.

5. Ben's grandmother works for a lot of charities. Do you think that she's charitable? Why or why not?

Ben's grandmother provides lots of comic relief. She is a hypocrite who supports the right causes, but doesn't really walk her talk. She can't tolerate Colleen, who obviously has problems, and she almost seems embarrassed about Ben's disability, for example, when he changes his hair she wonders aloud whether he isn't already conspicuous enough. She even sends him to invite Marcie to lunch after dark so his awkwardness will be hidden.

She's a cold woman. She may believe she has Ben's best interests in mind, as when she suggests they go to a series of concerts because they're important, but she's made her choices from her head, not from her heart. It's as if she's read a list of politically correct causes to support and beneficial activities for her college-bound grandson, and that's what guides her actions, not love.

6. Do you think that Ben's grandmother loves him? How should she treat him differently?

She probably does love him, which she shows by giving him opportunities. Thinking about making him less conspicuous may come from wanting to protect *him* from embarrassment. She may be someone who has walled herself off to protect herself and is somehow wounded herself.

7. Ben has decided not to look for his mother. Should he? What do you think he could expect if he found her?

Ben's mother might be surprised by his abilities. Maybe over time she will have gained the maturity to accept her responsibilities toward him. Ben would be foolish to expect to be welcomed with open arms. Sometimes these cases can be a standoff. She may assume he would never forgive her for deserting him, and he may assume she doesn't want to hear from him. If one could make the connection, the other might soften.

8. Marcie has made a documentary about heart transplant patients, and Ben makes "High School Confidential." What would you make a documentary about and why?

9. How does Colleen's attention change Ben? Marcie's? How does Ben change Colleen?

By forcing him into situations that he formerly would have avoided, Colleen has helped Ben realize that his life doesn't have to be as limited as it has been. He becomes less rigid. It gives him confidence and self-esteem to have her attention. Marcie helps him further by giving him a project that places him in social settings, and, at the same time, he can express himself and learning a skill. Her belief in his abilities enables him to rise to the occasion.

Colleen has to admit that there is something attractive about feeling like she's really in high school. Ben is a nice, intelligent, interesting person with a sense of humor. He treats her well. Her boyfriend, Ed, puts her in dangerous situations and ultimately gives her away. Because of Ben, she is able to stay straight for a short while; that's hopeful. Ben is Colleen's only real friend. He shows her that there's something worthwhile in her.

10. Why are reactions different when Colleen says that Ben laid down his Harley or got hurt rock climbing from what they would be if she'd said he has cerebral palsy?

It's interesting to explore perceptions of someone you'd imagine to have been hurt crashing a motorcycle or rock climbing versus someone who has a disability, but it shouldn't be so, and Ed is right when he tells Ben that he's tough. Think about making a column for each label (motorcycle rider, rock climber, person with cerebral palsy) then list adjectives under the label your group chooses, for example, daring, weak, sick, athletic, challenged, brave. Why do some people prefer the word "challenged" to "disabled" or "handicapped?"

By romanticizing the reason for his condition when they go dancing, Colleen makes it acceptable to talk about it. Why is it more acceptable to talk about an injury than an illness or disability? Maybe it's because an affliction that someone is born with will always be a part of him, but if the affliction occurs as a result of an accident, it's easier to see the person as separate from it. Accident is a telling word. If someone has an accident, some of the blame or shame is taken away. Although, we don't know why, there is a feeling that shame may be involved—maybe shame on the part of the healthy person for being healthy, and so that inhibits honest communication.

40

STUCK IN NEUTRAL
by TERRY TRUEMAN

Bibliographic information: HarperCollins, 2000; 128 pages,
Themes: Disabilities, mercy killing.

Genre: Realistic fiction.

Main characters: Shawn McDaniel, 14; Shawn's father, Syd.

Tips: Trueman has written a startling, important, and thought-provoking book that makes us question our assumptions about some kinds of disabilities. For teens who ask for readalikes suggest *Petey* by Ben Mikaelsen or *Johnny Got His Gun* by Dalton Trumbo.

SYNOPSIS:

Shawn McDaniel has the same interests as any average 14-year-old boy. He's probably brighter than most, and he has the unusual talent of remembering everything that he has ever heard. These are all things that even those closest to him don't know because Shawn has no control over any muscle in his body. A victim of cerebral palsy, Shawn can't even swallow or focus his eyes at will. So no one really knows him and people might assume that the seizures that wrack his body cause him pain instead euphoric freedom. Shawn's condition has changed the lives of his family members. His father, who has become famous because of a poem written about Shawn, has left the family because he can't bear Shawn's suffering. In fact, he's thinking about putting Shawn out of his misery.

DISCUSSION QUESTIONS/LEADER POINTS

1. What assumptions do we make about people like Shawn? Did this book change the way you will think about them or treat them?

To reconsider whether someone has awareness when a doctor has said he probably doesn't can be an astonishing idea. A doctor is often making his best guess, yet one might assume that the guess being correct is more probable than it actually is. Asking myself whether I would treat someone in Shawn's condition differently if I thought he might have awareness was sobering. I realized that I don't usually speak to someone with whom I can't make eye contact. Ask readers whether they do.

2. Does Shawn's father act out of love?

Shawn's father loves him, but his love seems to be filtered through a narcissistic lens. He has to leave the family because *he* can't bear to see Shawn suffer. He doesn't consider how this affects the other members of the family. He allows his own feelings to matter more than anyone else's.

3. Shawn's mother says that his father can't stand thinking that he may have awareness. Why does he assume that awareness would make Shawn's situation worse?

Shawn's dad assumes that awareness would mean that Shawn would be cognizant of his limitations and unhappy about them, but Shawn has never known another way of being. His dad can only think of what being in Shawn's condition is like from his own healthy point of view.

4. Shawn thinks that his parents love him because they're required to love him (p. 60). Thinking about Ally makes him think about loving as part of knowing. How are these two kinds of love different? Do you think that he is accurate in his assessment of parental love?

Parental love is mysterious, biological, and perhaps divine. You certainly don't have to get to know your children to love them. The love is usually there from the moment they're born or perhaps before. There is an added dimension when you love your children for who they are. Adoptive parents develop the same devotion; maybe it's being entrusted with a child that awakens that kind of love. Romantic love only comes from learning whom a person is.

5. What do you think of Shawn's dad's feelings about educating the uneducable?

Syd makes an interesting point about educating the uneducable, a good point to debate. Trueman makes an even better point: that we don't really know whether the experience is enriching or valuable to those who are the uneducable. Who's to say the social experience of being with other people isn't valuable, or the loving touch of a caregiver might not communicate to a disabled person on a level we can't discern.

6. When he's on the Alice Ponds Show, does Shawn's dad make a valid parallel between voluntary euthanasia and a child with a condition like Shawn's (p. 76).

Of course Shawn is unable to express his wishes, his desire to live, so it's not the same as healthy people saying they would want to die if they were to assume vegetative states. It could be argued that a person who suddenly finds her or himself in that state might then have change of mind about preferring death; how could we know?

7. Why do you think Shawn's dad is so interested in Colin Detraux's case?

Syd is interested in Colin Detraux's case because he can empathize with Colin. Also, he may be looking for either justification for killing Shawn or evidence that it would be a mistake. He wants an answer to the question that's haunting him.

8. Do you think that Shawn may appreciate life more than the average person? See the paragraph that starts on page 84 with "I love my mom."

Read this paragraph that begins on page 84 aloud. It shows that Shawn is aware of more detail than the average person and probably more grateful for simple pleasures many people overlook. How often do we fully experience things like the sensual quality of a hairbrush against our scalp, the hair falling like a soft curtain against our skin. We should ask ourselves how happy the average functioning person is as he blindly rushes through his day.

9. The fragments of Syd's Pulitzer Prize-winning poem are scattered throughout the book. Read them all together. What feelings do you think this poem evokes in readers? What feelings did it evoke in you? Is it a poem of worthy of a prize?

Syd's poem evokes sympathy and pity, but I almost feel manipulated. It lacks the quality of many truly great works that elevate us beyond ordinary human response to tragedy. The tone is maudlin. In describing his slide from joy to despair as he realizes his baby is abnormal, he slides into self pity. His images of he and Shawn as birds are not fully developed. Shawn is also compared to cooked spaghetti and a braying beast. Lindy's womb is tidal and loud which calls to mind sloshing water- loud sloshing water. Words are compared inexplicably to firewood and concrete, then to meringue. The free verse doesn't benefit from form or rhythm. The construction is loose and the images are inconsistent.

In your discussion you may want to print the complete poem and read it to the group. It's hard to get a feel for it in bits and pieces at the beginnings of chapters.

Ask why Syd chose birds to represent Shawn and himself. Ask the group whether they think this is a prize worthy poem and why/not. It's not particularly well-crafted. It is perhaps what made me least sympathetic toward Syd. It might be more poignant if he had written about Lindy's reaction and her grace in accepting responsibility for her damaged son or if he had written about the love that endures through the disappointment and heartbreak, but he only addresses his own self-pity.

10. What do you think that Shawn's dad will do?

One hopes that Syd will recognize some glimmer of consciousness in Shawn and will make peace with his son's condition. Ask readers how believing that Shawn might have an inner life would change Syd.

41

TOMORROW WHEN THE WAR BEGAN
by JOHN MARSDEN

Bibliographic information: Houghton Mifflin, 1995; 286 pages.

Themes: Survival, war, leadership.

Genre: Appocalyptic fiction.

Main character: Ellie, the teen narrator, and six friends.

Tips: The first time I held a book discussion on this book, I found a wonderful Web site that had facsimiles of news wires as they would appear if the story were true. Sharing the pseudo-news was an interesting addition to the discussion. The site doesn't exist any more, but it's always worth a search for material to supplement your discussion. While I didn't find exactly what I was looking for, I found the following:

http://english.unitecnology.ac.nz/resources/units/tomorrow/home.html/—one teacher's unit plan for this book.

http://English.unitechnology.ac.nz/bookcat/archive/war/home/—chat archive.

http://www.booklookloon.com/Database/Teens_Reviews_of_Tomorrow_When_the_War_Began_by_Marsden.html.

http://tomorrow.my-age.net/about.html/—study guide developed by ninth grade students.

SYNOPSIS:

When Ellie and her friends return from a camping trip, they find that their country has been invaded and their families are being held as prisoners of war. Following the instructions of a fax left behind by one of their parents, the teens take to the bush where survival and fighting back become their goals. This is the first in a series of seven books.

DISCUSSION QUESTIONS/LEADER POINTS

1. What is the significance of the title?

Tomorrow is in the future. Thinking about your country being invaded is a thing most people would think highly improbable. Like death. It comes or can come sometime in the unforeseeable future. The title implies that improbability has arrived.

2. Ellie is elected to record the group's experiences. What is it that makes people need to write things down?

Those who keep diaries or journals will understand the benefit of writing things down to keep a record or to make sense of things. Keeping a journal sometimes makes things that are hard to understand clearer. Ellie certainly has reason to try to make sense of what has happened and what happens to her and her friends as a result. The survival of the teens is questionable; keeping a record of their experience honors their work and may inspire others to continue the work Ellie and her friends have started. After Ellie and Lee find the hermit's box and discover the facts behind his exile, the importance of keeping a record is reinforced. The truth is often distorted by the version of events that endures through oral history.

3. In her letter to the hermit, Imogen Eaken wrote, "There is no stopping women once they begin to gossip, and I say it although I am a traitor to my sex, but there it is, that is the way of the world and no doubt always will be." Is it sexist or honest to assume women are the ones who gossip? Would public reaction have been different if the genders of those involved were reversed (if it had been the wife who shot the husband and child)?

This is an especially fun debate if you have a mixed group. Don't let things get too heated. Women certainly talk more than men, but whether they gossip more is unclear. Most readers will guess that public opinion would have been more sympathetic toward a woman, especially if the incident involved her own child. However, there are certainly examples in recent years of women who have killed their own children.

4. What makes Ellie and Homer rise to assume leadership roles?

Ellie and Homer assume leadership roles because they have leadership qualities including courage, intelligence, and ability to get along with the others. For well-done character studies of both, see—http://www.tased.edu.au/school/penguinh/1999/work/tomorrow/into.html.

5. Is it realistic for Ellie to be preoccupied by romance under the circumstances? Why or why not?

Romance may be the perfect antidote for dire circumstances. It reminds people of the joys of life and gives them extra energy. Romance is a great preoccupation of teens.

6. Ellie struggles to justify the deaths that she has caused. When is killing justifiable? What about the hermit's case?

Most readers will agree that killing is justifiable in self-defense and in times of war, but it always has consequences for the killer—a loss of innocence. The hermit's act was a mercy killing and is heartbreakingly justifiable.

7. Ellie discourses on people who believe implicity that they are right—almost envies the strength of their beliefs because she imagines it makes life easier (p. 218). Is her questioning, doubting nature a blessing or a curse?

Faith, or belief, is mysterious. Belief is having certain knowledge, and it is very comforting to have some of life's hard questions answered. The mysterious part is that some people just never stop questioning while others are utterly convinced. It takes a stronger character to live with doubt, to keep probing. Ask readers whether they would prefer to be a believer in something or one who constantly searches and why.

8. After hearing bits of radio broadcasts, the group speculates on the reasons for the invasion. Robyn expresses empathy for countries which have much less, although she doesn't believe it justifies the acts of the invaders. What do you think of "reducing imbalances" in the world as a preventative measure against war and terrorism?

The question really is how much responsibility do we have for spreading out world resources equitably. Ask readers whether they think working to reduce imbalances would be an effective way of reducing terrorism and weapons proliferation.

9. Is the takeover plausible? How would you expect the U.S. and allies to respond?

It is likely that whatever country overtakes Australia would be quickly dealt with by her allies. Most readers won't mind suspending plausibility. The complex, compelling characters and the abundance of action are enough to keep them engaged.

10. Is the end satisfying?

The end is not the end and leaves readers eager to read the next in this series of seven.

42

TUCK EVERLASTING
by NATALIE BABBITT

Bibliographic information: Farrar, Straus, Giroux, 1975;

Themes: Eternal life, exploiting a questionable product because of greed, taking a life, and breaking the law to protect the greater good.

Genre: Fantasy.

Main character: Winnie Foster, 10 in the book, 15 in the movie version.

Tips: While originally written for a younger audience, the recent Disney movie has piqued the interested of teens. It's a good title to use for a book and movie comparison. Teens might not love the book, but they'll enjoy comparing the book and movie and discussing the issues they bring to light. The changes made to the story when the book was translated to film and the attractive teen actors give it plenty of teen appeal. Winnie is 15 instead of 10 and Jesse and

Winnie definitely have some romantic chemistry. Most teens will pre-fer the movie over the book and like the changes.

SYNOPSIS:

Winnie Foster considers running away from home. While she is in the woods, she discovers the Tucks and the spring with the water that gave them immortality. The Tucks persuade Winnie to accompany them to their home, where they convince her not to reveal their secret. Unbeknownst to them, a mysterious man in a yellow suit follows, acquires the woods, and plans to exploit the spring for his own profit. When Mae Tuck kills the man, she is arrested. Winnie and the Tucks must help her escape so that their secret won't be revealed. Jesse leaves Winnie with a bottle of spring water and she must decide whether to drink it and become immortal.

DISCUSSION QUESTIONS/LEADER POINTS

1. Winnie says, "The ownership of land is an odd thing when you come to think of it. How deep, after all, can it go? If a person own's a piece of land, does he own it all the way down, in ever narrowing dimensions, till it meets all other pieces at the center of the earth? (p. 7)" What do you think of her thoughts? Can anyone really own land?

The question of land ownership is an intriguing one. It seems arrogant and naïve to think of owning a piece of land, a rock, or a tree, especially if you view the earth as a living organism. You might want to explain Gaia theory or talk about Native American beliefs about land.

2. Does the book give enough detail about Winnie's time with the Tucks to justi-fy her devotion to them? Does the movie do a better job of it?

The time that Winnie spends with the Tucks seems longer in the movie, and there seems to be the implication that time with them may have been magically expan-sive. In the book it's a little surprising that Winnie feels so devoted after spending only a day with them. There isn't much detail about the time they spend together.

3. How is the story enhanced or compromised by making Winnie older in the movie version?

The element of romance that Winnie's older age allows certainly makes the movie more appealing to teens. Love makes her choice more compelling, also. The movie also conveys a stronger a sense of Jesse's choosing to ask Winnie to drink the water because of who she is and his feelings for her than because she's the only other per-son who knows their secret about the Tucks.

4. What other differences are there between the book and movie and how to they affect the story?

In the movie, Winnie's very controlled life and the fact that she is going to be sent to finishing school give her a more believable motive for running away. Her situa-tion doesn't seem as serious in the book.

In the book, Winnie replaces Mae in her jail cell, but as soon as the constable approaches she reveals herself. Why is her being there preferable to an empty cell? It would have made more sense if she had covered herself with a blanket and feigned sleep to give the Tucks more time. The movie escape seems more realistic, with the trio distracting the constable instead of removing and replacing the window.

Most people would agree that the man in the yellow suit seems more sinister in the movie. Perhaps this is simply a difference in the media, or maybe the gentle tone of the book influences the reader's interpretation. Readers probably don't interpret the man to be as repugnant as Ben Kingsley did.

5. Why do you think Babbitt doesn't give the man in the yellow suit a name?

As for his namelessness, in an interview Natalie Babbitt said that she originally gave the man a name, then took it out because she thought not having a name would make him more mysterious and threatening—people tend to fear what's not identified (Scholastic online, 2003). A teen in my group guessed that the author might not have given him a name so that it would be easier to accept his death. The more detail known, the more of a person he becomes. We may have felt worse if we knew that he had children, for example.

My group expressed curiosity over the fact that the nameless man was dressed in yellow. One reader suggested that he was a gold digger. He was certainly in opposition to the simple, goodhearted Tucks who never aged; yellow is another sign of aging.

6. Does Mae do the right thing in killing the man in the yellow suit? Should she be punished?

Readers are likely to argue whether it was necessary to permanently silence the man in the yellow suit. Even if the Tucks had extracted a promise from him never to tell, he couldn't be trusted. Maybe the Tucks should have killed the constable, too, which would have solved the problem of Mae's having being arrested, although in the movie, there were more people who witnessed the killing. Another possibility was for the Tucks to hold the man prisoner indefinitely. As for being punished, it must be awful for gentle Mae to have committed the act of murder. Worse still is that she has all eternity to reflect on it.

7. Winnie remembers a line from a poem by Richard Lovelace, "Stone walls do not a prison make, nor iron bars a cage." How does this quote relate to the story?

8. Babbitt uses wheels and cycles a lot throughout the book. She describes the wood as the center of a wheel(p. 4). How is this so?

The quote describes well the prison of endless life. The spring and the Tucks are forever at the center of the wheel of life, but never part of the circle, the cycle of life from birth to death.

9. What do you think of Winnie's decision to sprinkle the toad with spring water? Is it cruel?

Winnie acts impulsively when she gives the toad immortality. Readers might assume that it has such limited consciousness that it wouldn't notice or mind living forever. Those who are concerned with all sentient beings might argue.

10. Would you have drunk the spring water if you'd had the opportunity? Would you have chosen a specific age to be forever?

Of course, the most interesting question is whether the members of your group would choose eternal life. Most teens will acknowledge the importance of family and friends in making life worthwhile, and how heartbreaking it would be to watch everyone you love die. Miles is a sterner and more bitter character in the movie, and the scenes of his lost family are particularly poignant. I wonder if I would have chosen to drink the spring water at 17. I was impetuous and did a lot of things then that I wouldn't choose to do now. Ask your group if they think any of their peers would choose eternal life. Who is the happiest Tuck? Is there a better age at which to be stuck?

In the book, Miles says that he wants to do something important with his life; one wonders what he's waiting for since he's already been alive longer than most people and is able bodied. It may be that if you have forever to do something, it takes away the motivation to accomplish things that comes from a finite life.

Some people may actually look forward to having a rest at the end of their lives; they get tired of living. Then again, death may be the best adventure yet. Most people believe that there's something after, so you'd miss a very significant part of life if you didn't die.

43

UNDER A WAR TORN SKY
by L.M. ELLIOTT

Bibliographic information: Hyperion, 2001; 284 pages.

Themes: War, resistance, survival.

Genre: Realistic fiction.

Main character: Henry Forrester, 19.

Tips: A wonderful complement to units on World War II, this book is also a study in the duality of human nature and the human heart. The atrocities of war bring Henry to pray to God that he may kill his enemy before he is killed, to protect him although those around him might die. He is reduced to a self-protective state. Meanwhile, the Resistance fighters, though some were certainly motivated by revenge, risked their lives to rescue strangers. The presence of remarkable evil allows the manifestation of remarkable good.

Elliott ends with an afterward of facts that inspired her story. More background on the French Resistance, the planes and missions of World War II, pilots, and heroes are obvious possibilities of enriching the discussion of this book.

SYNOPSIS:

Nineteen-year-old Henry Forrester is shot down on his fifteenth mission flying over occupied France in 1944. Assisted by members of the French Resistance, and holding closely to memories of his farm home in Virginia, his mother, and the girl next door, he begins his long and perilous journey home.

DISCUSSION QUESTIONS/LEADER POINTS

1. Perhaps the most moving moment of the book comes when Clayton realizes his son has come home and embraces him, a clear expression of his love. Were there times when Clayton was hard on Henry because he loves him? Were there times when he was just too hard?

Henry wouldn't be the first person to realize the benefit of growing up with a stern, unaffectionate father. At times Clayton's harshness borders on abuse, but it gives Henry the necessary strength to keep going in the most challenging circumstances. Clayton says, "Love's got responsibilities. Things you gotta do even if you don't want to. That's the kind of love a real man is capable of" (p. 208). Clayton has difficulty showing love, but he acts out of love, as when he criticizes Henry for throwing away his educational scholarship. His overwhelming desire must be to keep his son safe at home, but he is unable to be direct and say that.

2. What makes one risk his or her life to help save a stranger?

What truth does one momentarily realize in the instant of spontaneously risking one's life to save a stranger? History is full of these spontaneous acts. If one believes that human spiritual evolution is ongoing, then the altruistic response is on a higher level than the primitive self-protective or vengeful act.

3. Is Pierre's mother being a responsible parent in doing work that endangers her family's life?

The question of what responsibility we have toward others and whether we should be more responsible toward *some* others, like a son, are intriguing. If the measure of a good parent is to put her child first, Pierre's mother fails, but if being a good parent means living outyour highest values, she succeeds. Personally, I wouldn't risk leaving my child motherless, but I can't say that's not a purely selfish response. On the other hand, if you do something that takes you away from your child, someone else has to take responsibility for the child's care.

4. Should the author have translated more of the French dialogue or is translation unnecessary?

The use of French makes the story more authentic, and readers don't miss anything crucial by not knowing French. Sometimes the meaning is decipherable by the context. There does seem to be somewhat more than necessary, however.

5. What things in his past and personal attributes help Henry survive?

Henry learned to be tough and self-reliant because of his father's sternness. In contrast to Billy, Henry grew up on a farm and was used to hard work, so he developed strength and stamina.

6. The Resistance fighters consider shooting Billy because he is a potential liability. Would they have been justified?

Ask readers if they think sacrificing one person is justifiable if it will save many. How many makes it justifiable, a nation? What if saving Billy meant compromising the entire Resistance network?

7. How do you account for the pure evil of the Gestapo?

A big question. Why does evil exist? Can anything exist without its opposite? How could we recognize it otherwise? The evil of the Gestapo brought out the response of goodness in the Resistance fighters.

8. Henry and Claudette are both good, loving people, yet Henry kills and is glad he does and Claudette nearly kills the village girl accused of collaborating with the Nazis. What does this say about them?

One cost of war is a loss of innocence, the belief that one can be good under any circumstances. War makes people look at their shadow sides and recognize that self-preservation and revenge lie in every human heart; it's the will and conscience that determines whether we act from our shadow sides.

9. When Henry imagines finding Pierre and having his Ma adopt him, he thinks he might adopt him himself in a few years when he's an adult. Is it right to allow a boy to fight and not recognize him as an adult?

It is ironic that Henry is clearly doing the work of an adult, but doesn't have the rights of an adult. Much debated during the Vietnam war was the question of whether it was right to send a boy to war when he couldn't vote. The U.S. has since altered the practice. Should the drinking age be lowered using the same argument?

10. Did Henry betray Patsy in being intimate with Claudette?

War reduces people to their basest and most extreme instincts. In the instance of Henry and Claudette sharing intimacy, the author very poignantly illustrates the miraculous ability to express love in the direst of circumstances; it's a celebration of the human spirit. If Patsy had known, she may well have felt grateful for the comfort Henry got from the experience. Teen's may still debate whether he betrays her.

44

WAITING FOR CHRISTOPHER
by LOUISE HAWES

Bibliographic information: Candlewick, 2002; 224 pages.

Themes: Child abuse, parenting.

Genre: Realistic fiction.

Main characters: Feena and Raylene, both 14.

Tips: The ethics of the compelling premise don't really garner as much discussion as you might guess. The meatier issue here is the reality and responsibility of parenting.

SYNOPSIS:

When Feena witnesses the abuse and feigned abandonment of a toddler by his mother, she impulsively takes the boy. Taking care of Christopher seems to ease the loneliness of being new in town, her mother's remoteness, the absence of her father, and the remaining pain and bewilderment she suffered when her baby brother died. Her secret is discovered by one of the most popular girls in school, and Raylene becomes her ally and her friend. During the next few days, Feena becomes aware of the complexities of the situation. She makes the decision to return Christopher to his mother, and mother and child subsequently disappear.

DISCUSSION QUESTIONS/LEADER POINTS

1. Raylene says, "You and me, we've seen stuff. We know too much. We watched those towers tumble down like sandcastles on TV" (p. 141). Is Raylene being melodramatic about the impact 9/11 has had on the lives of teens? How has it affected you?

Hawes' references to 9/11 seem jarring and artificial. Most teens wouldn't speak this way. One wonders if the references were added as an afterthought to make the book timelier. Ask teens whether they feel the references added anything to the book. Be sensitive to the willingness and comfort of your group to discuss fears resulting from the attacks. It may well be that their generation has become less innocent, but, contrary to what Raylene says, the teens in the book are innocent to the point of naiveté at times. Are there additional events that may have made Raylene especially cynical? Maybe. Raylene has weathered the sadness of her mother's miscarriage and her father's absence, but we never learn enough about her to sufficiently explain her cynicism. Her popularity doesn't suggest that she is a depressed individual.

2. What would you have done if you'd witnessed Christopher's abuse and abandonment?

Readers may agree that teens do tend to act impulsively, but few are likely to take Christopher the way Feena does. Those who would take the boy probably would have considered the consequences soon afterward, at least sooner than Feena does. Raylene and Feena act as if their situation could go on indefinitely. Does their common experience of losing a sibling adequately explain their extreme behavior? Is loneliness a factor in Feena's impulsive kidnapping?

Of course the best thing Feena could have done would have been to alert the authorities or taken Christopher to the authorities. Ask readers how they think that Delores would have reacted to a visit by a social worker? Might she have disappeared sooner?

3. When Christy demands that Feena play when she can't, she becomes angry. Do you think of her reaction as reasonable? What understanding does it bring her?

Feena learns that caring for a child is more demanding than she anticipated. It always is. Young children can't empathize or control themselves in ways older people can. The caretaker's feelings aren't considered; she has to keep caring for the child regardless of her own perceived needs or desires. Feena begins to see the incredible commitment it is to be a parent, that there is no time off. While no one could condone Delores' treatment of Christopher, especially the burns, Feena begins to understand the frustration parents sometimes feel. Ask how Delores could have become a better mother. Possible assistance for her includes learning anger management, having help so she could have breaks, and alleviating stresses like her abusive relationship — all things she seems unable to acquire on her own.

4. Feena's mother says that not everyone is a natural mother and that we have pictures of a perfect mother in our heads that some people just can't live up to. What's your reaction to her statement?

The perfect mother ideal is pretty selfless and pretty hard to achieve 24/7. Ask readers where they get their ideas of what mothers should be like. Do we have unreal expectations?

5. Should Feena have returned Christy? What else could she have done?

Feena's hope and sympathy, perhaps her naiveté, in making a deal with Delores leads to their disappearance. We have to appreciate her forgiveness and her generosity in giving Delores a second chance, but her trust was misplaced.

6. What elements of the story do you find unrealistic?

Feena's and Raylene's mothers are surprisingly unquestioning about their daughters' whereabouts and companions. The girls seem to have a lot of freedom for girls their age. How could such a popular girl as Raylene skip school so often? Readers may also find the assistance of Mr. Milakowski unrealistic, although the author tries to make a case for his mistrust of authorities. Keeping Christopher hidden for three weeks stretches credulity. On the lighter side, Feena's not realizing diapers come in different sizes is surprising.

7. What's your reaction to Feena's mother's decision to move to make a new start?

Feena's mother is naïve in thinking that moving to a new state and new job would effect the change in her life that needs to take place on the inside. As long as she escapes in soap operas and alcohol, real change won't occur.

8. Do you think that Feena and Raylene would have become friends without Christopher? Why or why not?

Raylene and Feena are unlikely friends. Raylene is poised and popular. Feena is insecure and reserved. The only thing that they have in common, besides their enjoyment of reading, is Christopher. It is doubtful that they would have become friends without being bound by Christopher, but isn't it sometimes nothing more than a shared event that founds a friendship? Ask readers if they can think of examples.

One wonders at the racial composition of the school the girls attend. It seems odd that there is no mention of the race of anyone except Raylene, yet in all but the most utopian school, race does affect acceptance into groups and friendships. Ask readers what they think the author's motivation is in making Raylene African American.

9. How do you think Christopher's kidnapping and return will change his mother?

One hopes that the fear Delores must have experienced while Christy was missing will make a big impression on her, and that she will resolve to change her life. Her neighbor says that she doubts that the man Delores was living with would travel farther than the nearest bar, so there is some hope that at least she was out of that relationship. However, her move may have been to avoid being accountable.

10. What do the references to *Jane Eyre* and *Their Eyes Were Watching God* add to the book?

Unfamiliarity with *Jane Eyre* and *Their Eyes Were Watching God* doesn't diminish understanding of the story or characters. The comparisons Hawes tries to draw between the characters in these books and Feena and Raylene are slight and help define the characters in a very broad way. Many teens will not have read either and *Their Eyes Were Watching God*, especially, is not a typical choice for pleasure reading.

45

WHAT MY MOTHER DOESN'T KNOW
by SONYA SONES

Bibliographic information: Simon and Schuster, 2001; 259 pages.

Themes: Love, family relationships, friendship, peer pressure, popularity.

Genre: Realistic fiction, novels in verse.

Main character: Sophie, 14.

Tips: A great mother-daughter discussion title, this book also has great springboard potential for writing assignments. It's valuable for Sophie's discovery of what is truly satisfying in a relationship. Sophie is an admirable character who grows and retains her self-esteem amid the pressure of popular opinion and family dysfunction. Easy, quick reading and a diary-like point of view are among its charms. Recommend Virginia Euler Wolff's books, *The Brimstreet Journals* by Ron Koertge, *Learning to Swim* by Ann Turner, and *Girl Coming in for a Landing* by April Halprin Wayland, to name several in this growing category.

SYNOPSIS:

Writing in poems, Sones as Sophie, adroitly describes falling in love, then the experience of really falling in love amidst the backdrop of a dysfunctional family and typical suburban teenage girldom. The major dilemma is that the boy Sophie is truly in love with has a reputation with her classmates as a joke. A small amount of angst doesn't diminish the confection-like quality of the book.

DISCUSSION QUESTIONS/LEADER POINTS

1. How does Sophie's family use TV? What would happen if they turned off the TV?

In the book, Sophie's family watches TV during dinner to avoid talking to each other, especially her parents who are obviously having problems. The TV fills the uncomfortable silence that would no doubt ensue if it were off. Sophie's mother fills her days with TV, so she doesn't have to think or to face reality. Her way of dealing with problems is to avoid them. After she destroys Sophie's dress, she retreats and sulks rather than confronting the problem.

2. What do you think about Sophie and Dylan fighting over his haircut? Is it reasonable to consult your boyfriend or girlfriend before changing your look?

Without making judgments, some people would be very bothered by their boy or girlfriend's extreme change of looks, especially if the new look was considered less than cool. Looks are very important to teenagers. On the other hand, it may be argued that true friendship or love would overlook outside appearances.

3. When Sophie is going to meet Dylan's mother, he asks her not to mention that she's Jewish. How would you react if a boy asked you not to tell his mother that you were Jewish (Catholic, Muslim, etc.)?

Let's hope that your group members would not be as passive as Sophie is about Dylan's request. It's not uncommon to overlook red flags when you're in the throes of infatuation. Ask readers whether they've ever done so and what the results were—was it a lasting relationship or doomed from the start?

4. How is the time period important? How are your friendships like Sophie's?

The group I discussed this with thought the close friendship with girls within walking distance was unrealistic. These days many teens have less free time than Sophie and her friends do; they are involved in many organized activities and not home much. The kind of togetherness Sophie and her friends enjoy reflects an earlier time. Also, the friends daring in going to the diner in nothing but their coats seems tame and silly in our jaded world.

5. When Grace falls for Henry and tells her friends that they have a three-hour conversation, the other girls compare their relationships. Is that a reasonable thing to do? Why or why not?

It is not only reasonable, but a good measure of your satisfaction. If you find yourself envying a relationship, perhaps it shows where yours is lacking and gives you the opportunity to work on that area or decide it's not working for you. Meanwhile, you have to be cautious about having a "grass is always greener on the other side," outlook.

6. If you were to give Sophie advice about the men in her life, Dylan, Chaz, and Murphy, what would you tell her?

Don't be with someone who wants you to keep secrets about yourself? Remember that it's easy to lie on the Internet and lots of people do? It's best to fall in love with someone who could be your best friend, someone whom you can talk to for hours and with whom you can do the things that you enjoy doing by yourself? Is it easy to follow this advice when you fall for someone?

7. Were you shocked by Chaz's revelation (that he likes to jerk off in libraries)? Was this realistic? Why do you think that the author included this episode?

The Chaz Internet episode was jarring and one almost wonders whether the author includes it to remind readers not to trust what people say online. On the other hand, maybe Chaz, the fantasy boy, wouldn't excite Sophie if her relationship with Dylan were strong and healthy and the incident is actually a symptom of the relationship's failings. Or maybe her online tryst is a game she is playing with no real intention of meeting Chaz and no harm to her relationship with Dylan.

What is Chaz's motive in saying what he does? It's unusual for someone who has been communicating for a while not to backpedal when he realizes he has shocked his pen pal. Did Chaz say he liked to jerk off in libraries strictly to shock Sophie and possibly end their correspondence? If he were interested in continuing their correspondence, he would have written that he was just joking when Sophie suggested that he was. It did seem Sones' intent was to make him a repulsive character. While this incident might lead to a discussion of Internet safety, most teens are well aware of the issue and are frequently reminded.

8. How did Sones's format affect the story? Did it limit details? Character development? Did it make the book easier to read or more difficult?

This may be the first novel in verse read by some of your group, and it's an increasingly popular format. Some of the attractions of this format are that it's easy to read and it takes you into the experience and thoughts of the main character. It's like reading a diary, which is attractive to some for its intimacy. One drawback of telling the story in this way, and strictly from Sophie's viewpoint, is that supporting characters aren't very well developed. Sophie's mother is merely a soap opera addict (at least until the dress scene), and her father is a distant, constant traveler. Even her girlfriends are sketchy, although the intensity of their friendship comes across quite clearly.

9. Sophie's mother finds that she has been deceived by Sophie who bought and wore the dress she herself wanted instead of the one her mother chose. The mother then destroys the dress and sinks into a funk that lasts for days. What do you think of her reaction? Sophie's? Was part or all of what Sophie did wrong?

Sophie's mother reacts with violence and then sulks. The issue becomes her mother's hurt instead of them discussing why Sophie did what she did. Sophie is made to feel guilty and apologizes. She never gets to express her own hurt.

Sophie accepts her mother's choice of dresses in the first place because she doesn't want to hurt her mother's feelings or dismiss her desire to see Sophie as a flower. Instead of rejecting the dress her mother wanted her to wear, she accepts it and sets out to get what she wants by herself. In this she also accepts her mother's inability to empathize. Her understanding reveals her emotional maturity, which seems to exceed her mother's. Her mother's rejection of the dress Sophie wanted may have been motivated by her unconscious desire to keep Sophie from growing up; Sophie obviously looked more grown up and even sexy in the black dress. Is the dress inappropriate, or is her mother having a hard time with Sophie's growing up? Ask readers whether they have ever interpreted a parent's actions as an effort to keep them from growing up. Ask readers whether they believe that Sophie could forget about changing back into the flowered dress after the dance.

10. In the poem "Another Business Trip," Sophie is moved to hug her mother. When has Sophie learned to develop this compassion?

The last time in this book that Sophie's father leaves on a business trip, Sophie's mother is captured in a state of defenselessness. It's easy for Sophie to see how she's hurting, and Sophie rises to the occasion. The level of responsibility her mother's ineffectiveness requires from her, although it has made her strong and self-reliant, is disturbing.

11. All of Sophie's pals go on away on vacation during winter break, so Sophie

decides to vacation right where she is, in Boston, and do things a tourist would do. What would you do on a vacation in your city?

This would make an excellent writing exercise, and gives a fresh view of one's own surroundings. What kinds of things do we see so often that we don't see them anymore? What do we take for granted? Sometimes people never go to what tourists do in their cities. Have you been to the Rock Hall? The Museums? Have you taken a cruise down the Cuyahoga River? (Substitute your city's gems here.) Practice being in a tourist's shoes and see if your experience is richer.

12. How do you think that Sophie's classmates and friends will react to her and Murphy as a couple?

Readers can't help being optimistic about the future of Sophie and Murphy. Sophie appears to be beyond the influence of her less enlightened peers. Her true friends will get to know Murphy and realize what a great guy he is. Read Spinelli's *Stargirl* for an understanding of the negative pressure peers may exert when a popular teen falls for a quirky maverick.

13. Did this book change the way you think about poetry?

This is a wonderful book for anyone who has found poetry inaccessible. Be prepared with suggestions (some are under Tips, above) for further reading.

14. Why do you think the author chose the title?

The destruction of Sophie's dress by her mother is the most gut-wrenching scene and the one from which the title comes. As a coming-of-age story, the book shows Sophie maturing over the course of the story, and so the title not only refers to this incident but also to the intimate details of Sophie's life. Sophie's mother is more unaware of Sophie's life because of her own tendency to withdraw.

15. One of my favorite lines is Sophie's term for her period. She calls it "rebooting my ovarian operating system." Rachel calls it "riding the cotton pony" and Grace calls it "surfing the crimson wave." Do you think that what we call it influences our feelings about it?

This question is probably best to save for the end of the discussion because it can lead your group far afield. In my group, it took us into overtime, and we could have talked about related issues for another half hour or more. It was fun to share our terms for menstruation, our feelings about it, and stories of how to be discreet when talking about it at school. Ask readers whether they think what we call it influences how we feel about it emotionally, and maybe even physically. There has been quite a bit of literature about the mind-body connection during recent years. One teen in my group had read *The Red Tent* by Anita Diamant and talked about the very different attitude about menstruation presented in that book, one of celebration and power. Ask readers how they feel about their periods. Are they a bother or a blessing? If you have different generations in your group, compare reactions according to whether they are mothers or daughters. Does it make a difference?

46

WHAT'S IN A NAME
by ELLEN WITTLINGER

Bibliographic information: Simon and Schuster, 2000; 146 pages.

Themes: Popularity, homosexuality, peer pressure, names, parental pressure, identity, race.

Genre: Realistic fiction.

Main character: Ten teens whose lives intertwine during their senior year in high school.

Tips: There are a lot of issues to talk about with this book. It's a discussion dream. I have just touched on some, but another obvious discussion point is how the characters change during the course of the book. Also, you may want to ask with which character do readers most identify and why.

SYNOPSIS:

Ten interconnecting stories, each told by a teen, address the issues of identity and popularity against the backdrop of a campaign to change the name of their town from Scrub Harbor to Folly Bay. The characters' own perceptions of themselves are balanced against the perceptions of the other characters. The teens are diverse in class, race, sexual orientation, and nationality. Their problems include lack of self-esteem, cultural and language difficulties, controlling parents, confusion about plans for the future, and coming to terms with changing friendships and loyalties.

DISCUSSION QUESTIONS/LEADER POINTS

1. Which name is more appealing to you, Scrub Harbor or Folly Bay? Why? Is there a good reason to change the name of the town? What do you think about what Georgie's mother says on page 69: "Scrub Harbor sounds like a place where people work hard and appreciate the beauty of the spot they've settled in Folly Bay, on the other hand, sounds like a vacation spot for nitwits"? How do you think the author feels?

Teens will be quick to gravitate to their own camps regarding the preferred name of the town. Ask how names affect perceptions. Is Folly Bay a more attractive name to prospective tourists? Does Scrub Harbor sound more working class and unpretentious? The more pragmatic in your group will agree with Mrs. Pinkus, that the name change and campaign are a waste of taxpayer dollars, but what about attracting tourists brings in more revenue?

It may be telling that the author chose Folly Bay as the alternative name. The word folly connotes foolishness or frivolity. Would another name have been more attractive? How about Tranquility Bay? If you have time, readers will enjoy coming up with better names.

2. Why is Georgie so angry?

Georgie seems ashamed of where she lives and that she is not as well off economically as some of her friends. Does it matter to others? If it does, are they worth worrying about? She also carries a lot of anger about her father who deserted her. He calls to boast about his recent fortune, but is he serious about Georgie's visiting him? We may also assume that her innate personality is also a factor in her anger.

3. How do you think your classmates would react to an openly gay teacher?

It's unlikely that a teacher could be openly gay in most communities—not until antidiscrimination laws are in place. It makes too many people afraid. However, most teens will know of teachers whom they suspect are gay but don't advertise it, wisely, to protect their jobs.

4. Did the loneliness felt by Ricardo and Adam make you more thoughtful about how new students are treated?

Some teens will find that reading about difficulties new students face will make them more empathetic and supportive. Ask them to remember to reach out, even in some small way.

5. In his poem, O'Neill writes, "I am not my house, my clothes, my friends, my father, the country club, the town, my sexuality, my future. Who am I?" Adam wonders if "we're only who other people think we are" (p. 103). What gives people identity?

It is always interesting to talk with teens about what makes them who they are, to try get to the place beyond labels that is so mysterious and hard to pin down. Teens are often preoccupied with identifying themselves in ways that show their uniqueness and define them—piercings, tattoos, hairstyles, particular clothing. Ironically these efforts at individuality often make them part of a group who espouse the same look. Maybe the true nature of the self is ever changing, ever evolving. Ask readers whether they feel a need to define themselves and how it would feel not to have to. To know oneself is to allow oneself to be constantly becoming something else.

7. Adam thinks he has an opportunity to change what people think about him because he's new to town. How much are we influenced by how others see us? Do people see each other as constantly changing or as static and defined?

People do fall into the trap of defining others in certain ways and expecting constancy. We seem to require the reassurance of knowing what to expect. In reality, we can never know what to expect. Ask readers about an instance when a person close to them has surprised them, acted seemingly out of character. Was it really out of character or just different from their perception of that person? Ask whether they have experienced old friends thinking of them in old ways and not realizing the changes that have happened over the years.

7. Why is Christine able to accept being O'Neill's friend rather than his girlfriend, which she had hoped to become?

Christine shows remarkable maturity in accepting O'Neill as he is and what he can never be to her. Of course, she doesn't have a choice, but if her love for him were less mature, she might not be able to accept him as just a friend when she wanted him to be more. Surely some of your group members will share the experience of wanting a friendship to be more and not having those feelings returned.

8. Adam tells Nadia that she's too sure of herself; do you agree? Even though Nadia likes the town's name, she winds up handing out flyers in the rain to be with Nelson. What do you think about that?

Adam's assessment of Nadia as being sure of herself is ironic. She's chosen to pass out flyers in the rain so she can be with Nelson. She's compromised herself own feelings to try to attract a boy. If Nelson were interested in her, they would start out with dishonesty. While doing something for the sole purpose of impressing someone isn't a good strategy, many will admit to having done it.

9. Is the USISS program a good idea?

Programs like USISS that help disadvantaged students are well intended but may be idealistic and foster condescending attitudes. Ask readers how it would be to live in two such different worlds, constantly seeing kids with things you couldn't have. How would kids in her neighborhood view her being singled out? While it may be a good thing to give kids with potential opportunities they wouldn't have otherwise, it certainly puts a burden on them socially.

10. Does Shaquanda treat Nelson fairly?

Shaquanda's attitude is her worst enemy; she's convinced that others in Scrub Harbor look down on her. This causes her to reject Nelson without giving him a chance.

Nelson asks Shaquanda whether at some future point he might seem blacker to her. Is there sometimes a backlash against successful African Americans? Sometimes they are perceived as compromising themselves to fit into a white man's world. Recall the recent incident when Harry Belefonte referred to Colin Powell as a "house slave for President Bush." What did he mean?

11. Is Gretchen nice? What sacrifices does one make to be popular? Is it worth it?

Gretchen is a victim of her popularity. She is under a lot of pressure to maintain her image and fulfill her mother's expectations. Wittlinger makes popularity wonderfully unglamorous. Ask readers whether it be preferable to have a few good friends or to always be the one in the spotlight

12. At the end of the book, Gretchen stands up to her mother. What kind of changes do you see for her in college? Will she be as popular?

Gretchen will most likely welcome the anonymity of college and develop a small circle of friends. She has realized that she's been living her mother's dream, not her own.

13. Consider the reactions to O'Neill's coming out: Quincy's, his parents', and others', Gretchen says that somehow O'Neill is more normal than before. Was coming out a good decision?

O'Neill's decision to come out makes him more normal than before because there was always something hidden or wrongly assumed. People assume someone is straight and make all kinds of assumptions based on that. How would it be standing around with a bunch of friends and having them say things like, "Isn't she hot?" when you felt not? Is not expressing what you really feel being true to yourself, being honest? It might be easier for teens to understand how it would feel if you were straight and everyone assumed that you were gay. Would you feel the need to correct the mistake or just let people assume what they do.

Is it ever a good idea to keep a secret to protect others? Who is responsible for the reactions of others? If we act to protect them are we assuming their responsibility?

47

WHEN ZACHARY BEAVER CAME TO TOWN by KIMBERLY WILLIS HOLT

Bibliographic information: Henry Holt 1999; 227 page.

Themes: People as spectacles, friendship, shame, lies, the kindness of strangers, denial, a mother leaving her family to pursue her dream, small town life in the 1970s.

Genre: Realistic fiction.

Main character: Toby Wilson, 13.

Tips: Suitable for tweens.

SYNOPSIS:

It's 1971 and not much happens in the small Texas town of Antler, so when a trailer with the fattest boy in the world arrives, everyone lines up to take a gander. Fourteen-year-old Toby is having a tough summer. His mom has left to pursue her singing career in Nashville, the girl of his dreams remains out of reach, and the brother of his best friend, Cal has gone to Vietnam. Cal's interest in Zachary, at first annoying to Toby, turns into friendship when Zachary's guardian disappears and the town is left to care for the teen. The friendship of the boys changes each of them and the entire town.

DISCUSSION QUESTIONS/LEADER POINTS

1. Then Zachary arrives, the townspeople line up to view him. Why do people want to see freaks? Do they view them as people? How would you feel if you were in Zachary's shoes?

Curiosity is natural. It's what makes us slow down to look at accidents and watch reality TV. Perhaps the extreme variations of human presentation are intriguing just because they're different. The practice of viewing human beings as oddities is, however, ethically questionable. It dehumanizes them. Teens will easily empathize with Zachary's hostility since it's important to teens to fit in rather than stand out, especially if it's standing out because of some undesirable quality.

2. Do you think that Toby should be more understanding of his mother's need to pursue her dream of becoming a singing star? Does she act responsibly?

While it's unfortunate to feel as if one's dreams are unfulfilled, most readers will question Opalina's choice to leave her son. On the other hand, she was unhappy living in a small town and unhappy with her husband's choices. Maybe she expected him to change. Maybe she thought she could adapt to life in Antler. Ask readers if they think she could have compromised somehow. At the end of the book, Toby is going to visit her, so perhaps they will work out a shared-parenting arrangement that will be more satisfying to Toby.

3. Toby seems embarrassed that his father raises worms. Why do you think he feels this way?

4. Why does Toby hurt his father's feelings by refusing to eat his pancakes on delivery day?

Toby's embarrassment over his father's occupation has most likely been influenced by his mother. *She's* disappointed that he's not a lawyer and that he likes his quiet, small town life. Toby realizes that his mother was unhappy with his father's choices, so he temporarily blames him for her leaving. Isn't it common to try to blame someone for things that hurt us? Toby punishes his father by rejecting his pancakes.

5. Why does Zachary lie about the places he's been (not)?

In stark contrast to his confinement, Zachary imagines a glamorous life for himself based on things he's read. In reality, he would have a very hard time traveling because of his extreme size. That may be why Paulie leaves him behind. Zachary is probably embarrassed that he's had little life experience.

6. Why does Toby write a letter to Wayne from Cal? When is it okay to be deceitful?

Toby's deceit in writing to Wayne is an act of kindness. He loves Wayne and knows that he wants to hear from Cal. Cal puts off writing because he knows he won't have the opportunity for long.

7. Why does Cal want to take Zachary to the drive-in? Arrange his baptism?

Cal is from a very loving, supportive family. It's easy to imagine that he would have compassion for others. His good heart is nicely balanced by his nosiness. He asks questions that might be considered rude, but then acts in a caring way. Ask your group whether they think Toby would have become Zachary's friend without Cal's influence.

8. Why does Toby lie about what's happening with his mother? How are his lies similar to lies that other characters tell?

Not only is Toby not ready to accept his mother's desertion, he probably also feels some shame about it. He doesn't want people to know that she's chosen not to return either because it's not what mothers do or it makes him question his own worth. Shame probably motivates Zachary's lie about being baptized and Ferris lying about the self- inflicted wound that kept him out of the Korean War. Shame may also be a factor in Toby's writing to Wayne; he may be ashamed of Cal.

9. Why can't Toby go to Wayne's funeral? Why can't Ferris?

Like refusing to read his mother's letters and to accept the truth of her not coming back, Toby isn't ready to accept Wayne's death, so he can't go to the funeral. Wayne was his hero.

Ferris can't go to Wayne's funeral because it reminds him of what he didn't do. He must feel like a coward for not having gone to war. It would be hard for Ferris to face the town's dead beloved son knowing that he avoided his duty.

10. How is Antler changed by the presence of Zachary Beaver? How is Zachary changed?

Zachary's presence brings the people of Antler together. An unlikely alliance between Toby, Cal, and Kate is formed to chauffeur Zachary to the drive-in and to Gossimer Lake. Ferris is persuaded to revisit his first career path. Ask your group why he left it. Could he have reconciled his vocation and his conscience? Zachary's baptism seems to renew Toby as well as Zachary. Afterward Toby is able to read his mother's letters and begins to accept the reality of her leaving. The town's preoccupation with Zachary helps them to deal with their loss of Wayne. Zachary brings Cal and Toby together when Cal is angry at Toby for not attending Wayne's funeral. Zachary has probably lived more during his week in Antler than ever before. He's made friends, gone to a drive-in, and gotten baptized. He's participated in the annual release of the ladybugs. He is treated like a person instead of a freak. He's found goodness in people who were moved to care for him.

11. What makes the time period crucial to the story?

The 70s may have been a time of greater innocence and trust, or maybe small towns are still like Antler. The Vietnam War certainly is significant in the story, and it may be that people are more compassionate during wartime because tragedy is never far away and we're constantly reminded of how it can touch our lives.

It's doubtful that the fattest boy in the world would be paraded around these days the way he is in the story.

12. How do you think your community would react to the appearance and abandonment of Zachary Beaver?

Sadly, the group I discussed this book with felt that if Zachary had been left in a trailer in their suburban neighborhood, he would have been ignored or the police would have been called. Ask readers whether they think certain types of communities would respond differently to Zachary, and what type of reaction they would expect from a certain group.

13. What do Myrtie Mae's photos tell us about Zachary's story?

Myrtie Mae's photographic tribute to Zachary documents Zachary's progression from sideshow act to charity to friend to glory. The last photo of him in the cotton fields (yes, they are like an ocean) looking heavenward is reminiscent of his baptism. He's been saved by the goodness and fellowship of Antler.

There are so many moving moments in the story that you might want to ask for favorites. The image of the release of the ladybugs at sunset accompanied by Mozart is a beautiful image. Mrs. McKnight cutting and cutting her roses as the officials wait to tell her that her son is dead is heartbreaking. There are many humorous moments, too, such as when the Judge pelts Toby with apples.

48

A YEAR DOWN YONDER
by RICHARD PECK

Bibliographical information: Dial, 2000; 130 pages.

Themes: The Depression, country life, grandmothers.

Genre: Humorous fiction.

Main character: Mary Alice, 15.

Tips: *A Year Down Yonder* would complement a study of the Great Depression and nicely contrast with more serious accounts of that time period.

SYNOPSIS:

The year is 1937 and, like many others, Mary Alice's father has lost his job. Mary Alice is sent to live with her eccentric, formidable Grandma Dowdel for a year. During the year Mary Alice finds that her grandmother's stern, unapproachable exterior shelters a heart of gold, which shines as she metes out her own brand of justice throughout the community. Hilarious and ultimately poignant, this series of vignettes captures a city girl's adjustment to small town life during the Depression.

DISCUSSION QUESTIONS/LEADER POINTS

1. Is Grandma Dowdel justified in retrieving Old Man Nyquist's pecans? The Pensingers' pumpkins?

Grandma Dowdel's actions bring about desirable results, although her methods are often questionable. She's a sort of Robin Hood. The book provides lots of examples to discuss whether the ends justify the means. In Grandma Dowdel's mind, helping herself to someone else's pecans or pumpkins is absolutely justifiable. Why?

2. How would you have weathered the year in Mary Alice's place? What things would have been especially difficult for you?

It will probably be hard for modern teens to even imagine living in the time period before TV, computers, and cell phones. Ask for anyone who has been camping to talk about how that experience compares with normal life? How do you spend leisure time? How much harder is cooking? What about primitive bathrooms? What do you miss? Is it boring? Does it make you feel more peaceful? How?

3. What things about life in Chicago that it might be good to be away from?

You'll enjoy discussing the contrasts between city and country life. In this story one could certainly live more cheaply in the country. Grandma Dowdel is pretty self-sufficient. The pace of life is slower in the country; there aren't many people these days who don't feel overextended—teens included. Ask what the pros and cons of the anonymity the city provides versus the small-town life where everyone knows each other's business. The country people didn't have the means to be stylish, or even the access to information about current styles. You wouldn't have to worry about what to wear. How about the school Mary Alice attends. Where would she get a better education? What things does she learn in the country that she wouldn't have learned in the city?

4. Mary Alice describes her outfit on page 43: dungarees under a skirt, her grandpa's hunting jacket, a wool cap pulled down to her eyebrows. She says: "The longer I lived down here, the more I was starting to look like Mildred Burdick." She seems to care less about her clothes than she did. Do you dress to suit yourself or others?

Ask readers how it would be if they had no magazines, TV, and so forth, to show them what celebrities and everyone else in the world was wearing. How would they decide what to wear? Would their decisions be based solely on comfort and practicality? Is it a burden to be stylish, to have the next new look? How much time do we spend shopping?

5. Would you describe Grandma Dowdel as lovable? Affectionate? Why or why not?

Grandma Dowdel is absolutely lovable and her actions are very loving. She is generous and protective of the underdog. Her clever handling of Mary Alice's being bullied and her gift of shoes are two examples of her affection toward her granddaughter. She is the kind of person who works compassionately and covertly for justice. Ask readers if they know someone whose actions are loving yet they are unable to express them overtly.

6. Does Mrs. Weidenbach deserve the treatment she gets at the DAR tea? Why or why not?

This is a time when I think the basically good-hearted Grandma D. was a little too mean. I wish Grandma had exposed Mrs. Weidenbach privately. Ask readers whether it would have had the same effect on Mrs. Weidenbach. Why is it necessary for others to be witness to it?

7. Did the author give enough information on the time period? Were comments about ration cards and nylons confusing?

Be prepared to discuss everyday life during the depression and World War II. Ask readers for other details with which they are unfamiliar.

8. What was your favorite episode?

With so many humorous episodes to choose from, this is a natural topic of conversation. My own favorite is the snake episode.

9. Were you surprised by Mary Alice's decision to stay with Grandma Dowdel? Why or why not?

This book can be read as Mary Alice's story of falling in love with her grandmother. Peck does an excellent job of expressing Mary Alice's growing affection without saying so explicitly. Ask readers for evidence of Mary Alice's growing affection, the most apparent of which is when she helps Grandma D. with her trapping. Mary Alice begins to be protective of her grandmother. Is this a natural side effect of loving someone?

10. How has Mary Alice's year with her changed Grandma Dowdel?
Although she was always very involved with people, she kept them at a distance. Mary Alice has allowed her to be more intimate with another. Her heart has opened a bit.

49

THE YEAR OF MY INDIAN PRINCE
by ELLA THORP ELLIS

Bibliographic information: Delacorte, 2001; 212 pages.

Themes: Tuberculosis, convalescence, cross-cultural dating, death and dying, vanity versus wellness.

Genre: Realistic fiction

Main character: April, 16.

Tips: The paperback has a more attractive cover. The hardback makes the book look like a romance, and the teens in my group thought the portrayal of Ravi was "wimpy."

SYNOPSIS:

Instead of the year she was looking forward to (swim meets, senior prom, enjoying her father who has recently returned from the war), April finds herself in a tuberculosis hospital, desperately ill. During her internment she questions her relationship with her boyfriend; finds and loses a wonderful friend in her roommate, Nancie; and, unexpectedly finds romance with an Indian maharaja's son. When she doesn't respond to the "cure," April must decide whether to have risky surgery that will leave her scarred.

DISCUSSION QUESTIONS

1. What do you think of Mike's reaction to April's illness?
Mike and Dino are both very much influenced by their mothers. Mike is forbidden to see April, and Dino is urged to move on with his life. Their youth and short history together suggests that Mike and April were not deeply in love. Is it worth risking your health, and perhaps your life, to visit a girlfriend or boyfriend, or should she or he understand and not wish you to be exposed? While I didn't blame Mike for his fear, I think that he was disingenuous in asking April to go to the prom; I don't think he expected her to be well enough to go.

2. Do you think it's reasonable to expect a boyfriend/financé/husband to wait years for his sick loved one?
Is Dino and Nancie's case different from Mike and April's? Because they are older and engaged should he have been more committed to her? Should Eleanor's husband have stuck by her—even after seven years? Does it make a difference that they

are married and have a child? Some readers will be idealistic and believe that when you love someone, you should wait for them no matter what. Is the ability to do so more a reflection of one's love or one's character?

3. Do you think that Ravi leads April on? Does he realize that they will never end up together? Is he deceptive in waiting to tell April about his arranged marriage until after her surgery?

Ravi is infatuated with April. It's more of a love at first sight thing because he doesn't really know her. He may not think beyond the moment since it's not clear that either of them will recover. Although he expresses his wishes, he doesn't make promises to April. He must know that if he survives he will have an arranged marriage, as is the expectation of his culture. In waiting to tell April about his marriage until after her surgery, he has her best interest in mind; he doesn't want anything to interfere with her positive healing thoughts.

4. Is April in love with Ravi? How can you tell? Think about her reaction to his Christmas present. What does it reveal?

Maybe April's unappreciative reaction to the Christmas scarf is a reflection of her immaturity. How do you react when someone you really love gives you a less than desirable gift, especially if he exerted the effort to make it himself? How much does your mother treasure your first ugly, lopsided pot that you made in second grade? Another clue to April's lack of serious feeling for Ravi was that she comments on how she enjoys being out with *two* handsome men (Ravi and Boris) when she goes to the dentist. Also, she flirts with the art student.

5. Is it unwise for April and Nancie to sneak out with Ravi? Is their curiosity about the crematorium morbid?

April and Nancie need distractions like the outing with Ravi and their party to keep their spirits from sinking, and so they are worth the risk. Ask readers if they think that fun and laughter may have an effect on healing. The trio's curiosity about the crematorium is a way of facing their fear. It's empowering to stand in joy and in the company of friends and face your fear. Does Nancie's act of lying down in the crematory foreshadow her death or her defiance?

6. Both April and Nancie hesitate about having lobectomies because they will be scarred. Should that influence their decisions? What do you think of a man who would reject a woman because she has a scar? What decision would you make?

7. Does Boris take foolish risks with the lives of the patients? What qualities do Boris and Mrs. York have that make them good caregivers?

The patients were fortunate to have someone like Boris, also Mrs. York. Boris reminds his patients of the joys of life. It would be so easy to get depressed lying in bed for months. Ask readers to think about the last time they had a cold or the flu; how would they have felt if they thought it might go on for months or years? Wouldn't they be in dire need of fun?

Boris and Mrs. York, like many healthcare workers, have a call to serve. They find satisfaction in easing pain of and offering compassion to others. Mrs. York says it's a gift to serve. Do you agree? What are the rewards of service? Is it worth risking your life?

8. Nancie tells Dino's mother, "My blood's on your hands" (p. 102). What is your reaction to her statement?

While Dino's mother clearly wished for her son to break up with Nancie, she can't be responsible for Nancie's death. Dino has free choice even though he may have been greatly influenced by his mother. Nancie's statement indicates that she's giving up and not taking responsibility for herself. While she didn't have a choice about getting sick, she has a choice about whether to choose surgery and its effects or take her chances with bed rest. Her decision to remain unscarred for Dino isn't a decision she makes for herself. Should important life decisions be made solely on someone *else's* reaction?

9. What makes people react differently to illness? Compare Nancie and Rena.

Nancie isn't a fighter, especially when she no longer has Dino to fight for. Meanwhile, Rena is very proactive about her illness. She also seems deeply involved in life. Why do some people give up or cultivate a bitter "why me" attitude while others arm themselves for battle. Ask readers whether they think that Nancie believes she is a strong person. What about Rena? The reasons that make one react differently to adversity may include background, education, temperament, and grace.

10. Should Dr. Shipman allow Nancie to go home when she first asks (p. 111) ? Is he unduly strict with his patients?

Nancie was probably already resigned to her illness by the time she asked to go home. She probably wanted to go home to die, and if Dr. Shipman had allowed it, she may have died sooner. Sadly, her family wasn't supportive and positive enough to have a healthy influence on her. However, it may be argued that one should be allowed to die where she wants.

Shipman has a big ego and is arrogant. He may believe he is doing what's best, but he's forgotten to treat each person as an individual. His belief that what worked for him is the only possible cure makes him narrow-minded. One wonders if the doctor upon whom this character is based felt kindly about his characterization.

11. Did you find the ending satisfying? Why or why not?

Some readers may wish that Ravi and April had ended up together, but their recovery is the real happy ending. Ask readers whether they were afraid that one of them would die. How will having been seriously ill affect their outlook in the future? After such an experience is life dearer? Can there actually be a benefit to what seems an unfortunate event?

50

YOU DON'T KNOW ME
by DAVID KLASS

Bibliographic information: Farrar Straus Giroux, 2001; 272 pages.

Themes: Child abuse, identity.

Genre: Realistic fiction.

Main character: John, age 14.

Tips: The abuse is graphic and may be hard to handle for some readers, but overall it's nicely balanced by humor and John's resiliency.

SYNOPSIS:

Nothing in John's life is as it seems. His homework is not his homework because his teacher assigned and will grade it, so it's her homework. His friend is not a friend because they are interested in the same girl, whose name is not Glory Hallelujah. John views the contradictions of life with clarity and great humor. If it weren't for his sense of humor and ability to distance himself, his would be a completely grim existence. Convinced that no one knows him, especially not his mother, he endures physical abuse at the hands of the man who is not his father. John lives in a war zone, but in the end he finds love unexpectedly in the person of Violent Haynes (or is it Violet?), whose saxophone may or may not actually be a monitor lizard; and deliverance in the person of his band teacher who recognizes John's talent and need for help.

DISCUSSION QUESTIONS/LEADER POINTS

1. John thinks that his mother sees the man who is not his father "through a filter of tiredness and nostalgia," that she has surrendered. He questions whether her surrender is justified and deserving of sympathy or whether it is cowardly (p. 45). What do you think?

When I discussed this book with a group I was surprised at how unanimously unforgiving they were of John's mother. Perhaps this is the belief of children with attentive parents—that their parent will always rescue them. I was the only one who thought she really would have gotten rid of her boyfriend if she had known that he was abusing John. It is hard to know, since the only picture we get is through John's eyes. He presents her as tired and worn down. *He* obviously doesn't feel that she'd choose him if he confessed; otherwise, wouldn't he? Maybe he doesn't even consider that there is a choice and just stoically accepts his life as it is. You'll probably return to the debate over whether John's mother is simply unaware or in denial during the course of your discussion. Remind readers that even the dog cowered in the presence of the boyfriend, and she should have noticed that even if John hid his own feelings.

2. Mr. Steenwilly recognizes that John lives too much in his head. What are the advantages and disadvantages of this practice? How does it affect the readability of the book?

John truly lives in a world of his own. Often the reader is propelled along in one of his fantasies and abruptly brought back to reality. Usually this is a source of humor, but some readers may find it unsettling and confusing. We are given a ringside view of a very busy, creative mind. John appears to be gifted. Even though his inner world keeps him from being a good student and giving teachers his full attention, he is able to point out a mistake his math teacher makes. His vocabulary is impressive. The world of the Lashasa Palulu is a wonderfully creative construction, as are his alternative names for people. His inner world is a comfort and an escape and a place where he has control. When he calls his teacher Moonface, he has temporarily confused the line between his inner and outer world. He is so used to calling her Moonface in his head that it slips out. This is also a sign of his growing distress.

3. Why do you think that John sometimes talks about himself as if he were observing himself from outside his body?

John's distancing himself from reality by speaking of himself in third person is a defense to help him deal with an intolerable situation. If he is separate from the one experiencing distress, he keeps himself from feeling.

4. What does the Lashasa Palulu tribe represent to John?

The Lashasa Palulu is an ideal society where the nonsense John perceives around him doesn't happen. In contrast to reality, which is out of John's control, he has complete control over the world he creates. Half believing in an orderly, predictable world probably helps John to survive.

5. What do you think about John's assessment of how students act when they do or don't want to be called on in class?

Klass' descriptions are hilarious and right on target. Ask readers what their own strategies are for not being called on in class.

6. What do you think of John's habit of throwing in "whatever that means" when he exercises his impressive vocabulary?

John may be expressing real uncertainty about whether he's using words correctly, but I doubt it. The words are always used correctly. It may be an effect of his humility; he's downplaying his intelligence because he assumes he's unexceptional because of the way he's treated at home. Another possibility is that John has an audience of the average "everyteen" in mind and he's trying to express himself on that level. We can also read it as an expression of his uncertainty about everything.

7. John shares the simple, frightening truth that "your real enemy is someone who knows you" (p. 147). Do you agree or disagree and why? What about yourself? Is John his own enemy sometimes?

The simple frightening truth that those closest to you can hurt you the most is true because someone who knows you well knows your tender parts, the things you fear, the things you regret. The cruelest thing the man who isn't his father does to John is to remind him that his own father doesn't even care to see him. This may be worse than the physical abuse.

8. Until the night when the man who is not his father takes him to load TVs, John has never called him "sir" (p. 150), yet he uses the term for every other man he meets. How do you explain this irony?

Until the night of loading the TVs, John is able to exercise a subtle form of rebellion in calling everyone but his mother's boyfriend "sir." He is expressing his lack of respect for the boyfriend—that everyone else is more deserving of respect. John's acquiescence on the night of the TV loading is a sad victory for his tormentor and a sign that John is broken.

9. Why is Violet a good match for John?

The love story between John and Violet is sweet. Their feelings begin with genuine caring in contrast with Gloria, who is an attractive package with nothing on the inside. The crossover from friends to couple is gradual and realistic. While I thought that Gloria was unrealistic, the teens I discussed this book with assured me that they knew someone like her who would date or hang out with people just because it fed her ego. Ask your group what they think.

10. Why is Mr. Steenwilly at John's house on the night of his brutal beating? What could he have done differently to prevent the beating?

Personally, I thought Steenwilly's impeccable timing was a coincidence that might stretch readers' acceptance. However, his concern was apparent; it wasn't inconceivable that he would routinely drive by John's house. Steenwilly is an endearing character. Should he have reported his suspicions to authorities? Bruises alone don't constitute proof of abuse. John could have fallen or gotten bruised playing sports. The seriousness of reporting suspected abuse can't be downplayed. An investigation could have a devastating effect on an innocent person's life. Steenwilly did the only thing he could have done by talking to John and giving him an opportunity to confide in him.

11. In describing Mr. Steenwilly's composition John says, "Forlorn and cautionary as it started out, and muddled and painful as it became in places, it was, in the end, a love song." (p. 262) Is "The Love Song of the Bullfrog" John's story?

"The Love Song of the Bullfrog" is a touching summary of John's story. It not only describes his relationship with Violet, but his relationship with life. Having the truth out in the open and living in a safe world, John may begin to live his love song with life. The presence of Violet's large, gentle, and loving father and of Steenwilly makes John's future more hopeful. He has at least two good male role models.

12. Are all of the elements of the story meant to be taken at face value, or are some exaggerated by John as narrator? What is the purpose of exaggerating?

Can anyone be so vapid as Gloria? Are we expected to believe that someone who hates the teen generation as much as Mr. Kessler would be a vice principal? How about the Bulldozership—is he anything more than a caricature? And can we believe that an average-sized teen squeezed himself through a pet door? John's home situation is dreadful and dangerous, yet the humor in John's exaggerations make us laugh out loud, which may be just right for a book concerned with things not being what they seem. It may be hard for readers to reconcile the very realistic and horrific elements of John's existence with the silliness of the incident in Gloria's basement, but it's a relief. Maybe his sense of the absurd keeps him sane.

REFERENCES

Anderson, William W. (1995) "Launching the Freshman Year." *Liberal Education* 81, no.3 (Summer): 42-47.

Daniels, Harvey. (2002). *Literature Circles: Voice and Choice in Book Clubs and Reading Groups*. Portland, Maine: Stenhouse.

Jaeger, Linda and Shelia N. Demetriadis. 2002. "Book Club on a Budget: Who Says Everybody Has to Read the Same Book?" *School Library Journal* 48, no. 3 (March): 47.

Lehman, Barbara A, and Patricia L. Scharer. (1996). "Reading Alone, Talking Together: The Role of Discussion in Developing Literary Awareness." *The Reading Teacher* 50, no.1 (September): 26-35.

Saal, Rollene. (1995). *The New York Public Library Guide to Reading Groups*. New York: Crown.

Scieszka, Jon. (2002). Guys Read. [Online]. Available: www.penguin putnam.com/static/packages/us/yreaders/guysread/content1.html.

Vandergrift, Kay E. (1993). "Vandergrift's Reader Response Criticism." [Online]. Available: www.scils.rutgers.edu/~kvander/readerresponse.html

Ward, Caroline. (1998). "Having Their Say: How to Lead Great Book Discussions with Children." *School Library Journal* 44, no. 4 (April): 24-29.

FOR FURTHER READING

Birnie, K. Joan. (2002). "Broken Bow Book Discussions." *NLA Quarterly* 33, no.1 (Spring): 6-7.

Brouse, Ann, ed. (1999). *Talk It Up: Book Discussion Programs for Young People.* New York: New York Library Association.

Dodson, Shireen. 1997. *The Mother-Daughter Book Club: How Ten Busy Mothers and Daughters Came Together to Talk, Laugh, and Learn.* New York: HarperCollins.

Fineman, Marcia. (1998). *Talking about Books: a Step-by-Step Guide for Participating in a Book Discussion Group.* Rockville, Md.: Talking about Books.

Greenwood, Monique. (date) The Go On Girl! Book Club Guide for Reading Groups. New York: Hyperion.

Knowles, Elizabeth, and Martha Smith. (1999). *More Reading Connections: Bringing Parents, Teachers, and Librarians Together.* Englewood, Colo.: Libraries Unlimited.

Slezak, Ellen, ed. 2000. *The Book Group Book: A Thoughtful Guide to Forming and Enjoying a Stimulating Book Discussion Group.* Chicago: Chicago Review Press.

Smith, Michael W., and Jeffrey D. Wilhelm. (2002). *Reading Don't Fix No Chevys: Literacy in the Lives of Young Men.* Portsmouth, N.H.: Heinemann.

AUTHOR INDEX

TITLE INDEX

THEME INDEX

ABOUT THE AUTHOR

Constance Dickerson earned her MLS at Kent State University in 1990 and has worked in public, school, and academic libraries in Texas, Colorado, and Ohio. Most of her 20 years of library experience has been with teens and children. A BA in humanities from Hiram College, where she minored in theater arts fostered her love of writing and performance art. Leading writers' groups and hosting teen book discussions have been highlights of her career. She is currently supervisor of Children's Services at the Beachwood Branch of Cuyahoga County Public Library in Ohio.